Psychology
and the
Christian Faith

Erratum

The last paragraph on page 24 should read as follows:

There is, on the other hand, a wide spectrum of methodologies which do reflect the type of integration discussed here. They include Crabb's (1977) approach to counseling, which he calls biblical counseling. Though Crabb does clearly intend to integrate psychology and Christian faith, his attempts at integration seem at times to be rather halfhearted, and his approach must also be faulted somewhat for its premature definition of itself as *the* biblical approach to counseling. Other attempts at integration from this perspective include Frank Lake's (1966) massive attempt to relate psychoanalytic and Christian thought. McLemore's (1982) helpful book endeavors to relate Christian faith to a variety of issues which commonly arise in the conduct of the psychotherapeutic enterprise.

Psychology
and the
Christian Faith
An Introductory Reader

Stanton L. Jones, *Editor*

BAKER BOOK HOUSE
Grand Rapids, Michigan 49506

For **Brenna** . . .

"The heart of her husband trusts in her,
And he will have no lack of gain.
She does him good and not evil
All the days of her life."

(Prov. 31:11–12, NASB)

Contents

Psychology
and the
Christian Faith

Preface

As an undergraduate major in psychology at a prominent public university, I instinctively followed a pattern of separation between my studies in psychology and my Christian faith and experience. I enjoyed the intellectual challenge of my studies and found the subjects to be intrinsically interesting. But I was constantly troubled by the apparent and real conflicts between what I studied at the university and what I believed. The silence of personality theory and developmental psychology regarding the religious dimension of life seemed to suggest that the insights from these areas were incomplete and somehow distorted. The reductionism of behaviorism that made all of the complexity of human life to be instances of either respondent or operant conditioning was suffocating. The implicit determinism of all of the psychology I studied left me with a feeling of despair as I considered my life as possibly the inevitable result of predetermined choices. These are only a sampling of the tensions I experienced.

To cope with these tensions, I separated my faith from my studies, effectively compartmentalizing my life into the spiritual part and the secular part. I vacillated between the position that, on the one hand, there must be at least a tangential relationship between the two parts and that the tensions I experienced must be of an illusory nature, and the antagonistic position that psychology and Christianity are in fact incompatible views of reality which must be ever in conflict. I also experienced an undeniable desire for a wholeness to my intellectual and spiritual life. Instinctively, I rightly knew that I should not draw rigid boundaries between the various parts of my life, and that somehow I as a Christian should be able to study psychology with integrity and excitement.

In my struggles, I turned for help to Christian writers. I began to devour the writings of anyone who claimed to be an orthodox Christian and who was addressing a topic in any area related to psychology. Frankly, many of these writings served to intensify my struggles. As I read some authors who argue that only the Bible teaches true psychology, I found their theories to frequently stretch the bounds of responsible interpretation of the Scriptures. In general their theories proved to be quite inelegant and uncompelling, especially when compared to those of secular theorists. I also encountered those who attempted to explain (or explain away) religion in terms of contemporary psychological theory, and found these sources to be equally unacceptable and disturbing.

I then came across a number of books about "integration." I found the writings of Collins (1977), Myers (1978), Jeeves (1976), and Carter and Narramore (1979) to be quite helpful in my struggles. The concept of integration, of bringing a wholistic unity to my thinking about psychology as a Christian, was what I had been hoping for in my studies.

Since those early days of struggle, I have benefited from many excellent books and articles by Christians in this field. The major drawback of the majority of these works for the person just embarking on the study of psychology is that they either tend to talk about the concept of integration without sufficient help as to how to go about it, or they tend to be rather focused volumes dealing with integration in specific areas. These focused volumes are a great help in their specific areas, but frequently do not give the student a sense of the variety of ways in which Christians relate their faith to their studies in the diverse subfields of contemporary psychology.

This volume is meant to fill that gap. Its intended audience is the person interested in or studying psychology at the general level. It is meant to be read alongside a standard introductory psychology text, either as an assigned supplement at a Christian college or university, or on an individual basis by the Christian who is studying psychology at a nonreligious school. It will also be of use to those simply reading to help develop their understanding of the nature of integration.

This book of readings is a sampler of topics in integration, and should not be regarded as a "Christian introduction to psychology." It does not attempt to systematically cover the content of all the various subdisciplines of this field. Rather, the challenge to the authors was to take a general area of psychology and demonstrate how we can interact as Christians with the content of some aspect of that area. This book does not represent the completion of the task of struggling to relate faith to psychology; rather, it provides some good examples of how people are conducting that task. It is a book of examples of how scholars are effecting integration.

The student who is reading this book in conjunction with an introductory psychology text should be aware of the parallels between the content of this book and that of the typical text. The nature of psychology as a science is discussed in chapter 1, and less directly in chapters 2 and 3. Chapters 2 and 3 deal with the basic psychological processes which are assumed to undergird all human action. Chapter 4 deals with emotion. Developmental psychology in relation with Christian faith is the focus of chapter 5. Chapters 6 and 7 deal with Christian considerations in the study of personality theory, but should be applied more broadly as speaking to all studies of the person. Chapters 8 and 9 deal with the area of counseling and psychotherapy. Chapter 10 introduces the reader to a topic not frequently dealt with in the study of general psychology, that of psychology of religion. Chapter 11 examines some of the findings of social psychology. Finally, chapter 12 looks at community psychology, one of the many disciplines of applied psychology.

In chapter 1, I attempt to describe the major ways in which Christians approach relating their faith and the field of psychology. I argue that scholars approach this task in quite different manners because of the different ways they may conceive of psychology or of the nature of integration. In fact, the contributors to the present volume have approached their respective chapters in fundamentally different ways. They may explicitly identify their approaches to integration, or the reader may have to discover the author's approach by carefully considering the methods he uses and the very questions he asks of his faith and the particular area being discussed. It is my hope that this volume will aid readers to understand and appreciate the different approaches to integration, and to formulate their own conception of how faith and psychology should be related.

It will be noted that the authors represent a wide spectrum of disciplines. The reader might ask what a theologian (McDonald), philosophers (Evans, Roberts), and a specialist in Christian education (Steele) can have to say about psychology. After a long period of isolation, psychologists are recognizing that the study of human nature is of necessity a multidisciplinary one. There is a need even for experts within the discipline to hear the wisdom of those who, perhaps due to their position outside the discipline, have some clear insight into an area of psychology. Another reason for the broad authorship is that a significant number of Christians see one of the fundamental tasks of Christians in psychology to be the reformulation of the presuppositions we bring to study in this area. The disciplines of theology/religion and philosophy engage in such activities, and thus those scholars may have much of value to say to students of psychology.

One of my few regrets in editing this book is the absence of women authors from the final product. Women have historically made major contributions to the field of psychology, and their impact is being increasingly felt today. Three eminent women psychologists were approached about contributing to this book, but unfortunately none was able to participate in its completion. It is my hope that the lack of women authors will neither be interpreted as an instance of sex bias nor discourage female psychology students from taking their place among productive Christian scholars in this vital field.

I wish to express my deepest thanks to Steve Moroney, who as my research assistant devoted a great deal of time and energy to helping me with this project during the period of greatest effort in putting it together. My thanks go also to Mrs. Carol Blauwkamp and Mrs. Marcy Bump for their cheerful and skilled work as typists.

The time is ripe for Christians to have a formative impact on the field of psychology. There has never been a greater need for self-consciously Christian thinkers to be productive and distinctive in their chosen field of study, especially in light of the seeming collapse of the Judeo-Christian world-view in contemporary America. It is the hope of the editor, and I am sure of each of the authors, that this volume will contribute substantively to the furtherance of work in integration among a new generation of Christian students and scholars in psychology.

References

Carter, J., and B. Narramore (1979). *The integration of psychology and theology: An introduction*. Grand Rapids: Zondervan.

Collins, G. (1977). *The rebuilding of psychology: An integration of psychology and Christianity*. Wheaton, Ill.: Tyndale.

Jeeves, M. (1976). *Psychology and Christianity: The view both ways*. Downers Grove, Ill.: Inter-Varsity.

Myers, D. (1978). *The human puzzle: Psychological research and Christian belief*. San Francisco: Harper & Row.

Relating the Christian Faith to Psychology

Stanton L. Jones

This chapter introduces the reader to the nature of the task of integrating religious faith and the study of the social science of psychology. Stanton L. Jones (B.S., Texas A & M University; Ph.D., Arizona State University) is associate professor and chairman of the undergraduate and graduate divisions of the Department of Psychology at Wheaton College.

Christians studying psychology frequently have several reactions to the field. On the one hand, they may be struck by the way in which their studies in psychology illuminate or expand on some Christian truth, or by the way in which their faith illuminates or expands on some finding in psychology. On the other hand, Christians frequently wonder at the apparent conflicts between what psychologists say about people and what the Christian faith implies about them. They are also frequently struck by the fact that the psychologist's theories omit important religious truths about people. The Christian faith asserts important things about ourselves and others that psychology does not deal with, and vice versa. How do we relate these different views of the person? How do we understand the wonderful compatibilities between them? How do we handle the conflicts between the two?

The focus of this volume is the relating of Christian belief to the discipline of psychology. There are many approaches to this task, which has come to be called the "integration of psychology and theology" or "of psychology and the Christian faith." Whole volumes have been written just classifying various approaches to the task (the interested reader may find the volumes by Carter and Narramore [1979] and Collins [1981] helpful in this regard). Rather than present a wideranging description and analysis of all the possible approaches to integrating Christian belief and psychology, I would like to simply describe the two most common approaches Christians take. I will use the typology of C. Stephen Evans (1982) as my starting point. The two different approaches as explained here are in a sense pure cases which few individuals conform to in every way, and the reader will probably note that none of the contributors to this volume is a perfect example of either category. Nevertheless, we must examine some pure cases to understand the issues at stake in relating religious faith and social science.

Limiters of Science

According to Evans (1982), the limiter of science contends that there are limits to what psychology as a science and Christianity as a religion can each respectively explain. Some limiters of science maintain that certain areas of reality are not appropriate for scientific, or on the other hand religious, study. Evans calls these persons "territorialists," by virtue of their limiting of science and religion to different territories of focus. More typically, however, limiters of science argue that science and religion see, study, and attempt to explain the same aspects of reality from different, nonoverlapping, independent perspectives or levels. Evans calls these persons "perspectivalists." A perspectivalist might follow the behavioristic psychologist B. F. Skinner in choosing a particular methodology in psychology, but would never argue that psychological explanations of human behavior can replace religious explanations. Rather, the religious and psychological are separate, independent levels of explanation, and obviously neither can replace the other.

Donald MacKay (1974), an evangelical Christian and leading brain scientist, gives a vivid analogy of what he means by different levels of explanation. He points out that an electrician can give an exhaustive and true account, from the perspective of an electrician, of the operation of an electric signboard (such as those proclaiming the score of a football game). Such an explanation, though it might exhaustively explain the electrical aspect of the signboard, will probably neglect the meaning communicated by the illuminated light bulbs on the sign. It is precisely this meaning of the score showing on the board, however, which is of interest to the football enthusiast, who could not care less at the peak of the game about the functioning of the capacitors, resistors, and other elements which make up the mechanical side of the signboard. For MacKay, science can explain (even exhaustively) a phenomenon at the scientific perspective or level without robbing the phenomenon of meaning at a different perspective or level. As an example, a psychologist might produce a useful, persuasive, and even exhaustive scientific explanation (i.e., leaving no room for other scientific factors in the explanation) of a human phenomenon such as the conscience without denying the validity of the religious interpretation of that phenomenon.

The practical implications of adopting the position of the limiter of science will differ depending upon whether one is engaged basically in academic research or in professional practice of applied psychology. The task of academic psychologists is to use the tools of the discipline of psychology to understand the results of their research from the psychological perspective. Those academic psychologists who are perspectivalists will see integration as exploration of the interface between psychological and religious levels of explanation.

Malcolm Jeeves (1976) is a good example. In the preface to his book *Psychology and Christianity: The View Both Ways*, as he discusses conflicts between psychology and Christianity, he notes:

> On closer scrutiny, however, it sometimes turns out that supposed conflicts between what psychologists have discovered and what Christians believe have arisen through not pausing long enough to establish precisely what the psychologist is and is not asserting, and what a biblical faith does and does not encourage us to believe. One of the main aims of this book, therefore, is to show how Christian beliefs and the statements of behavioral scientists concerning the same set of events may be related, so that neither is abused and both are given full weight. [p. 7]

So the task of integration for the academic psychologist is that of relating distinct entities, psychology and Christianity, which frequently view the same phenomena from independent perspectives.

As an illustration of this approach, Jeeves argues that it is perfectly valid for social psychology to attempt to explain religious conversion as an interpersonally based change in attitude. From this perspective, conversion can be viewed as a change in beliefs similar to the types of changes in beliefs we all go through when we switch political affiliations, decide to buy a Ford instead of a Dodge, or alter our attitudes toward those of another race. Such a view of the phenomenon of conversion is quite different from the religious view, which sees conversion as a fundamental change in our existence, especially in terms of our relationship with a real God. The theologian uses the terms *salvation, justification,* and *regeneration* to explain this change.

Is there a conflict between these views? Not for the limiter of science, because explanation from one view or level does not mean that other perspectives on the same phenomenon are not valid. To suggest that explanation at one level excludes all other explanations is to engage in what MacKay (1974) calls the logical fallacy of "nothing buttery," the claim that the phenomenon is "nothing but" what is entailed in the explanation offered from one perspective. According to Jeeves (1976, p. 142), the two perspectives (the religious and scientific) are complementary in that the scientific perspective attempts to explain "the mechanisms whereby" psychological changes take place while the religious perspective attempts to explore the "personal significance" of those changes.

The practitioner of applied psychology who is a limiter of science functions in a similar fashion. The mandate of the professional psychologist is to apply psychology to promote human welfare, whether the practitioner is a clinical or counseling psychologist, an industrial or organizational psychologist, a school or educational psychologist, or some other brand of specialist. In the process of applying psychology, one is frequently confronted with the areas of interface between psychology and religion, as when a client struggles with his psychotherapist regarding the meaning of life or an organizational psychologist asked to aid a management group to increase production by dehumanizing means must decide whether to go along with or protest such policies. The specialist in applied psychology who is a limiter of science is committed to the essential separation of scientific psychology and religious belief as addressing different questions. However, he or she also acknowledges the insufficiency of the scientific view of human behavior when examined in isolation from other perspectives on humanity.

How are these limitations of the scientific perspective on human behavior handled? Some professionals who are limiters of science feel strongly that their professional commitment to psychology entails a commitment to limit themselves to dealing exclusively with the "psychological" aspect of human existence and not to dabble in "religious or spiritual" questions. Thus, they might address religious issues only by highlighting points where psychology has contact with religious issues. The essence of this position is its hands-off approach to religious issues.

Others go a bit further in exploring the interface of psychology and religious belief by arguing that psychology as a science answers empirical questions and that religion addresses nonempirical issues such as values. They recognize that applied psychology cannot function without such nonempirical input, but still hold separate the areas of influence of scientific psychology and religious belief. Some argue that religious beliefs shape our values and thus our goals in the professional tasks of applied psychology, and also provide the base for our reasoning in the area of ethics. Scientific psychology then determines empirically how to achieve the goals dictated by our values. So Christian faith is seen as addressing ethical and other nonempirical issues inherent in the applied tasks of the practitioner. This is essentially a restatement of Jeeves's assertion that religion dictates significance, while science studies and clarifies mechanisms.

It is appropriate at this point to briefly offer some evaluative comments on this position on integration. First, there is much merit to the notion that an exhaustive biochemical description of a behavioral event such as the blinking of an eye may be of value to science without exploring all dimensions of that event (e.g., its possible meaning as a flirtatious gesture). The limiters are also on firm ground in suggesting that we need to be acutely aware of what our religious beliefs really assert (remember the trial of Galileo when the church claimed the Bible teaches that the earth is stationary) and what science can really prove (that a scientist says that God does not exist does not mean that science has proven that God does not exist).

But the position of the limiters of science also has some difficulties. The first concerns the degree to which levels of explanation can really be considered to be separate. Does religion really deal with a separate and independent spiritual world which is completely unrelated to the empirically accessible world of the psychological, or is there some overlap between the two? On the face of it, we must surely disagree with Jeeves and assert that religious beliefs do more than dictate the significance of psychological changes—the Scriptures address many issues relevant to the mechanisms and methods of change, as well as make some strong claims about factual matters. It is also increasingly recognized that science in the very way it is defined and practiced embodies some strong premises concerning values. So we must deal with some overlap between science and religion that cannot be resolved by sending each back to its respective corner.

This leads to the second criticism. The position of the limiters of science does not help us to work out the real conflicts that can emerge

between psychological and religious views, such as the conflict between the views of conversion as a mechanistic change in attitude on
the one hand and as a responsible act of a repentant human being on
the other. Jeeves in essence asserts that conflict arises when science or
religion or both have overstepped their bounds. But if we recognize
some overlap, we must develop creative ways of resolving the conflicts
that might emerge from integrative work. The limiter of science cannot help us here.

Finally, this position is based upon a view of science as "value neutral" and objective. But many today doubt that either the research of
the academic or the professional tasks of applied psychology can in
any way be considered to be purely objective and scientific. For a
presentation of these issues, the interested reader is referred to the
recent debate in the journals of the American Psychological Association (Bergin [1980]) which explored the broad and pervasive impact of
religious and philosophical beliefs upon the professional tasks.

Humanizers or Christianizers of Science

There is a second major perspective on the nature of integration. To
borrow ideas from Arthur Holmes's discussion of "Christian philosophy" (1975, p. 56), an integrated psychology will be defined by the
differences that Christianity makes to the person of the psychologist,
the content of his thought, and his methodology. We can synthesize
these factors by saying that Christianity should alter the person of the
psychologist and the basic approach he takes to his task. What should
Christian faith do to the person of the psychologist in his functioning
as a psychologist? Ideally, a sincere commitment to the Christian faith
should motivate the psychologist to seek and understand truth, increase his confidence in the accessibility of truth, bring unity to his
thought life, increase his perceptiveness and sensitivity, deepen his
scientific commitment to honesty and integrity, and increase his wisdom
and empathy for others.

The more controversial aspect of integration is the impact which
faith is presumed to have on the basic approach the psychologist uses.
Faith is seen as affecting the scientist's task by providing new thought
content and by influencing one's method as a psychologist. Many
scholars today argue that all sciences are shaped by a multitude of
nonscientific factors. This recognition in general terms leads to a
"humanized" science attuned to the extrascientific factors that shape
it. An attempt to build science on explicitly Christian presuppositions
would produce a "Christianized" science. This is true even of the

"hardest" of the sciences such as physics. If this is true of physics, it is even more true of psychology.

Nicholas Wolterstorff, a prominent Christian philosopher at Calvin College, addressed exactly this point in his book *Reason Within the Bounds of Religion*. His argument (which is very much like the arguments of others) is basically as follows: The idea of an objective, neutral science which is unaffected by nonscientific beliefs perseveres because some imagine that science is built upon a foundation of absolute certainty which consists of certain facts known to be true without recourse to other facts. In other words, science is seen in this conventional view as built upon truths that are absolutely certain and not dependent for their validity on any mere beliefs. Furthermore, the proponents of this view insist that the way to gain this certainty about the core facts is to put aside all preconceptions, assumptions, "biases and prejudices," and become "purely objective." Empiricists throughout history have in one form or another argued that our sense experience provides this foundation of certainty. For example, they might suggest that I can know for certain and without inference from other facts that as I write I am wiggling a smooth, black pen in my right hand and holding Wolterstorff's book in my left. On the basis of such certainties, we can build science.

One historic answer to such empiricist certainty is to point out the relativity of sense perception. Am I so certain of my facts if my limbs are numbed due to frostbite, or if the light is dim, or if I am fatigued and nodding off to sleep? Such personal factors will have a bearing on how much I can view as certain. More importantly, Wolterstorff argues that even if we could find some set of agreed-upon facts, they would not be sufficiently numerous to support the broad enterprise we know as science. He demonstrates (pp. 42–51) how, under the relentless questioning of the skeptic, the facts or indubitables can be progressively whittled down to a group of statements about what we experience. For instance, my claim regarding the factual existence of the black pen I hold in my hand can be reduced to the statements that "I experience blackness," "I experience smooth hardness," "I experience cylindricalness," and so forth. The only certainties are my experiences; they do not constitute the objective reality necessary for the foundation of science as we know it. Surely it is obvious that this set of "facts" is a meager lot. Thus, philosophers of science today generally acknowledge that absolutely certain facts do not form a broad enough foundation for what we know today as the broad enterprise of science. Mahoney (1976, pp. 128–40) discusses in more detail the many problems of the conventional view of science.

Wolterstorff is not saying that we cannot know truth at all. He is instead suggesting that knowing is a profoundly human enterprise wherein what we accept as true is determined by certain "control beliefs" which we accept as fundamental to our way of viewing reality without total proof of their truth. In regard to my previous example of my pen, I make many an additional assumption, including that of the validity of my sense experience, to move from "I experience black roundness" to "I am holding a pen"! Control beliefs, then, shape what we see as facts. In this analysis, it is presumed that in science, like all forms of human knowing, everyone brings certain implicit notions to the act of knowing and the process of inquiry. This is widely acknowledged today among philosophers of science. According to Thomas Torrance (1981), the great physicist Einstein recognized this a half century ago, and referred to these control beliefs as "intuitive and religious in nature" (p. 58). What Wolterstorff argues, then, is that it is critical for us as Christians to allow our faith to shape our scientific work by having our Christian beliefs act as control beliefs for our scientific work.

What is basically being proposed by the humanizer of science, then, is a restoration of the unity of knowledge, a recognition that our religious beliefs are not segregated from and unrelated to either our philosophical reasoning or empirical investigation. The meaning of such a move can be made clearer in principle by quoting extensively from Wolterstorff (1976):

> Since his fundamental commitment to following Christ ought to be decisively ultimate in his life, the rest of his life ought to be brought into harmony with it. As control, the belief-content of his authentic commitment ought to function both negatively and positively. Negatively, the Christian scholar ought to reject certain theories on the ground that they conflict or do not comport well with the belief-content of his authentic commitment. And positively he ought to devise theories which comport as well as possible with, or are at least consistent with, the belief-content of his authentic commitment. . . . Only when the belief-content of the Christian scholar's authentic Christian commitment enters into his or her devising and weighing of psychological theories in this way can it be said that he or she is fully serious both as scholar and as Christian. [pp. 72–73]

I would add that Christian belief will not only, as suggested by Wolterstorff, influence devising and evaluation of theories, but that it will in addition have a direct influence on what questions we see as relevant and important to study, what data we regard as real, and what methods of study we consider valid (following Kuhn [1970] and Mahoney [1976]). Koch's (1981) conclusion that "psychology is necessarily the most philosophy-sensitive discipline in the entire gamut of disciplines that claim empirical status" (p. 267) is one more of many possible examples of recognition of the importance of nonempirical assumptions and reasoning in the empirical science of psychology.

The Christian humanizer assumes that Christian control-beliefs will alter the conduct of psychology as a discipline in direct proportion to the degree to which these control beliefs differ from non-Christian control-beliefs. Radical and crucial differences will lead the Christian psychologist into nontraditional avenues of research or professional practice; trivial differences or functionally equivalent control-beliefs will leave the Christian and non-Christian psychologist essentially indistinguishable upon casual observation.

Theologian Emil Brunner (1946) asserted that sin will have a greater and greater distorting effect on the thought life of non-Christians the closer their thoughts bring them to the central issues of life. He made this assertion in light of the biblical references to the blinding and deceiving effects of our sinful natures. Following the reasoning of Brunner, we might predict that in areas of little direct relationship to the central issues of human existence, such as the functioning of a specific part of the brain in a hooded rat or the validity of one form of statistical analysis over another, Christian control-beliefs will produce little departure from the work of secular psychologists because these areas, while important, are not central to human life and hence the effects of sin in these areas will be minimized. On the other hand, in areas more central to human life and thus more likely to be influenced by sin, Christian control-beliefs might lead the Christian psychologist committed to integration to radically depart from the methods and conclusions of his nonbelieving colleagues. Obvious examples might include the psychological understandings of an identity crisis, of a person's emotional conflict over a perceived purposelessness in life, and (in an academic discussion) of the basic motivations which we all share as human beings. Such a gulf between Christian and non-Christian scholars would probably rarely be so profound as to make communication and understanding between the two groups impossible.

As with the position of the limiters of science, the impact of the position of the humanizers will vary depending upon the professional activities of the psychologist. Remember that the perspectivalist saw his integrative task as that of relating complementary but independent perspectives on our human condition. The humanizer of science also sees limits to what psychology can tell us and hence feels a need to relate the separate perspectives of psychology and religious belief. But in addition, the humanizer sees his task as the restructuring of psy-

chology to allow for a more direct impact of Christian belief upon work
in this field. In academic research Christian commitment will shape
the psychologist's control-beliefs, and hence his perception of data,
generation of hypotheses, choice of methodology, and all aspects of the
scholarly task. Collins (1977), Farnsworth (1981), and Van Leeuwen
(1982) are examples of psychologists who are attempting to understand, from a humanizer's perspective, how Christian commitment
will shape the face of academic research. All three have suggested, for
example, that Christian control-beliefs have led them to embrace a
wider spectrum of research methodologies than most non-Christian
psychologists regard as valid.

For the practitioner of applied psychology, the effect of Christian
belief is equally profound. The professional task is seen not as a purely
or merely scientific one, but rather as a profoundly human one informed by humanized scientific grounding and research. Thus, Christian control-beliefs become the major anchoring points of one's
approach to the professional task, and in this sense the person is practicing a "Christian psychology," that is, an approach to psychology that
is intentionally and thoughtfully directed toward being compatible
with the Christian faith.

Many of the methodologies of Christian psychology or Christian
counseling which at first glance appear to be examples of this approach are in fact not; they are, rather, attempts to ignore psychology
in favor of a purely Christian approach to enhancing human welfare.
They are basically anti-integrationist. For example, due to their failure
to interact with psychology as a discipline, Adams's (1970, 1979)
nouthetic counseling, Solomon's (1971) spirituotherapy, and Captain's
(1984) theory of human development should not be considered inte-
grationist.

There is, on the other hand, a wide spectrum of methodologies
which do reflect the type of integration discussed here. They include
Crabb's (1977) approach to counseling, which he calls biblical counseling. Though Crabb does clearly intend to integrate psychology and
Christian thought. McLemore's (1982) helpful book endeavors to relate
Christian faith, his attempts at integration seem at times to be rather
halfhearted, and his approach must also be faulted somewhat for its
premature definition of itself as *the* biblical approach to counseling.
Other attempts at integration from this perspective include Frank
Lake's (1966) massive attempt to relate psychoanalytic and Christian
thought. McLemore's (1982) helpful book endeavors to relate Christian
faith to a variety of issues which commonly arise in the conduct of the
psychotherapeutic enterprise.

The humanizer's position must also be critically evaluated. The r. jor charge that has been directed at it is its potential to lead to a degeneration of the scientific enterprise into never-ending squabbles about whose control beliefs are better and a resulting unwillingness to be influenced by what the data tell us about reality. It could be that questioning and even downplaying the objectivity of the scientific method will lead to a parochialism and fragmentation of psychology into, for example, secularist psychology, Buddhist psychology, and Christian psychology, or even into Baptist psychology and Reformed psychology. Psychology has struggled to establish its credibility as a discipline for many years. It is quite possible that too heavy a focus on the influence of control beliefs will fragment it and hinder its further development. Another criticism leveled at the humanizer's position is that objective truths cannot really be so easily bent by our control beliefs. Surely we have such beliefs, but perhaps the humanizer's view of integration exaggerates their importance.

Arguments Against Integration

There are many who are dismayed about the attempts to relate a scientific discipline like psychology and Christianity. "What do the two have to do with one another?" they ask. Many people do in fact doubt that the two have anything in common. They say, "Science deals with facts; religion is just a matter of beliefs or suppositions or values. Why would you want to muddy up your facts with all that religious garbage?" Among religiously conservative people, on the other hand, we might hear exactly the opposite, including comments like "Christianity tells us how to live a good life and gives us everything we need to do precisely that. Psychology is the pseudoscientific speculations of a bunch of atheists. Why mix up the true faith with that psychology garbage?" Both of these responses argue that the two entities, science and religious belief, are incompatible. By exposing the inadequacies of each of these views, we can further our understanding of the nature of a proper integration of Christian belief and psychology.

The anti-integrationist scientists

The belief that science should have little or nothing to do with religion is quite prevalent. Mahoney (1976) offers the following list of what are commonly supposed to be the characteristics of the scientist: intelligence, creativity, logical reasoning skill, experimental acumen, objectivity, neutrality, loyalty to truth, humility, and willingness to suspend judgments until the facts are in. Religious persons have been characterized by some as embodying the opposites of several of these qualities, in that religious belief (so the argument goes) requires suspending logical judgment, rejecting humility in favor of premature certainty, and sacrificing objectivity and neutrality to claim the "real truth."

B. F. Skinner, the prominent Harvard behaviorist, is one example of this mind-set in psychology. Skinner (1953, 1971) argues that psychology as a science must study exclusively the effects of external events (such as a particular form of grading student work) on observable behavior (student performance), and not study such internal variables (the traditional interests of psychologists) as need for achievement, test anxiety, and religious belief unless those variables can be redefined as concrete behaviors. Many psychologists, Christian and non-Christian, agree with Skinner on this point. Some go along with Skinner because they believe that such methods are the most suitable ones for a scientific psychology, and not because they believe that other types of explanation are superfluous. But Skinner and many of his followers go much further. They suggest that other forms of explanation of human behavior are unneeded and in fact interfere with acceptance of the scientific explanations of human behavior. Thus, Skinner (1971) argues that scientific explanations must replace "prescientific views" (p. 22) such as the theological or religious. Psychology, as science, must supersede myth (i.e., religion). Such a program, Skinner (1953) suggests, will require a set of characteristics much like those described by Mahoney (1976).

Thus, in this conventional view of science, scientists must at the very least separate their religious beliefs from their work as scientists, because religious beliefs inappropriately compete with a scientific account of human behavior. Some, such as Skinner, would go as far as to argue that religion and science are competitors in explaining human existence, and that science must unseat or replace "religious myth."

There are two prominent assumptions here that must be examined more closely. The first is that scientific perspectives on reality have primacy over all other perspectives, especially religious ones. The second is that religious belief is fundamentally different from scientific knowledge. Religion is viewed as mere opinion, conjecture, supposition, or, as it is prominently labeled today, a matter of mere values. Science, on the other hand, is assumed to deal with neutral facts, verified assertions, or truth. It is assumed that science can be and is conducted in a neutral, objective context separated from the dangerous subjective values of lesser mortals.

The belief that a scientific view of reality has primacy over all other views has already been discussed and refuted in our section on the position of the limiters of science. Science, as they have argued, is a way, not the way, of looking at ourselves and our world. Skinner's assertion that we are nothing more than biological mechanisms acting out our determined lives in accordance with universal, unvarying laws of behavior is nothing more than that, a bare assertion. No conclusion that broad and sweeping could ever be proven scientifically; it is, rather, merely one way of looking at the world. The scientific view does not necessarily supplant the meaningfulness of other views; an understanding of light refraction does not explain the fragile beauty of a rainbow.

Regarding the second assumption, we should note that the common distinctions between scientific and religious knowledge have been breaking down steadily in the past three decades. On the side of religious knowledge and belief, prominent philosophers such as Alvin Plantinga (1982) have been arguing that some types of religious belief are as basic to the human being as the trust in our physical senses which forms the foundation of the empirical natural sciences. That is, Plantinga argues that a belief in God is no less justifiable than a belief that one's senses are reliable. Plantinga does not argue for some form of irrationalism wherein people are justified in believing whatever they may choose without regard to reason or evidence. Rather, he suggests that people who are rationally led to believe in God are engaged in the same human task as are people who are led to believe there is a floor beneath their feet because they can see and feel it.

It is even more important, however, to be aware of the errors of the conventional view of science as a purely objective activity, one that is thus totally different from religious belief. The thinking of many contemporary philosophers, sociologists, and psychologists of science has been converging for years toward a view of science as a profoundly human enterprise. This thinking has already been surveyed for the reader in the preceding section on the humanizer's view of science. To briefly summarize the argument presented, science must be seen as a human task profoundly shaped by the prescientific and religious control-beliefs which we bring to the scientific task.

Philosopher Ian Barbour (1974), drawing on this understanding of science and religion, has challenged the rigid distinctions made between the two, arguing that the two differ in degree and emphasis, but are not fundamentally different human activities. Both science and religion, argues Barbour, are influenced and shaped by the facts or realities of human experience (though science is more directly and immediately influenced by the facts). Further, neither scientific theories nor religious beliefs are susceptible to pure logical falsification, though both are accepted or rejected in part on the basis of their ability or lack thereof to help us understand reality. Finally, a host of nonempirical factors shape acceptance and rejection of both scientific theories and religious beliefs. In summary, science is not purely objective, mental, factual, and empirical, and religion is not purely subjective, biased, and dogmatic. Thus the scientific anti-integrationists have an inadequate view of religious belief and of science.

Before progressing, let me emphasize that I am not suggesting that we should be unconcerned about objectivity and bias in science. Rather, we must acknowledge the fact that science is a profoundly human endeavor which is shaped by our most fundamental convictions about the nature of our existence. To be a responsible scientist is to be open, honest, and self-critical about our basic control-beliefs as well as about our methods.

The anti-integrationist Christians

Many Christians react with suspicion, distrust, or even outright repugnance to the idea of relating psychology and Christianity, though for quite different reasons than do Skinner and other pure scientists. For example, R. J. Rushdoony (1977) asserts that psychology as we know it today is shot through with humanism; it is "now in its death-throes, and we leave it to the dead to bury their dead. . . . Psychology properly is a branch of theology" (p 1). Philip Captain (1984) "rejects the idea of accommodation with secular psychology. . . . Too many Christians are seeking answers to spiritual questions from secular men who have constructed secular theories. . . . As Christians, we need to go beyond integration" (pp. ix–x).

The objections of the anti-integrationist Christians are quite different from those of the scientists, and thus must be dealt with separately. Rushdoony and others like him bring to their assessment of contemporary psychology two critical assumptions which must be evaluated. The first is the assumption that the Bible is sufficient to answer all important questions in psychology, thus making psychology "a branch of theology." This assumption is based on Scripture passages like 2 Timothy 3:16–17: "All Scripture is inspired by God and profitable for teaching, for reproof, for correction, for training in righteousness; that the man of God may be adequate, equipped for every good work" (NASB). Anti-integrationist Christians argue that this verse tells us that Scripture is all that is needed by the devoted believer to answer the important psychological questions of life. Thus, Adams (1979, p. 46) calls all integration sinful because it shows a lack of trust in the sufficiency of Scripture to meet all the needs of the Christian.

The second assumption is that there are two sources of counsel in the world, that of God and that of Satan, and that any counsel which is not of God is necessarily of Satan. Christians who make this assumption contend that to learn from secular psychologists is to "walk in the counsel of the wicked" (Ps. 1:1, NASB). On the basis of such reasoning, Richard Ganz (1976) states: "It takes an unpolluted spring to form an unpolluted pond. Likewise, the only way to have a nonpolluted system of counseling is to fill it from an unpolluted source. That source is the Scriptures" (p. 196).

There are some merits to this view. It draws our attention to several critical realities which we must remember; namely, the infallibility and utility of the Scriptures and the ever-present and detrimental force of evil and error. But the problems with this view far outweigh its merits. Its first assumption, that Scripture provides a sufficient source for answers to all important questions of psychology, seems overblown in that there are many issues which Scripture never addresses. Tonight, as I bathed my two-year-old son, we had a terrific game of "make-a-splash." Soon, however, he was splashing too energetically, and I had to decide what to do about it, given that I am told in Scripture to discipline my child yet not to exasperate him. Should I have ignored the splashing, left the room, screamed at him, spanked him, struck him with a stick, or what? Small but important decisions such as these fall between the cracks of the large planks laid down in Scripture which guide our behavior. Similarly, in my activities as a psychologist, whether helping a client or trying to understand a particular aspect of the human experience, I am challenged to broaden my understanding beyond what is given to me by revelation in the Bible. My deliberations and decisions in many areas have to be based on reason informed by Scripture and by experience interpreted in the light of scriptural truth.

In essence, then, I am arguing that God's revelation in the Bible is a necessary basis for the development of a wholistic knowledge of human behavior, but that it is not all-sufficient. Its place in life can hardly be overemphasized, but we must remember that it is a revelation of limited scope with particular purposes. We need to fill in the specifics between some of the broad truths which Scripture gives us. If we stand firmly within and upon the basic tenets of our Christian faith as revealed by God in the Scriptures, we can fill in these specifics by using our reason and experience, learning from Christians and non-Christians alike. Filling in the specifics this way is precisely the task of the Christian social-scientist. So to learn from sources other than the Bible does not necessarily entail a denigration of the importance of that divine revelation. This seems to be the best interpretation of 2 Timothy 3:16–17.

This brings us to the second assumption of the Christian anti-integrationists, which is that all non-Christian thought is the counsel of Satan and hence unacceptable for use by the Christian. There are major problems with this assumption. First, it exaggerates the apprehension of truth by Christians. Their grasp of the truth is regarded as absolutely pristine and pure. Such a view is surely exaggerated. Christians make errors too. Perhaps we need to be reminded occasionally of the medieval church's dogged insistence, on biblical grounds (so they thought), that the earth was flat and the center of the universe, and also of the fragmentation of the modern church wherein numerous subgroups of the body of Christ all lay claim to *the* truth, even though their respective dogmas conflict.

Secondly, acknowledging the eternal conflict between God and Satan does not inevitably commit us to viewing every word of the Christian or every interpretation of Scripture as the counsel of God and every pronouncement of the non-Christian as the counsel of Satan. Rather, *truth wherever found should be seen as God's counsel* and falsehood wherever found should be regarded as the counsel of Satan. We must reject the reasoning that says that to heed the voice of a nonbeliever is to "walk in the counsel of the wicked." This reasoning would lead us to reject the counsel of any nonbeliever, whether it is true or not. Thus, if I were to pull up to a roadblock and the flagman were to say, "You can't go any farther because there's a bridge out ahead," my critical question would not be, "Is he telling the truth?" but rather, "Is he a Christian?" If he is not a Christian, then by this absurd reasoning I would be morally obligated to ignore his advice and proceed down the road in order not to be guilty of "walk[ing] in the counsel of the wicked." This is a ludicrous example, but it points up for us a more compelling interpretation of Psalm 1: it is telling us not to follow wicked *counsel*. That is, the critical question is whether the counsel itself is wicked, not whether or not the counselor is a Christian. So we must listen discerningly to the counsel of both believers and nonbelievers alike to make sure that we are pursuing God's truth.

This line of argument is by no means unique. The great thinkers of the Christian faith have consistently shown a deep appreciation of truth wherever it has emerged. Many of the early church fathers (e.g., Clement of Alexandria, Tatian, and Justin Martyr) as well as Augustine, Thomas Aquinas, Martin Luther, and others all wrote eloquently about the value of the truths and insights God has spread abroad to Christians and non-Christians alike according to his divine grace. This indiscriminate spreading of his blessing of truth has been called God's "common grace" by theologians and biblical scholars. Perhaps one of the best statements of this concept is in Calvin's (1981)

Institutes of the Christian Religion (2. 2. 15): "The human mind, however much fallen and perverted from its original integrity, is still adorned and invested with admirable gifts from its Creator. . . . We will be careful . . . not to reject or condemn truth wherever it appears." He cites examples of marvelous insights which pagan thinkers have had on nature, politics, medicine, mathematics, and philosophy (which included the psychology of the day). Surely Calvin, one of the fathers of the Protestant Reformation, cannot be accused of having a deficient view of Scripture or of being unaware or unconcerned about evil, yet he praised and searched for truth "wherever it appears." Examples of similar statements could be multiplied to fill an entire volume.

While we must recognize that non-Christians can apprehend truth, and may do so so well as to put Christians to shame, we must also remember that non-Christian thought will necessarily contain error, especially in areas where unbelief directly confronts matters of Christian truth. I earlier drew upon Brunner (1946), who argued that the closer we come to dealing with issues at the core of human life, the greater is sin's effect on our knowledge:

> The nearer anything lies to that center of existence where we are concerned with the whole, that is, with man's relation to God and the being of the person, the greater is the disturbance of rational knowledge by sin; the farther away anything lies from this center, the less is the disturbance felt, and the less difference is there between knowing as a believer or as an unbeliever. [p. 383]

Brunner recognized the critical fact that as beings created in the image of God, we all, Christians and non-Christians, have some capacity to see truth, and that wherever it is appropriated, truth must not be dismissed. He also recognized that apprehending truth is an intensely personal enterprise which is affected by the alienation from God which is a part of all human experience, but especially that of the non-Christian.

So in summary, the Christian anti-integrationists exaggerate the extent of the important psychological knowledge which God reveals in the Bible, and they exaggerate the impact of evil upon the revelation of truth in the writings of nonbelievers. Scripture is intended by God to serve as the cornerstone, the essential foundation of all human activity. But because it is a revelation of limited scope, Christians must necessarily extend their knowledge beyond the words of Scripture by exercising their reason and learning from experience (i.e., science), with both of these latter activities continually subjected to the authority of God's special revelation (see Greidanus [1982] for an excellent discussion of these issues). They must be ready to separate truth from error in the thought of Christians and non-Christians alike, recognizing that non-Christians may be especially prone to error in areas of particular relevance to the central concerns of human existence, such as the ultimate meaning of life. Awareness of the presence of error should not, however, lead us to throw out the true baby with the erroneous bathwater. Holmes (1977) has provided an articulate defense of this position that "all truth is God's truth."

The task of integration is one of great excitement and challenge. Its complexity belies easy summarization, so I will not make the attempt. In closing allow me to encourage the readers of this book to commit themselves to the task of integration as a lifelong endeavor, one which will prove personally rewarding and will be glorifying to the Father if it is conducted faithfully and with integrity. For the Christian, a commitment to the pursuit of truth entails a necessary commitment to the task of integration. Further, a commitment to the cause of Christ also entails a commitment to integration. Why? Because "He is the image of the invisible God, the first-born of all creation. For in Him all things were created. . . . And He is before all things, and in Him all things hold together" (Col. 1:15–17). With Christ the living God at the center of the universe and of human life, surely only an approach which integrates scientific and religious truths can rightly bring him the glory and honor which he so richly deserves.

References

Adams, J. (1970). *Competent to counsel.* Grand Rapids: Baker.

———— (1979). *More than redemption: A theology of Christian counseling.* Phillipsburg, N.J.: Presbyterian and Reformed.

Barbour, I. (1974). *Myths, models, and paradigms.* New York: Harper & Row.

Bergin, A. (1980). Psychotherapy and religious values. *Journal of Consulting and Clinical Psychology* 48: 95–105.

Brunner, E. (1946). *Revelation and reason.* Translated by O. Wyon. Philadelphia: Westminster.

Calvin, J. (1981). *Institutes of the Christian religion.* Translated by H. Beveridge. Grand Rapids: Eerdmans (original work published 1559).

Captain, P. (1984). *Eight stages of Christian growth.* Englewood Cliffs, N.J.: Prentice-Hall.

Carter, J., and B. Narramore (1979). *The integration of psychology and theology: An introduction.* Grand Rapids: Zondervan.

Collins, G. (1977). *The rebuilding of psychology: An integration of psychology and Christianity*. Wheaton, Ill.: Tyndale.

———— (1981). *Psychology and theology: Prospects for integration*. Nashville: Abingdon.

Crabb, L. (1977). *Effective biblical counseling*. Grand Rapids: Zondervan.

Evans, C. S. (1982). *Preserving the person*. Grand Rapids: Baker (originally published 1977).

Farnsworth, K. (1981). *Integrating psychology and theology: Elbows together but hearts apart*. Washington: University Press of America.

Ganz, R. (1976). Nouthetic counseling defended. *Journal of Psychology and Theology* 4: 193–205.

Greidanus, S. (1982). The use of the Bible in Christian scholarship. *Christian Scholar's Review* 11: 138–47.

Holmes, A. (1975). Christian philosophy. In *Encyclopaedia Britannica* (15th ed.).

———— (1977). *All truth is God's truth*. Grand Rapids: Eerdmans.

Jeeves, M. (1976). *Psychology and Christianity: The view both ways*. Downers Grove, Ill.: Inter-Varsity.

Koch, S. (1981). The nature and limits of psychological knowledge. *American Psychologist* 36: 257–69.

Kuhn, T. (1970). *The structure of scientific revolutions* (2d ed.). Chicago: University of Chicago Press.

Lake, F. (1966). *Clinical theology*. London: Darton, Longman, & Todd.

MacKay, D. (1974). *The clockwork image: A Christian perspective on science*. Downers Grove, Ill.: Inter-Varsity.

McLemore, C. (1982). *The scandal of psychotherapy*. Wheaton, Ill.: Tyndale.

Mahoney, M. (1976). *The scientist as subject: The psychological imperative*. Cambridge, Mass.: Ballinger.

Plantinga, A. (1982). The Reformed objection to natural theology. *Christian Scholar's Review* 11: 187–98.

Rushdoony, R. (1977). *Revolt against maturity*. Fairfax, Va.: Thoburn.

Skinner, B. F. (1953). *Science and human behavior*. New York: Free Press.

———— (1971). *Beyond freedom and dignity*. New York: Bantam.

Solomon, C. (1971). *Handbook to happiness*. Wheaton, Ill.: Tyndale.

Torrance, T. (1981). *Christian theology and scientific culture*. New York: Oxford University Press.

Van Leeuwen, M. (1982). *The sorcerer's apprentice: A Christian looks at the changing face of psychology*. Downers Grove, Ill.: Inter-Varsity.

Wolterstorff, N. (1976). *Reason within the bounds of religion*. Grand Rapids: Eerdmans.

2

Brain Research and Human Responsibility
Donald M. MacKay

Without question, scientists have made great strides in recent decades in their understanding of the modes of operation of the human brain. Study after study has revealed the compelling beauty and startling complexity of the brain's functioning.

Donald M. MacKay has been in the forefront of that revolution. He has also devoted considerable efforts to informing the Christian world about these advances and helping us to understand their implications. In this chapter he clearly articulates why Christians should not fear these advances in basic brain research. The responses which he here develops to the concerns expressed in many circles that the findings of the brain sciences refute or are in some way incompatible with the Christian view of the person are in distinct contrast with those offered by C. Stephen Evans in chapter 7.

MacKay (B.A., St. Andrew's University) took his Ph.D. from the University of London in physics. His interests moved over time from radar to analog computing and finally via information theory to the organization of the brain as an information system. He founded the

This chapter is a revision of "Brain Research and Human Responsibility" by Donald M. MacKay from *Horizons of Science* edited by Carl F. H. Henry. Copyright © 1978 by Carl F. H. Henry. Reprinted by permission of Harper & Row, Publishers, Inc.

Department of Communication and Neuroscience at the University of Keele, where he is research professor emeritus. He has published many books for Christian audiences, several of which are listed in the reference section of this chapter.

Scientists are like exploratory mapmakers. Their mapmaking, like that of geographers, may require them to feel their way where few others have gone before, to pry into territory in which many others claim an interest, and to exercise discretion as to whether, when, and to whom to disclose what they discover. Their aim, of course, like that of modern geographers, goes far beyond mere description. The purpose of their explorations is to understand what must be reckoned with in the world around them, to discover the motive forces of what they study, to identify resources that may be tapped by future mapusers. Their maps, in a word, are *functional*. Their duty is to guide intelligent agents and not mere sightseers. Brain scientists are not exempt from any of these obligations. Their chosen domain has an organized structure more complex than any other known to man. New tools of investigation create constantly expanding frontiers of pioneering effort. Every one of their fellow human beings claims a natural interest in the territory they explore. The proper use of their knowledge is thus for brain scientists a matter of constant and inescapable concern.

The Authority for Brain Research

Fundamental for anyone in this position is the question of *authority*. By what authority are the maps being made? To whom are the mapmakers accountable? Whose is the territory they explore? For the Christian, the answer is clear. The world is God's. It is to him that we are ultimately accountable. It is by his authority that we are commissioned to explore and have dominion over the works of his hands, not in a spirit of arrogant exploitation, but of humble and compassionate stewardship. In contrast to the pagan image of the gods as jealous of their secrets and resentful of man as an inquisitive interloper, the biblical emphasis is on man's duty to apply his mind to the understanding of the natural world, as an expression of reverence for its Creator and in gratitude for the benefits that deeper understanding can bring.

Inasmuch as the human brain is one of the works of God's hands and a part of the natural world, the Genesis mandate to "subdue" nature

presumably makes brain research not just a legitimate but an oblig-
atory sector of our responsibility to our Creator. But there are two
singular features that set the human brain apart from other objects of
investigation. First, mapmakers of the brain are in a certain sense
mapping (or trying to map) part of themselves; and the logic of such an
enterprise must present certain difficulties and pitfalls that mapmakers of other domains can escape. Second, our common experience
in choosing and acting, let alone the Christian doctrine of the human
soul, might seem to raise a question as to whether the human brain is
in fact a purely "natural" object, conforming to the same physical laws
as the rest of the natural world.

It must be said straightaway that this last question is still an open
one. Despite all recent advances in brain science, our ignorance of the
causes of brain events still vastly exceeds our knowledge. Nobody can
rule out on scientific grounds the possibility that some events in the
human brain may violate the physical principles that apply in other
parts of the natural world. What I hope to show, however, is that it
would be both unnecessary and dangerously misleading for Christians
to try to defend any such theory in the interests of the biblical doctrine
of man. It would be unnecessary, I believe, because nothing in biblical
teaching requires the brain to be exempt from normal physical principles; and dangerously misleading, because such an emphasis would
deflect attention away from the distinctive points that the Bible does
make about our human nature and destiny.

In this context, then, my title has an obvious double meaning.
First—and vital for a healthy relationship between brain research and
Christianity in particular—there is the question of our human responsibility to explore, map, and gain understanding of the vastly mysterious territory in which we are embodied as conscious agents. Have we
any right to probe the mystery that surrounds the springs of human
action? The biblical answer to this, I have suggested, is in principle
straightforward. If there is need to be met, and good to be done, by
gaining knowledge of God's world not forbidden us by him, then we
would need a good excuse to neglect its pursuit. We have not merely a
right, but an obligation to our Creator and our fellows, to learn all we
legitimately can about the way the brain works, the ways it can go
wrong, and the ways it may be mended. Increasing knowledge will of
course bring enlarged responsibility for its proper use, but to gain that
knowledge, in that spirit, is a matter of obedience.

This, however, in turn raises the much more complex question implied in my title, namely, that of the implications of what we learn
about the brain for our concept of human responsibility itself. Science
has a long-standing reputation for demonstration that things are not

always what they seem to common sense. Brain science is likely to be no exception. Is there not a risk, then, that it may eventually show up as "illusions" those very aspects of our commonsense view of man that make meaningful our idea of responsibility? Might not brain science, for all its biblical warrant, lead to a debunking of the biblical view of our human nature? It is this second question that will occupy us for most of the present essay.

Major Developments

The great surge forward in brain science in the present century has resulted from a coincidence of advances on many different fronts. Developments in microscopy, including the art of selective staining of nerve cells, have told us more about the way cells interconnect than we know how to use. The rise of electronics has produced a whole battery of sensitive tools that allow us to stimulate, record, and analyze the chatter of electrical activity that goes on in the ten-thousand-million-strong neural population and even in the minute individual members of it. Workers in biochemistry and related fields have begun to trace intricate patterns of chemical interaction that add a new dimension to our already complex map of the brain and greatly enlarge the cabinet of drugs whereby its behavior can be modified for good or ill.

But perhaps the most far-reaching influence on brain science has come from quite another direction. The need for automatic machinery to take the place of human operators in dangerous, boring, or otherwise undesirable occupations has forced engineers and psychologists to cooperate in an unprecedented effort to understand and specify the mechanisms of intelligent action. Although this hybrid "cognitive science" (whose components go by such names as "automata theory," "autonomics," "communication and control theory," "cybernetics," and "artificial intelligence") is only a few decades old, it has already revolutionized the way in which brain scientists think of their problems. Let me emphasize that this does *not* mean they draw detailed analogies between brains and present-day computing machines. Our present electronic computers work on quite different physical principles from those governing the nervous system, and the differences between computers and the brain are probably more significant than the resemblances. What it does mean is that the *habits of thought* of the automation engineer have powerfully shaped the kind of question brain scientists ask, and the kind of answer they may accept as satisfactory. It now comes as second nature to them to think of the brain as a protoplasmic way of engineering the kinds of information-processing functions that we have found necessary to produce intelligent, goal-directed behavior in our automata. The brain may well be *more* than that, but it is at least amenable to a great deal of detailed explanation in these mechanistic terms. Hypotheses framed in such terms have led to an astonishingly fruitful crop of experimental results, and they show every sign of continuing to do so. Conversely, the merchants of artificial intelligence keep on producing formal written instructions for ever more sophisticated tasks. In working out their ideas, they find that a computer serves as an invaluable "test bed," because it can relentlessly expose any flaws in a hypothetical model and allows them to discover (or obliges them to face) unexpected as well as expected consequences of their speculations.

Room for the Soul?

In biblical thought, man is distinguished from all other animals as "made in the image of God." What this means in theological depth has been the subject of unending debate (Berkouwer [1962]). For our present purposes, however, we can extract three essential ingredients:

1. Man has rational faculties capable of apprehending not only concrete facts of his immediate environment, but also abstract ideas, including truths revealed by God.
2. Man's death on earth does not annul his relationship (whether of love or rebellion) with his Creator.
3. Man is *answerable* to God for his actions: he can be *called to account* by his Creator.

Our question in this and the following three sections is whether, and if so, how, these ingredients mesh with the kind of understanding of man being developed in brain science, particularly in its mechanistic aspects.

In tackling this question we must beware of a presupposition that has no basis in biblical doctrine, but is widely accepted, even by some Christians, as "common sense." According to the mechanistic model, which was popularized by Descartes, the brain and body are to be thought of as a steerable machine, like a car or an aircraft. The "soul" is then thought of as the invisible pilot, exerting quasi-physical influences on suitably sensitive parts of the machine. I am not concerned here to argue that this model is wrong. Our ignorance of brain mechanics is so great that nobody can dogmatize about the details of its control system; and no less an authority than Sir John Eccles, Nobel Prize winner for his work in neurophysiology, has opted for something very like the Cartesian picture (1970).

What I do want to emphasize, however, is that this model is not required by the biblical data. The teaching of Genesis 1 is that man "became" a living soul, not that a "soul" was coupled to his body as an extra *part*. The mechanistic notion of the soul as an invisible and independent entity, capable of exerting *forces* on parts of the brain, goes far beyond anything taught in Scripture. It implies, in addition, that unless there are suitable "gaps" or indeterminacies in the chain mesh of physical cause-and-effect patterns in the brain, there can be no effective connection between the workings of the soul (so conceived) and the activity of the body. It suggests that if brain science were ever to swing in a completely deterministic direction, the soul would find itself squeezed out, having no effective part in determining human behavior.

Christians brought up to accept a bipartite (if not a tripartite) idea of man may at this point feel restive. Surely body, mind, and spirit are biblically distinct concepts? How can we do justice to them if we do not postulate forcelike connections between the body and the soul?

Oddly enough, I think that the example of computer technology itself illustrates the answer. When mathematicians say their computer is "solving an equation," they mean that the behavior of the machine is *determined* (note the term) by that particular equation. This does not imply that there are "gaps" in the physical cause-and-effect chain mesh linking its components through which some invisible entity called an "equation" exerts quasi-physical influences on the transistors. Indeed, the electronic engineer in charge of the machine will insist that every physical event in it is *determined* (note the same word) by other physical events in its depths. Far from contradicting this, the mathematicians will insist that they *rely* on its being true as the basis for their own claim that the behavior of the machine as a whole was determined by their equation! They will insist equally strongly that computer hardware and mathematical equations are distinct concepts, in quite different categories.

Any appearance of conflict here is of course illusory. A computing machine is simply one example of a situation that *needs explanations at more than one level* in order to do it justice. Each explanation may specify in its own terms what determines the behavior at its own level *without necessarily conflicting* with the claims of another. No matter how complete the electronic engineer's explanation, the mathematicians' is *necessary* if we are not to miss the whole point of what a computer is and does. The equation determines what the network of transistors do, not by prodding them with quasi-physical "forces," but by *being embodied in it*.

The point of this illustration is not of course to argue that computers have minds, still less that men are "nothing but" computers. (I have discussed the fallacies of such arguments elsewhere [1962, 1965b, 1979, 1980].) Its purpose is only to suggest an alternative way of doing justice both to biblical data and to common experience, by regarding body, mind, and spirit as entities recognizable at three different *levels of significance* of our mysterious and complex human nature, rather than as three different kinds of "stuff" that somehow exert forces on one another. According to this alternative view, which I like to call *comprehensive realism,* mental activity determines brain activity by being *embodied in it.* This does not mean that these are only three names for the same thing, nor that mental activity is "nothing but" brain activity. That is an example of the fallacy of metaphysical reductionism, or "nothing buttery," and is as absurd as to suggest that the equation embodied in the computer is "only another name" for the transistor network, or that mathematical relations are "nothing but" relations between computer parts. If there were any conflict here, it is our immediate experience as conscious agents that would have to take priority over any explanation at the level of our brains and bodies, however persuasive. But the point is that there need be no conflict. Each explanation bears witness to solid facts, although at different levels of significance. As we shall see, this way of thinking about man— as a unity with at least three levels of significance—is, if anything, more consonant with biblical emphases than is the Cartesian (tripartite or bipartite) model.

The moral I wish to draw is, not that we should all espouse comprehensive realism (although I personally do), but only that there exists at least one viable alternative to *Cartesian interactionism,* the doctrine that the mind or soul *interacts* with the brain or body by exerting *influences* on certain physical parts. The alternative we have considered, moreover, has nothing to fear from advances in mechanistic brain science; it can indeed positively welcome them. If that is so, then Christians have a responsibility to avoid giving the contrary impression, as if the biblical doctrine of the soul logically required some breakdown of physical cause-and-effect relationships in the brain. Here, as on so many other scientific questions, our Christian duty is to keep both our minds and our eyes open and obedient to whatever further data God may give us.

Lower Animals and Automata

If our capacity for conscious experience depends so directly on the structure of our brains, what are we to say of the capacities of lower animals, or, for that matter, of automata? The nerve cells making up the brain of a monkey, a dog, or a cat are very similar to our own. The principles on which our behavior is organized can, to some extent, be imitated by automata. Is there not then a "thin end of the wedge" argument for attributing some kind of mind or soul both to such animals and to automata?

Once again, our concern here is not to decide the issue one way or the other, but rather to evaluate the *logic* of such arguments from continuity. I see no biblical reason to deny that animals have conscious experience and (limited) mental ability; indeed the term *nefesh*, translated in Genesis 2:7 as "living soul," is elsewhere applied to lower animals. Recent work (Gardner and Gardner [1971]; Thorpe [1974]) has shown that even the rudiments of symbolic communication are within the capacities of chimpanzees trained to use the deaf-and-dumb alphabet. Similarly, as I have argued elsewhere (1965c, 1980, 1985), the Bible offers no objection in principle to the possibility that artificially constructed "brains" might embody some kind of conscious mentality—however speculative and impracticable such science-fiction notions may be. But the "argument from continuity" by itself is quite invalid. To take an obvious counterexample, a weak mixture of gas and air may contain the same kinds of molecules and lie on the same continuum as a richer mixture that burns; but this does nothing to prove that some kind of flame must be possible in the weaker mixture. Below a certain minimum concentration, the mixture is simply nonflammable. By the same token, the fact that a human brain organized in a specific way can embody conscious mental and spiritual life does nothing to prove that similar mental and spiritual capacities must be present in the brains of animals, still less in the artificial brains of automata built of different elements.

Now that this negative point has been made, it is important to put it in perspective. Why do so many atheistic propagandists try to make anti-Christian capital out of advances in the scope of artificial intelligence? Why have some Christian apologists felt it to be in their interests to minimize the powers of lower animals or of automata? I suspect the reason may be, on both sides, a hangover of the same "nothing buttery" thinking. If the biblical claim were that man is distinguished from lower animals and automata by having a brain sensitive to nonphysical influences, and that these nonphysical influences are what make his behavior essentially human, then of course the question of the capacities of animals or automata built of ordinary physical matter would become crucial. Once this claim is recognized as without biblical foundation, however, the polemical pressure disappears, and the whole issue becomes one of marginal interest to the biblical apologist, whose primary duty regarding it is to keep an open mind.

Immortality

So far, our discussion has been tied strictly to experience here and now. But the example of the computer, with its two levels of significance, seems to raise a difficulty when we face biblical teaching regarding the hereafter. After all, if a computer were destroyed physically, that would be the end also of its mathematical significance. Does not this suggest that when our brains are destroyed at death, our mental and spiritual life ends too?

Although such arguments from analogy must be handled with care, I believe that this one has an element of truth in it. There is a real biblical sense in which death is the end of our agency in this space-time framework. But the very same example suggests a possibility which, in fact, seems more in harmony with the biblical emphasis on resurrection of the body than does the Cartesian solution. If a computer solving an equation is destroyed, the mathematicians can, if they wish, set up the very same equation again in some new embodiment. This need not be a computer identical to the old, and certainly need not reuse the original components in order to be recognizably an embodiment of the same equation.

In 1 Corinthians 15, which gives our most explicit teaching on the Christian hope of eternal life, we find a remarkably similar emphasis. We are given no promise of *physical* continuity, let alone identity, between our present body and the resurrection body. As when a grain of wheat is sown, the blade that rises from the ground is a quite different structure, so at death we are "sown as an animal body, . . . raised as a spiritual body" (1 Cor. 15:44, NEB). The continuity implied is, rather, at the level of our personal relationship with God; the personality that is ours will find expression in a new embodiment, perhaps unimaginably different from our present one, but still having the same essential structure of dispositions and interrelationships, both internal and external, that identifies and distinguishes us as individuals here and now.

Attempts have been made to discredit the biblical doctrine by suggesting that such a resurrected individual ought to be regarded as a mere *copy* of the original. This argument seems strangely perverse. Nothing is more universally accepted than our daily experience of waking up to find ourselves *the same individuals* who went to sleep the night before. Despite all kinds of metabolic changes in bodily tissues, nobody in his senses would argue that he is today a "mere copy" of what he was last night. Mysterious though the idea of resurrection may be, there would seem to be no basic *logical* difference between the problem of personal identity upon waking up in another world and personal identity upon waking up in this world. The objective reference in either case must of course be ontologically to the *fiat* of our Creator, to whom we owe our continuing identity moment by moment, day by day. If he knows and recognizes us in the resurrection as those whom he knew in the days of our flesh, then by the same token, that is who we are in fact, for it is our Creator who alone determines and gives being to what is the case.

Even the most mechanistic brain-science, then, offers no objection in principle to the possibility that our Creator might bring into being a sequel to our earthly career and in that sequel bring to eternal fruition (for good or ill) the solemn consequences of our dealings with him here and now.

Responsibility

Here (if not before) someone may be inclined to protest. Even if mechanistic brain-science has no valid objections to the biblical doctrine of the soul or of the resurrection, surely it must question whether we as individuals can be held *responsible* for "the deeds done in the body." If my brain were as mechanical as a computing machine, would it not be physical forces, rather than my decisions, that determine my actions?

I have discussed this question at length elsewhere (1960, 1965a, 1973, 1974, 1979) and must here be brief. I believe that it rests on a fallacy—the same fallacy of "nothing buttery" that we noted earlier. The question presupposes a certain exclusiveness: *either* my actions are determined by my decisions *or* they are determined by physical forces. But where we are dealing with explanations at different levels, this assumption of exclusiveness is baseless. At one level a computer's behavior is determined by the equation it is solving; at another level it is determined by physical forces. To suggest that if one of these explanations is true, the other must be false or redundant, is to talk sheer nonsense.

It is equally nonsensical, and for the same logical reason, to argue that my brain processes *must* be inexplicable in mechanistic terms if my actions are determined by my decisions. This ignores the possibility that the brain processes are precisely the *necessary correlate*, at the mechanistic level, of the mysterious process I know in conscious experience as "making up my mind." In view of our present ignorance, nobody can say whether, in fact, my brain workings always proceed entirely according to physical laws; but even if they did operate in that way, I could not on those grounds rationally deny, or be denied, responsibility for my actions.

But, you may say, if physical laws ruled all my brain workings, would not the outcome of my making up my mind be inevitable? Here we must make a crucial distinction. *For an observer* who is physically incapable of interfering with me, the outcome of my decision process could well be inevitable, in the sense that (by definition) he could do nothing to affect it and might even be able *(ex hypothesi)* to predict it with certainty. But—and this is the crucial point—even though inevitable-for-him, the outcome would not in general be *inevitable-for-me*. *Inevitability* is essentially a *relative* term. An event inevitable-for-A need not be inevitable-for-B. In particular, we shall see that there will be some events in B's brain that would not be inevitable-for-B, even if his brain were as mechanical as a computer.

The proof of this is quite short, though the result digs deep. According to brain science, there must be some mechanism in B's brain which represents by its physical state *what B believes*. Let us call this mechanism M. By definition, no change can take place in what B believes without a correlated change in M. It follows that no completely detailed specification of the present or immediately future state of M would be equally correct whether or not B believed it. (If it were correct *before* B believed it, then it must be incorrect in some detail *after* B comes to believe it; conversely, if the specification were adjusted so that it would *become* correct if and when M were changed by B's believing it, then it would not be correct *unless* B believed it.) In this strict sense, then, the immediate future of M is not *inevitable-for-B*. By this I mean that no complete specification of it exists, unknown to B, with an *unconditional claim to B's assent*. The truth is, rather, that in some details at least, the immediate future of M is *up to B*, in the sense that what B thinks and believes will determine the correctness or otherwise of any purported specification of it, and there is no unique specification of it that B would be logically bound to accept as inevitable, to the exclusion of all others, if only he knew it. The details in question are *logically indeterminate* for B.

It follows that B cannot logically argue that any decision causally dependent on those details of M was inevitable-for-him. The truth, rather, is that such decisions were strictly *up to him* in the foregoing sense, no matter how physically determinate the workings of his brain.

Note that so far we have been discussing a normally functioning individual in whom the process of deciding and acting depends directly or indirectly on what he knows and believes. If through brain damage, drugs, *force majeure*, or the like, the normal link between M and the action centers of the brain is cut or overridden, then the outcome may cease to be logically indeterminate for the agent, and may become inevitable for him. To the extent to which this happens, there would then be logical grounds for denying or diminishing the responsibility we attribute to him for that outcome. One of the challenges offered by brain science to Christians especially is to clarify the rationale of arguments for reducing the accountability of criminals for their actions, arguments which are often quite inadequately based on claims that "physical causes" or "psychological causes" made them "inevitable." In the light of the foregoing, there is a clear need to distinguish two questions. The first concerns the strength of the alleged evidence for causal connections between particular factors and behavior. The notorious "XYY-chromosome" abnormality, for example, seems to have been much overrated as an indicator of criminal tendencies (Borgaonkar and Shah [1974]; Hook [1973]). Explanations of behavior in social terms are often even more shaky. It would be a great mistake, however, to imagine that such explanations ought to be minimized *in order* to maintain a belief in human responsibility. The force of the argument above is that even if causal explanations of behavior in such terms were complete, this would not necessarily diminish the responsibility of the human agent.

The relevant question highlighted by the argument is not whether (or how far) an action was *predictable* (by a detached observer) in practice or in principle, but whether and to what extent it was *inevitable for the agent*. All too often, an answer to the first question is taken (by both sides) as if it were an answer to the second. The foregoing argument makes clear that it is not. Christians accustomed to living responsibly under divine sovereignty should not find this too surprising.

The Damaged Brain

Despite the delicate intricacy of the nervous system, a remarkable amount of damage can be done to certain large areas of the brain without causing death. A bullet wound in the occipital lobes at the back of the head, for example, may merely leave the patient with a permanent localized "blind spot." Excision of tissue to remove a tumor from so-called association areas may have still less easily detected effects. Even after such a drastic operation as the separation of the two hemispheres by cutting the millions of connecting fibers in the corpus callosum, a patient may seem surprisingly normal to superficial observation.

If the brain embodies the human personality in the sense we have been exploring, a Christian is bound to ask the effect of such brain damage on the spiritual status of the individual and the spiritual significance of any resulting changes in his personality. Whereas damage to the occipital lobes of the brain may make no more difference to the personality than the loss of sight in an eye, a corresponding loss of brain tissue or connecting fibers from the frontal lobes (above the eyes) can turn a formerly civilized and restrained individual into an uninhibited and inconsiderate boor (Teuber [1964, 1972]). Damage to one of the parietal lobes (roughly above the ear) can lead to a patient's completely neglecting the opposite side of his body, and even denying that it is his. Most dramatically of all, after the split-brain operation mentioned above, it is possible for the opposite halves of the brain to develop *incompatible* goals (Gazzaniga [1970]). One unfortunate patient found that when he was buttoning up his trousers with his right hand, his left hand would push past the right and unbutton them again!

Startling though such observations are, it would be a mistake to regard as novel the issues they raise. Mankind has known since the discovery of alcohol that damage to the functioning of the brain (in this case via its blood supply) can radically transform personality. Because drunkenness is normally a reversible condition, we tend to solve the problem by associating the identity of the individual with his sober state, saying that he is "not himself" when drunk. Deterioration of the brain in senility presents a different, though equally long-standing, problem. Here we find ourselves having to say that the patient is "not the man he was."

Doubtless, as we grow more accustomed to the newer forms of personality disturbance caused by brain surgery, we shall develop verbal ways of coping with the mystery of the resulting transformation. A mystery, however, it remains: a mystery of which death itself is the ultimate exemplar. In a case of sudden death we are spared the need to speculate about the status of half-mangled personalities. What cases of brain damage force us to consider is the possibility of the death of a personality without the death of the body that once expressed it, leaving a half-personality that may be so different as to lack essential spiritual continuity with the one who is no more.

In this context what the Christian must recognize is that the entry into eternal life offered by Christ is something far more and other than a mere extrapolation of the personality as it exists at the point of death. The stuff of eternal life, as the Gospel of John in particular makes clear, is the relationship formed in our present life with the eternal Son. It is by virtue of this relationship that we can be known by the Father and can be welcomed to eternal bliss in the resurrection. The events in our lives that have sealed our relationship with Christ are in no way annulled by death. Thus if, through brain damage, the death of our personality takes place by stages, there is no more reason to fear the eternal consequences than if those stages were telescoped into one. What matters is always and only the covenant of grace entered into while the personality was entire and undamaged.

I am painfully aware that this does not answer all the theological questions raised by the aftereffects of surgery on or accident to the brain; but I believe that, for spiritual purposes, the general principle of focusing on the relationships formed with God while the individual was capable of them, and thinking of brain damage as a first installment of death, is fully consonant with biblical teaching. If no one can snatch from Christ's hand those to whom he has given eternal life, we may be sure that no brain damage can do so either, however horrendous the behavioral consequences of that damage for the remaining span of bodily existence.

The Challenge to the Christian

Let me end by mentioning a few summary implications of what I have said.

1. It is vital that Christian apologists for the dignity of man should not rest their case upon arbitrary "postulates of impotence" such as, "You'll never find a scientific explanation for such-and-such." We may or may not in the end succeed in explaining or predicting the bulk of human behavior on a scientific basis; but to pretend that there are any *biblical* grounds for predicting failure would be totally unwarranted. Christianity has no stakes in our ignorance of the physical causes of brain events. Its concern is that we should see and reckon adequately with what they *mean* at the personal level.

2. We must beware of confusing claims about *brains* with claims about *people*. For example, it is not brains but people—conscious cognitive agents—that think. Their brains doubtless go through corresponding motions, embodying their thoughts much as a computer embodies an equation; but it makes no sense to describe the brain (or the computer, for that matter), *qua* physical mechanism, as "thinking." Similarly, it is people, not their brains, who make choices, freely or otherwise. As we have seen, there need be no contradiction in saying that a person's brain is physically determinate, and saying that the person (as a cognitive agent) has several possible courses of action— any more than in saying that a computer is physically determinate, yet

the equation that determines its behavior has several possible solutions.

3. One of the greatest temptations of Christian apologists is to *go beyond their biblical brief* in their eagerness to erect would-be lines of defense. With regard to those aspects of human nature that concern the scientist, the biblical data are much more reticent than is commonly supposed. As Reijer Hooykaas has remarked in another connection (1972), we are all too ready, like Uzzah, to put out our hands unbidden to steady the ark (2 Sam. 6:6). We cannot remind ourselves too often that our brains, like the rest of our world, are God's workmanship in all their intricate detail. He is affronted if we presume to tell him in advance how they must—or must not—function in order to leave room for our spiritual nature and eternal destiny.

4. In contending with destructive reductionism, or "nothing buttery," one of the best services that Christian apologists can render is to remind people of simple ontological priorities. For biblical theists, the only ultimate reality is God; what is real is what God holds in being. It is God who brings into being and holds in being the world in which we find ourselves, including our own brains. It is he who gives us moment by moment the flux of our experience as conscious agents. Since it is only in and through that experience that we gain scientific (or any other) knowledge of the world of physical objects, including our own brains, there can be no question of our scientific knowledge throwing in doubt the reality of ourselves as conscious agents. If there were any conflict, the doubt would have to be the other way around! Even in science it is to the conscious experience of other observers that we appeal in order to resolve questions of objectivity and reality. Thus the practice of science itself is built on a recognition that people have ontological priority over things: our fellow scientists, as conscious beings, are more indubitably "real" than anything we may collectively believe about the world around us. Nothing could be more fraudulent than the pretense that science requires or justifies a materialist ontology in which ultimate reality is granted only to what can be weighed and measured, and in which human consciousness is reduced to a mere epiphenomenon. Even apart from biblical considerations, this is to stand reality on its head.

5. But the greatest challenge offered by brain research, I suggest, is not so much to our theoretical understanding of ourselves as to our practical compassion for our fellow human beings. Once the nonsense of "nothing buttery" has been exposed, each advance in our knowledge of brain processes is to be welcomed in principle as enhancing our sensitivity to one another's vulnerabilities, as increasing our respect for one another's strengths, and as extending our capacities to do one

another good. The fateful effects of malnutrition on infant brain development (Wurtman and Fernstrom [1974]); the vital importance of social and environmental factors in the maturation of personality (Jeeves [1978, 1984]); the risks of unethical manipulation, whether by psychological or physicochemical means (Wolstenholme [1963]); the possibilities (as yet, alas, primitive and limited) of scientifically based psychotherapy (Bergin and Garfield [1971])—our rapidly growing knowledge under these and similar heads daily adds fresh dimensions to our responsibility both to discern its right use and to guard against its abuse. Here science as such is not enough. Although knowledge of the scientific "map" is essential, and would-be guides who are ignorant of its details can be a menace, the choice of a route is not exclusively the business of the mapmaker. Christians can claim no monopoly of wisdom in such a task, but they surely have a special duty to contribute positively and constructively to the effort to do it justice, as in the sight of God its giver.

References

Bergin, A., and S. Garfield, eds. (1971). *The handbook of psychotherapy and behavior change*. New York: Wiley.

Berkouwer, G. (1962). *Man: The image of God*. Grand Rapids: Eerdmans.

Borgaonkar, D., and S. Shah (1974). The XYY chromosome male—or syndrome? In *Progress in medical genetics*, vol. 10, ed. A. Steinberg. New York: Grune & Stratton.

Eccles, J. (1970). *Facing reality*. New York: Springer-Verlag.

Gardner, B., and R. Gardner (1971). Two-way communication with a chimpanzee. In A. M. Schrier and F. Stollnitz, eds., *Behavior of non-human primates*, vol. 4. New York: Academic Press.

Gazzaniga, M. (1970). *The bisected brain*. New York: Appleton-Century-Crofts.

Hook, E. (1973). Behavioral implications of the human XYY genotype. *Science* 179: 139–50.

Hooykaas, R. (1972). *Religion and the rise of modern science*. Edinburgh: Scottish Academic Press.

Jeeves, M. (1978). Psychological knowledge and Christian commitment. In C. Henry, ed., *Horizons of science: Christian scholars speak out*, pp. 193–216. San Francisco: Harper & Row.

_____, ed. (1984). *Behavioural sciences: A Christian perspective*. London: InterVarsity.

MacKay, D. (1960). On the logical indeterminacy of a free choice. *Mind* 69: 31–40.

_____ (1962). The use of behavioural language to refer to mechanical processes. *British Journal of the Philosophy of Science* 13: 89–103.

_____ (1965a). Information and prediction in human sciences. In S. Dock and P. Bernays, eds., *Information and prediction in science*. New York: Academic Press.

_____ (1965b). A mind's-eye view of the brain. In N. Wiener and J. P. Schade, eds., *Cybernetics of the nervous system*. Progress in brain research, vol. 17. New York: Elsevier.

_____ (1965c). From mechanism to mind. In J. R. Smythies, ed., *Brain and mind*. London: Routledge and Kegan Paul.

_____ (1973). The logical indeterminateness of human choices. *British Journal of Philosophy of Science* 24: 405–08.

_____ (1974). *The clockwork image: A Christian perspective on science*. Downers Grove, Ill.: Inter-Varsity.

_____ (1979). *Human science and human dignity*. Downers Grove, Ill.: Inter-Varsity.

_____ (1980). *Brains, machines, and persons*. Grand Rapids: Eerdmans.

_____ (1985). Machines, brains, and persons. *Zygon* 20.4: 401–12.

Teuber, H. (1964). The riddle of the frontal lobe function in man. In J. Warren and K. Akert, eds., *The frontal granular cortex and behavior*. New York: McGraw-Hill.

_____ (1972). Unity and diversity of frontal lobe functions. *Acta Neurobiologiae Experimentalis* 32: 615–56.

Thorpe, W. (1974). *Animal nature and human nature*. London: Methuen.

Wolstenholme, G., ed. (1963). *Man and his future*. London: Churchill.

Wurtman, R., and J. Fernstrom (1974). Nutrition and the brain. In F. Schmitt and F. Worden, eds., *The neurosciences: Third study program*. Cambridge, Mass.: MIT Press.

Perception, Relativity, and Knowing and Doing the Truth

Bert H. Hodges

The study of the psychology of human perception is a humbling experience during which one is confronted with all the foibles of the human capacity to know. Research into illusions, bias in perception, and related phenomena undermines one's confidence about whether we can really know anything for certain.

For the Christian, these findings produce some special tensions, in that we fancy ourselves to know the truth. Perhaps only partially, perhaps imperfectly, but we do believe that we are able to know truth. One should recognize that such findings create real problems for the scientist as well, who is in the business of finding out what this world is about. It is a curious thing for scientists to be conducting studies in perception which call into question their own capacity to know anything truly.

It is to these issues that this chapter is addressed. It will prove challenging, but the reader who mines its depths will find in it some very good suggestions for struggling with these complex issues.

Bert H. Hodges (B.A., Wheaton College; Ph.D., Vanderbilt University) is professor of psychology at Gordon College. A social

This chapter is a revision of "Perception Is Relative and Veridical" by Bert H. Hodges in *The Reality of Christian Learning*, edited by Harold Heie and David Wolfe (Grand Rapids: Christian Universities Press, in press).

*psychologist with specialized interests in social cognition, he has pub-
lished a variety of journal articles and contributed chapters to a number
of books. He has also served as a visiting research professor at the University of California at Santa Barbara and at Rutgers University.*

Introductory psychology textbooks often do a strange thing.
In an early chapter they state that psychology is a science and proceed
to describe science as an objective, impersonal, and bias-free method
for determining the truth about reality. Then in a later chapter they
state that perception is the process by which the sensory inputs from
ears, eyes, and other receptors are organized so that they become
meaningful. The perceptual processes, particularly vision, are usually
described in ways that stress their subjective nature, their proneness
to bias as a result of personal needs and beliefs, and their susceptibility
to illusion and error. In short, introductory texts tell us that we can
trust science but cannot always trust our own perceptions. It seems
not to have occurred to the authors of these texts that much of the
"objective" scientific activity they praise is based on the "subjective,
error-prone" perceptions they bemoan.

I want to suggest that science is more subjective and perception is
more objective than introductory accounts usually indicate. In fact,
what I really want to suggest is that we would do well to rethink the
whole idea of objectivity and subjectivity if we want to understand
how people know the truth, both in everyday perception and in science.

This is a lot to try to do in a short chapter, but I hope at least to help
the readers appreciate the mystery of perception and to encourage
them to ask new questions about knowing truth. College students
often express frustration over the continual questioning characteristic
of a liberal-arts education and the lack of clear, certain answers.
"Asking a better question" is not what they came to college for. But, as I
will argue later, the humility of asking questions, even if they are new,
or difficult, or disturbing ones, is a necessary discipline for any saint,
scientist, or student who wants to know the truth. The truth of reality—God, the world, and ourselves—is always mysterious. True science and true Christianity encourage us to notice and value these
mysteries. Take, for example, something as commonplace as breathing. Science helps us appreciate the awesome complexity of this activity which we take for granted, and the Bible makes plain that
breathing is a grant, a gift from God that should be returned to him in
praise and service. So if this chapter gives its readers a sense of mys-

tery about perception, science, Christianity, and truth, I will be glad. It is the reason I wrote it.

Relativity and Perception

Relativity as a problem

By the time we get to college most of us have figured out that we do not know "the truth, the whole truth, and nothing but the truth" about the world. What we may not have thought about carefully is why this is so. Let me offer three reasons why our perceptual knowledge is not perfect.

First, the world is complex and the information available to a perceiver may be ambiguous. When I was in first grade we were asked to draw a robin with our crayons. When I colored the breast of my robin orange, I was informed by my teacher that robins are red-breasted. We argued. I was horrified at her ignorance, and she, no doubt, was horrified at my impudence. Part of what led to our unfortunate disagreement was that there is no precise boundary where red stops and orange starts, only a fuzzy one. Most of the perceptual categories we use daily have such fuzzy boundaries (Labov [1973]; Rosch and Mervis [1975]).

Second, perceivers are finite and can attend to only a tiny fraction of the information available to them. Shelley Taylor and Susan Fiske (1975) had two persons carry on a conversation that was prearranged to be equal in almost every measurable way. As shown in Figure 1, six persons sat around the conversants and listened. Typically, observers A and B thought that person Y had dominated the conversation while observers E and F thought that conversant X had dominated. Observers C and D tended to see the conversation as the equal exchange that it was. Why? Taylor and Fiske argue convincingly that the focus of attention for observers A and B was Y (they could see her face), while the focus of E and F was X, and that we are biased in our perceptions toward the focus of our attention. In short, what we pay attention to affects our judgments more than does what we do not notice. Humans, by virtue of being finite, are forced to be choosers; we must notice some aspects of reality and miss others.

Third, perception is constrained by the prior experience of the perceiver. Lack of prior experience may make it difficult or impossible to pick up available information. If a person has never seen Chinese people, never listened to rock music, or never drunk wine, he will probably be quite poor at recognizing the differences between particular Chinese people, rock songs, or wines. They will all look alike, sound alike, or taste alike. On the other hand, prior experiences often set up "expectancies" that cause us to "see" what is not there, as the following story

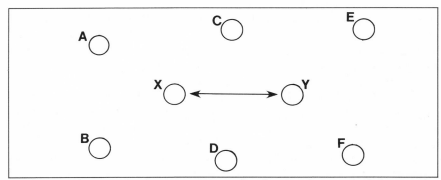

FIGURE 1. **The seating arrangement in the Taylor and Fiske study.**
Adapted from "Point of View and Perception of Causality," *Journal of*
Personality and Social Psychology **32: 441.**

illustrates. A woman shopping for groceries heard a young child
scream, "Stop, stop, you're killing my father!" She turned the corner
(with definite expectancies) and saw a large man on top of another
man whose head was all bloody. Thinking she had witnessed a mur-
derous assault, she ran for help. When she returned she discovered that
the "murder" she would have sworn in court she had seen was not a
murder at all. The man sprawled out on the floor had had an epileptic
seizure and fallen, hitting and cutting his head. The second man had
tried to prevent further injury by loosening the victim's tie and holding
his head up. The woman realized on her second look that there was
only a small amount of blood from a quite minor cut, and that the
"murderer" was rather small and a neighbor of hers (Coon [1977]).

Introductory treatments of perception often raise the kinds of issues
I have just illustrated. They usually do *not* mention these problems in
regard to science, but they should. Science can be thought of as a
community perceiving some aspect of reality from a particular point
of view. Like everyday perception scientific perception is limited and
imperfect. The reality it seeks to explain is complex and often ambiguous. And scientific research is finite: selected observations employing
limited methods under particular conditions are used to answer specific questions. Scientists do not and cannot look at everything. Finally, how informative research is depends on the prior knowledge and
expectations of the scientists doing the research.

Another way of saying what I have just described is to say that
science is inherently theoretical. The traditional view of science that
says, "Collect all the facts and let them speak for themselves," is simply
naive. What facts are we to collect? Facts, as we call them, cannot even
be identified, much less described or explained, independently of the-

ory, as the following example illustrates. Which of the following data are relevant to the question, "What causes nosebleeds?" The astrological sign under which a person was born? The current phase of the moon? The color of a person's eyes? The temperature of the room? I would have been unlikely to pick phases of the moon as relevant data, but I once read an article in a psychiatric journal that proposed that the phases of the moon and nosebleeds are causally related. Now the point of this example is not that psychiatrists propose crazy theories (although they sometimes do!), but that they, like any scientific observers for that matter, do not know what to notice, measure, or describe unless they have some theory. The "nasal tides" theory may be wrong, but lots of scientific theories we now find sensible once sounded like the fantasies of lunatics. (And on the very subject of lunatics, testing the theory that the full moon is related to bizarre behavior would itself involve the researcher's *theories* as to what constitutes bizarre behavior!)

Since facts are defined, related, and explained only in theoretical contexts, scientific research can never absolutely and logically prove or disprove any scientific theory. The logic of this argument can be shown with a simple, nonscientific example. Suppose you are a detective hired to explain the dead body lying on the marble floor of Dame Edith's mansion. You suspect foul play (theory has already crept in) and after preliminary questions prompted by your suspicion you theorize that "the butler did it." On the basis of your theory you hypothesize that if the butler did it the bloody footprints next to the corpse should be those of a man. You measure the footprints and decide they are those of a man. (Note that your methodology involves a theory regarding footprints: their measurements relate to the gender of the person who left them.) Can you conclude the butler did it since the evidence supports your theory? Obviously not (although I find it surprising how many students will make this mistake if the example is a scientific one further removed from their everyday experience). On the other hand, suppose you decide the bloody footprints are those of a woman in high heels. Would your "the butler did it" theory be falsified? Perhaps not. Maybe the butler is a transvestite! Or maybe he is just cunning and wore the high heels to make you think Dame Edith or the scullery maid is the culprit. In any event it is unlikely that you will easily relinquish your theory. If and when you do give it up, it will probably be in favor of a better theory, not simply because of inconsistent facts. At least this is what Thomas Kuhn (1970) argues is historically true of scientists. Theory testing is always a choice among competing theoretical statements: "No theory forbids some state of affairs specifiable in advance; it is not that we propose a theory and

Nature may shout NO. Rather, we propose a maze of theories, and Nature may shout INCONSISTENT" (Lakatos [1968], p. 162).

So far I have illustrated that perception and science are *relative*, that they depend on the perceiver (whether scientist or layman) as well as the information available to him. In this sense perception and science are *subjective*. Notice that the emphasis so far has been on what the perceiver or scientist *cannot* do, on what limitations, omissions, or distortions might occur in perception or science. So far we have implied that relativity is a *problem*. Now it is important to note these limitations imposed by our being finite, but it is equally important not to jump to inappropriate conclusions regarding our ability to know the truth about the world. The temptation is to turn relativity into relativism, the view that we all live in our own make-believe worlds, that we may see, or hear, or theorize anything we wish. Richard Gregory (1972), a well-known perceptual psychologist, seems to hold such a view: "Normal everyday perceptions are not selections of reality but are rather imaginative constructions. . . essentially fictions." To counter the view that relativity means relativism we will now flip the coin of relativity over to show its more profound and positive side.

The value of relativity

If one looks at the perceptually guided actions of organisms, for example, walking through a cluttered room without barking one's shins, or threading a needle, or recognizing an old friend's voice or face after an absence of two decades, it appears that they are enormously successful in adapting to their environment. Theories of perception should account for the fact that perception is generally *veridical* (true to the world). However, most theories of perception have assumed that the information available to the senses is too impoverished or ambiguous to specify adequately the nature of the environment. For example, these theories note that the tiny upside-down image on the retina of an eye does not contain information sufficient for the perceiver to know unambiguously the three-dimensional layout of his environment. The insufficient information is assumed to be supplemented in some way by cognitive operations (e.g., inference, memory, imagination) so that the character of the world can be known. Thus, traditional theories stress that perception is *indirect:* certain things (e.g., a retinal image, the state of our nerves) come between us and the objects and events of the world we wish to know so that vital information is either lost or distorted.

In the next few pages I will outline several key points of a theory of perception that is radically at odds with the traditional theories described in most introductory texts. It tries to do justice to the fact that perceiving is an activity that puts us in touch with the world instead of hiding the truth of the world from us. And it takes the relativity of perception even more seriously than do traditional theories. The theory of which I speak is James Gibson's (1966, 1979) ecological theory of perception. Gibson argues perception is *direct:* the information available in light and sound, for example, offers a sufficient specification of the properties of the world to allow a properly tuned perceiver to adapt meaningfully to his or her environment. The media in which the information is embodied (e.g., light, the nervous system) are transparent to the information. For example, we do not see light but the objects off which it bounces; light is transparent to the optical structure of the world. Perceivers need not infer or mentally construct what the world is like; they are in direct contact with it whether they are touching, looking, or listening.

There are several reasons for focusing on Gibson's ecological theory of perception. The theory is rarely described, or at least described well, in textbooks. In fact many texts do not provide a coherent account of any perceptual theory, so this account may help organize things a bit for the reader. A second reason for my use of Gibson's theory is that I think it is more adequate than alternative theories, even though it is not without its problems and flaws (some of which I will mention). Finally, the themes that the ecological theory highlights are ones that naturally relate to larger questions about truth and faith.

I will outline three main themes of the ecological theory: (1) invariants, (2) affordances, and (3) effectivities. To put these themes in everyday language: (1) perception depends on a true relationship between an organism and its environment; (2) perception is meaningful; and (3) perception depends on action to be accurate and action depends on perception to be effective.

1. Invariants: the clarity of perception. For Gibson perceptual systems are attuned to *invariants,* unchanging patterns within the general flux of energy (i.e., of light, sound, etc.). For example, the horizon is a reference line "perpendicular to the pull of gravity" by which a person judges when something is upright or tilted, including oneself (Gibson [1979], p. 164). The invariant horizon can also specify the sizes of objects, for it cuts objects of the same size into the same ratio. No matter how close to or far from the observer, objects divided by the horizon into the same ratio are the same height. Moreover, the horizon cuts objects at the height of the observer's eyes. Thus in Figure 2 tree B is three times the height of the observer's eyes (⅔ is above the horizon), while trees A, C, and D are only twice the height (½ is above the horizon).

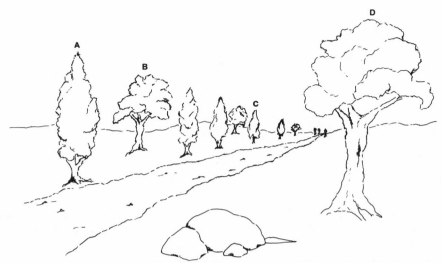

FIGURE 2. **Which of the trees in this scene is the tallest? See the text for the answer.**

The previous example involved object perception. There are invariants of event perception as well. If, for instance, every part of my visual field begins to move outward as illustrated in Figure 3 (this is called optical outflow), what I am perceiving is that I am moving forward through a stable environment. Vision alone indicates self-movement even without feedback from muscles and joints. Even more significantly, where I am going is indicated by the unmoving center of the optical outflow. This center of optical expansion is the reference point by which I can control my locomotion.

Perceptual invariants demonstrate that the world is structured in nonarbitrary ways that allow us to know what is true about our environment as we relate to it. Veridical perception is made possible by these "absolute" reference points (lines, relations), and many of these invariants appear to hold universally, for all humans and many other animals. While much is variable in the world, some things do not change. Invariant relationships provide the *clarity* of perception.

Some of the examples of ambiguity in the first part of this chapter seem less severe when reexamined in this light. For instance, we may disagree about whether robins are red- or orange-breasted, but no teacher would have told me that robins are green-breasted! Research (Berlin and Kay [1969]; Heider [1972]; Rosch [1973, 1975]) has shown that colors are perceived much the same the world over even though there are fuzzy boundary disagreements and even though some languages do not have specific terms for certain colors (e.g., green, brown,

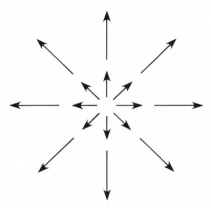

FIGURE 3: **An optical expansion pattern that, when occurring over the whole visual field, specifies movement of the observer toward the point at the center.**

pink). The errors and disagreements about the world are real and sometimes serious, but they do not occur in an amorphous, undifferentiated world. The world may not be black and white but it is not a dull, undifferentiated gray either.

2. Affordances: the coherence of perception. Gibson's ecological theory says that what organisms perceive is "information," invariants detected over temporal and spatial transformations. Information is something specific to an object or an event that differentiates it from other objects or events. The punch line is: something can be known only *in relation to* something else. Knowledge is relative.

Even the invariants illustrated in the previous section are relative; all involve relationships. The information gleaned from the invariant horizon was related to the height of the perceiver's eye and expressed in ratios, the mathematical term for relationships. Events are movements by one or more objects through space over a period of time. Time and movement are inherently relative. For example, a melody is an invariant set of temporal and tonal relations. Since invariants are relative, the absolute values (e.g., G above middle C) of the members of the relationship are irrelevant. Thus, we can transpose a melody across keys and play it on different instruments: the melody of the opening line of Beethoven's Fifth Symphony is the same when played by a violin or trumpet, sung by a soprano or a bass, performed in the key of C or E-flat. All of these are different embodiments of the same melodic structure; their differences are irrelevant to the melody.

If the absolute value of an element in a relationship remains unchanged but the relationship changes, we perceive a change. A simple example is that the same color can be perceived differently: when an orange of a certain wavelength is put on a black background, it appears to be a different shade from when it is placed on a white background. We perceive relationships, not objects in isolation.

What an organism perceives and *how* it perceives it cannot be described unless we know the organism that is doing the perceiving (Shaw and McIntyre [1974]). What can be detected by one animal cannot be detected by another. Heat patterns identify warm-blooded prey for rattlesnakes, and ultraviolet radiation patterns locate nectar for honeybees. What is information for rattlesnakes and bees is not information for humans. Even when two animals can both detect the same thing, it may be perceived differently. For my cat a window sill "affords" sleeping. It does not for me. Even for two animals of the same species, the "affordances" attended to may differ depending on their ecological habitat and their behavioral purposes. Indeed, the same organism may perceive the same object in different ways at different times. A fry pan can be perceived as a means of cooking fish or a weapon to fling (which affordance the individual notices depends on whether one is hungry or angry).

"The *affordances* of the environment are what it *offers* the animal, what it *provides* or *furnishes*, either for good or ill" (Gibson [1979], p. 127). Thus, the affordance of an object or event is the *meaning* it has for a given animal. Meaning is neither subjective nor objective, but relative to both the animal and its environment; it is the *coherence* between an animal and its ecological niche. When an animal perceives the meaning (affordance) of an object, it is detecting what behaviors it can enter into with respect to the object (e.g., whether it can eat, sit on, or throw the object).

An object can have multiple meanings because it can enter multiple relationships. As noted earlier, a frying pan can be used for (can mean) quite different things. Objects afford much more than we notice, but there are constraints on the meanings an object can have. Some constraints are relative to the organism (e.g., I cannot lie down on a window sill), while others reflect environmental relations (e.g., household scissors do not afford cutting sheet metal no matter how strong I am).

3. *Effectivities: the comprehensiveness of perception.* Traditional perceptual theory has assumed that movement makes perception more difficult; however, Gibson's theory suggests that movement makes it possible to see the truth more clearly, not less. G. Johansson (1973) has provided an elegant and important demonstration of the role of movement in visual perception. Imagine that you are looking at a film showing a random arrangement of lights. Suddenly the lights move and you see not a random collection of lights, but a person, a person

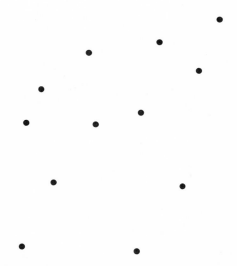

FIGURE 4.A.   "Random" pattern of lights attached to a nonmoving person (adapted from Michaels and Carello [1981], p. 29).

walking! Even the distinctive gait and the gender of the walking individual can be quickly and accurately detected (Cutting and Koslowski [1977]; Koslowski and Cutting [1977]). J. Maas (1971) has made such a film, and its effect is as fully dramatic as I have attempted to describe. As Figure 4 shows, the effect was created by attaching lights to the major joints of a human body dressed in black and filming in the dark. When the movement stops, the person seems to disappear and the impression of random lights reappears.

A fascinating set of experiments reveals that motion is a *necessity* for vision, not just a convenient way of resolving ambiguity. Due to the antagonistic muscle sets holding the eye in place, there is a constant slight movement of the eyes. Roy Pritchard (1961) and others have found that if an image is continuously projected onto exactly the same receptors of the retina, the perceived image disappears after a few seconds. The visual system will literally respond only to relationships, some temporal or spatial discontinuity. If the world held perfectly still and our eyes did not move, we would be blind.

The most important movements by which we discover the objects and events of our environment, however, are not the slight physiological movements of the eyes. The visual system includes a pair of eyes, which can move together, in a head that moves, attached to a body that moves. Since we are finite we have to move around in our

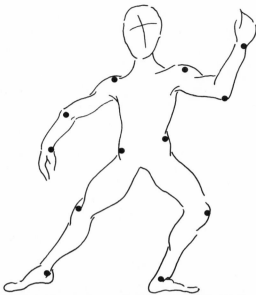

FIGURE 4.B. **Diagram of where lights were attached in Johansson experiments (adapted from Michaels and Carello [1981], p. 29).**

environment if we want to discover the invariants that reveal its true structure. For example, walking around the corner of an object we discover (literally uncover) optically another side of the object. If we look at it from all sides we begin to have a *comprehensive* view. The distorted room pictured in many introductory psychology textbooks where people appear to vary greatly in size has its effect precisely because we are allowed to look at the room from only one perspective. If we were allowed to look at the room from multiple perspectives, we would have no trouble discovering the truth that it is oddly shaped.

To discover the absolutes of the world, its invariants, we must *relativize* our perspective on it. Again Gibson sees and writes clearly: "Seeing the world at a traveling point of observation, over a long enough time for a sufficiently extended set of paths, begins to be perceiving the world at all points of observation, as if one could be everywhere at once. To be everywhere at once with nothing hidden is to be all-seeing, like God" (1979, p. 197). No one perspective on an object or event is as good as multiple perspectives for comprehending (visually grasping) the truth of the world. But knowing takes time and active exploration. Commitment is required to discover truth.

The truth of the world can be known by any observer who moves through it and extracts the invariants. Although two people cannot be in the same place simultaneously, they can share the same path of locomotion, and thus have available to them the same invariants (at least for those objects or events that are stable over time). Consequently, public knowledge is possible: we can all know the same world, although incompletely, as well as be aware of our own place in it.

Not only is action necessary to perception, but the reverse is also true; the primary purpose of perception is *effective action*. First, let us clarify the term *action*. Different animals can engage in different actions: a snake can slither, a bee can make honey, and a human can throw, but none can do the other two actions. The possible actions of an organism are called its *effectivities* (Michaels and Carello [1981]). Even members of the same species have different effectivities. I will probably never be able to play a sonata on a violin although some people can, but I can do psychological theorizing and research most people cannot. Effectivities are limited by biology (some people simply cannot run fast), our particular stage of development (first graders are not ready to read Shakespeare), and lack of learning (most people have not studied enough psychology to be good at it).

Effectivities are the flip side of affordances. If affordances are what the environment means to me, then effectivities are what I mean to my environment. Gibson's theory stresses that an organism and its ecological niche go together as part of a whole system. While traditional theories treat perceivers as independent of their environment and view meaning as something that an organism *invents* and *imposes* on a neutral environment, the ecological theory of perception treats meaning as objective, as something that is *discovered* by the organism as it interacts with its environment.

Second, how can we know if an action is "effective"? Only by knowing the purposes of the organism, what it *values*. As Clarence Lewis (1946) has put it: "The primary and pervasive significance of knowledge lies in its guidance of action: knowing is for the sake of doing. And action, obviously, is rooted in evaluation. For a being which did not assign comparative values, deliberate action would be pointless; and for one which did not know, it would be impossible" (p. 1). Every finite animal has to make choices and those choices reveal the organism's values. If an animal values living in the dark, then actions that move it into the light are ineffective. Actions guided by values are *behaviors*. To describe and explain the behaviors of an animal or person requires knowing something about the *identity* of the organism and the *purpose* of its existence. It is not hard to see that how a scientist answers the questions of identity and purpose depends on his or her values. This is an example of the general principle that scientific description is theory-dependent and value-laden, as I have discussed. Although theories of perception (and most scientific theories) ordinarily avoid asking these questions, proponents of the ecological theory of perception have raised them (e.g., Shaw and McIntyre [1974]). If they are pressed, the usual answer scientists, including psychologists, give to the question, "Why does this particular organism perceive what it does the way it does?" is "survival." I will argue later on both ecological and biblical grounds that this appeal to evolutionary theory and biological survival is an inadequate answer. But ecological theory is at least honest enough to raise the question.

Some implications

Subjective and objective. What we usually call "subjective" and "objective" are really only differing "poles of attention" (Gibson [1979]). The boundary between subjective and objective is a shifting one. Tools which are separate from us when they are not in use become part of us when in use. For example, we can *feel* the cutting action of the blades when we use a pair of scissors. A blind person using a white-tipped cane feels the sidewalk or grass as it is tapped. What is perceived (noticed) in these instances is information about an event (cutting) or an object (the sidewalk). One can, however, shift attention to the hand and its sensations as it cuts or taps; such a shift is from an objective perspective (what is the world like?) to a subjective perspective (what am I doing?).

To perceive is to know both the world and the self. An organism cannot be separated from its environment without losing its identity. To discover my environment is to discover how something relates to me; to discover who I am is to discover what I can know about my environment and do to it. Thus, meaning is neither mental ("in my head") nor impersonal (out there, unrelated to me). Knowing is ecological, both personal and true to the world.

Tacit knowledge. Perception is an activity, not an experience in consciousness. According to Gibson (1979), "perceiving is an achievement of the individual, not an appearance in the theater of his consciousness. . . . Perception is not a mental act. Neither is it a bodily act. Perceiving is a psychosomatic act, not of the mind or of the body but of a living observer" (pp. 239–40).

Perceptual knowledge of the world is *tacit*, to use Michael Polanyi's (1966) term. Tacit knowledge is what we know without necessarily experiencing it consciously or being able to describe it. Knowledge in general is more a matter of *knowing how* to do something (e.g., walk in a cluttered environment) than *knowing about* the doing. For example, a typist's knowledge is "in her fingers"; consequently, answering a verbal question about the keyboard (e.g., where is the colon?) is harder than actually typing. This example suggests a more general principle. Knowledge is embodied and dispersed. Knowing is a skilled interaction with the world and is dispersed throughout the body of the knower. Thus, knowing involves a restructuring (a constraining) of the body, its muscles, nervous system, and so on, not just an appearance in one's consciousness. In fact, if a typist thinks too much about what he or she is doing, speed and accuracy decrease. To learn about the world and act effectively in it often require that we be unselfconscious.

Most of our perceptual skills are tacit: neither the invariant relationships that make perception possible nor our perceptual activities in detecting those relationships are things of which we are ordinarily aware. When someone learns a new perceptual skill (attends to previously undetected invariants and their affordances), the new information *restructures* the perceiver so that he or she is a new person (i.e., has new effectivities). "The consequence of personal experience is not that the old animal has new knowledge, but that it is a new animal that knows better" (Michaels and Carello [1981], p. 78).

Error and truth. The ecological approach to perception does not rule out all ambiguity in the world or the possibility of illusion, but it does suggest a reassessment of what is meant by "error." What are the standards by which we judge truth or error in perception?

First, truth or error in perception can be identified only by comparison to what a more sufficient (comprehensive) sample of the available information has revealed to be true. Second, the truth (or error) of an animal's perception and the consequent effectiveness (or ineffectiveness) of its action must be evaluated with regard to the animal and its purposes. In this sense, what is true is relative, relative to the particular occasion. A prosaic example is provided by my two-year-old daughter who is struggling to understand why I call her a big girl one day and a little girl the next. Of course, it all depends on whether I am comparing her to a baby or a ten-year-old. What is big depends on both the organism that is doing the perceiving and its present purposes. The appropriateness of this sort of relativity is easily seen, but that other physical measurements must be ecological, not animal-neutral, is less well appreciated. An ecological approach to the phenomenon of color contrast (p. 60) suggests that wavelength, the classical and animal-neutral criterion by which physicists define color, is an inappropriate criterion for human perception of color. Other physical definitions, too complex to describe here but which take into account the relationships of all the wavelengths presented in a given situation (Land [1977]), seem better for describing the invariants that afford color vision in humans. Thus, a spectrometer which ignores relationships and reads out that two oranges, one on black and one on white, are identical is no truer a description than is a human's perception of the oranges as different. Spectrometers detect one invariant relationship; the human visual system detects another.

Finally, truth or error in perception can best be judged by focusing on the perceiver's actions over an extended period of time. If we were to define perception as the conscious awareness that results from the momentary activity of a single set of receptors (e.g., the eyes), perception would often be erroneous. However, such a definition is unecological and inappropriate, as we have seen, because perceiving involves activity over time and is primarily aimed at producing effective action rather than conscious ideas. For example, if I am in a desert and I become aware of a shimmering oasis in the distance, which is really a mirage, my conscious percept is erroneous. But if I walk toward the oasis, my perceptual systems will sooner or later reveal that it is only "more sand affording walking but not drinking." It is not clear that my walking toward what turns out to be a mirage should be called a mistake, however. As Michaels and Carello (1981) point out, if one were thirsty, "the mistake would be to take no action" (p. 95).

Truth, then, is more a matter of long-term action than momentary belief. In addition, truth for us and other animals is always relative and pragmatic rather than absolute and complete. Truth for us is a matter of *faith*. What is demanded by God and the world is not contemplative certitude, but action that "hunts for comprehension and clarity" in the interest of living. Humans have to *work* to know and live: they must grow, and learn, and persevere if they are to discover truth.

Science. The ecological approach suggests scientific knowledge is (1) limited and self-critical, (2) social, (3) tacit and dispersed, and (4) contextually constrained and value-laden. First, science is no different from ordinary perception in being finite and relative. Scientific theories are not absolutely comprehensive and clear; they do not capture all of the details and relationships of the world as known at the time. Aware of this limitation, Walter Weimer (1979) has argued that the rationality of science is found in "comprehensive criticism":

> Knowledge claims, whether scientific or otherwise, are always *fallible;* anything in both common sense and the "body of science" is subject to criticism and consequent revision or rejection, *at all times and for all time.* . . . Nothing in science is immune to criticism or justified fideistically, by appeal to authority. . . . The only way to defend fallible knowledge claims is by marshaling other fallible knowledge claims. [pp. 40–41]

Even the claim that the rationality of science is embodied in comprehensive criticism cannot avoid critical scrutiny. It too is a fallible knowledge claim!

Weimer's (1979) "comprehensively critical rationality" does *not*, however, rule out commitment:

> But is [a comprehensively critical] rationality "nothing but" the idea of being constantly critical? The answer is emphatically "no." . . . [For] what *counts* as criticism . . . is far from *obvious*. . . . In a broad, vague sense, to criticize a position or theory (scientific or otherwise) is to work within it, to explore and articulate it and examine its consequences. . . . Indeed there are times when being *committed* to a position (even dogmatically) may be an effective means of being critical. [pp. 48–49, 41]

Comprehensive criticism does not rule out faith commitment, only "blind faith." It is an indication that the rationality of science resides in humility; only individuals and communities that know their limits, that admit to errors and the need to learn more, can learn more.

Second, science is intrinsically social: it can be done only within a community. A communal character is necessary for at least two reasons: (1) the sheer enormity and complexity of the subject which any science tries to describe demand multiple perspectives; and (2) scientists must communicate with each other to share their perspectives and to engage in comprehensive criticism.

Third, scientific knowledge is tacit and dispersed. Scientists are not able to specify an explicit set of methodological rules that will guarantee them success. Scientists know more than they can tell. Like other human skills science can be learned only by doing (that is why it must be practiced in a laboratory). Since knowledge is dispersed as well as tacit, the community as a whole knows more than does any of its members (that is why publication of studies is so important). Furthermore, since scientific knowledge is dispersed, it defies "conscious planning and explicit control" (Weimer [1979], p. 91) by scientific, political, and religious leaders.

Finally, the ecological approach to science suggests that the various disciplines are mutually constraining and cannot be done comprehensively and clearly without reference to each other. Physics needs psychology (e.g., the concept of the observer is important in quantum mechanics—Weimer [1982]) as much as psychologists need an ecological physics (e.g., an ecological approach to the phenomenon of color contrast [see p. 65]). Physics is not more basic or real than is psychology.

Science involves choices. Unless these choices (of research questions, methodologies, and explanatory theories) are to be capricious, random, and thus irrational, they will be based on the scientist's values. These values are influenced by everything from economic conditions to religious world-views (Wolterstorff [1976, 1980]). Most of these values are implicit, but scientists and philosophers need not cringe when these hidden values are discovered. Only comprehensive criticism is then required.

Knowing and Doing in Biblical Perspective

A theological analysis of truth, knowledge, and meaning contextually constrains a psychological analysis and vice versa. This is just a specific case of the general principle that all disciplinary perspectives mutually constrain each other, that our knowing is ecological and not based on some foundational discipline. In general the theology embodied in our discussion of perception has thus far been implicit; now parts of it will be made explicit. Perhaps the view afforded by these two perspectives on perception and truth will enhance the depth of our understanding.

Finiteness

All perceivers, human and animal, are finite, creatures of the infinite God who brought them forth from the dust and water of the earth (Gen. 1:20, 24; 2:7, 19). As creatures all animals are limited, subject to God and his purposes and constrained by their place in the earth environment. As a consequence, their knowing and doing are limited; omniscience and omnipotence do not characterize creatures.

The finiteness of perception forces a cognitive economy on organisms: they must be selective. And choices always mean tradeoffs. For example, looking at a computer-printed replica of an art masterpiece at close range causes the masterpiece to disappear and the typing characters to become prominent, but choosing to view the printout from across the room causes the typing characters to vanish. Both are true views of the work, but they are different. Clarity of the typing characters must be sacrificed if one is to have a comprehensive view of the masterpiece.

The need of organisms for clarity, definition, and precision is constrained by the competing need for comprehensiveness, extension, and flexibility. What organisms need is truth, clarity that is comprehensive. Alas, organisms are finite; neither clarity nor comprehensiveness can be fully realized. A tension must be maintained between the values of clarity and comprehensiveness if we are to hold on to truth (Hodges [1985]).

For example, a recurrent problem within Judaism and Christianity has been the tension between freedom and responsibility in moral conduct. Legalists have great clarity (their rules prescribe precisely the correct thing to do), but Jesus condemned them for their lack of comprehension ("the sabbath was made for man, not man for the sabbath"—Mark 2:27, RSV) and comprehensiveness ("you tithe mint and dill and cummin, and have neglected the weightier matters of the law, justice and mercy and faith"—Matt. 23:23, RSV). There can be multiple embodiments of the same truth, but legalism restricts the biblical flexibility (Rom. 14). On the other hand, the "libertines" have so adapted to the hedonism of the culture that they have lost their definition (clarity) as Christians. They are salt which has lost its taste (Matt. 5:13).

Since truth can be embodied in multiple ways (the same truth appears in different forms) and we cannot grasp its comprehensiveness (we cannot know everything) as well as its clarity (we cannot know perfectly), it is relative for us. Only a God that is omnipresent (comprehensiveness) and holy (clarity) will be ultimately true ("in him all things hold together"—Col. 1:17, RSV). For finite humans, truth means knowing and doing with sufficient clarity and comprehensiveness to fulfil our God-given and environmentally constrained mandates. Compared to the perfection of God's perceiving and doing, human perceptual efforts are incomplete, always in need of growth. God calls humans to learn. What is sufficient knowing and doing for a child is not for an adult, and what was adequate perceiving and acting for previous generations is inadequate for the current one. The biblical evidence suggests that humans will be judged by relative standards (e.g., "to whom much is given, of him will much be required"—Luke 12:48, RSV). But the biblical evidence also suggests all humans have fallen short of an absolute minimum standard (e.g., Rom. 3:23), and this "fall" presents a major complication for knowing and doing the truth.

The human rejection of creaturely status

The crux of the biblical story of the fall is that humans rejected their creaturely status as beneath their dignity. They were not content to be finite perceivers: they wanted to know "like God" (Gen. 3:5). This rejection of the finiteness of their perception was a moral rebellion with profound, puzzling consequences. The first one noted in the Genesis account is that humans became painfully self-conscious (3:7). Then they became afraid (3:8–10). Then social cohesion and trust were ruptured (3:12). Finally, humans became alienated from their own environment (3:17–19). Ironically, their attempt to know more led to a lessening of their ability to know and do. Self-consciousness hinders rapid, accurate perception and action. Fear keeps one from seeking the information afforded by multiple perspectives. The loss of communal trust among humans likewise reduces each individual to his or her own perspectives with a consequent loss of comprehensiveness. And the environmental dislocation of humans has led them to think of the environment as something "out there" that cannot be trusted.

One of the distressing consequences of humans' rejecting their creational responsibilities (they were created to obey God, take care of the earth, and love each other) is that they have lost their identity. The identity, the meaning, of any given human is the relationships he or she has (through knowing and doing) with environmental objects and events, other persons, and the Creator. Since the fall distorted those relationships, human identity has been lost and needs to be re-created (redemption) and rediscovered (conversion).

The biblical account suggests inadequacies in the various theories of perception. Even Gibson's ecological approach does not articulate adequately the effects of human evil on perception. He seems not to consider the possibility that perceivers do not always "hunt without rest" for comprehension and clarity. A perceiver may choose to be passive rather than to multiply perspectives; and even if the perceiver is motivated to seek the truth, other humans may inadvertently or even deliberately restrict the perceiver's perspectives or divert his or her attention. Gibson is right to argue that perceptual errors can usually be avoided by sufficiently sampling the available information, but perceivers often engage in inadequate sampling. In the most sophisticated version of the ecological theory of perception, Shaw, Turvey, and Mace (1982) claim, "One cannot know the good (veridical) and do the evil" (p. 224). This implies evil action (or inaction) does not occur except when our knowledge is limited by our finiteness. The biblical view, on the other hand, holds that humans do not always seek to know and do the truth, but may stifle the truth (e.g., Rom. 1) and deceive themselves and others (e.g., Jer. 17:9).

Epistemologies, Christian and otherwise, often seem to ignore the finiteness of perception in a search for absolutely certain knowledge. Despite enormous differences, each epistemology proposes some knowledge (e.g., biblical revelation, empirical givens, self-evident analytic axioms) that escapes the relativity of finiteness and achieves the status of indubitable and perfect truth. If I have not misread Genesis 3, this search for absolute certainty that has characterized evangelical Christians and analytic philosophers alike is a modernized recapitulation of the original sin. Scientists in their theories and Christians in their theologies have wanted to be like God. The ecological theory and the biblical data suggest that the humility evidenced by submitting to comprehensive criticism might be more appropriate. The biblical call to knowledge and wisdom, as in the Book of Proverbs, requires faith, not total certainty.

In discussing the constraints of finiteness on *who* humans are and *what* and *how* they perceive, I have assumed but not described *why* humans engage in knowing and doing. Biologists use evolutionary terms to answer the question why we perceive: adaptation to the physical environment is necessary to survive. The biblical data make it clear, however, that biological survival alone is not sufficient to answer the why of knowing and doing: man shall not live by bread alone but by all the words of God (Matt. 4:4). Theologically, we perceive so we can "listen to," "taste," and "see" God, the ultimate environment. If we ignore the biological environment, we die. Similarly, if we ignore other real-world structures, we can die psychologically, historically, aesthetically, and theologically as well. The value of what we know and do is measured not just by whether it furthers the survival of the individual or the species, but by whether it allows us to enjoy God, other persons, and the creation, and to love them. Enjoyment (knowing) is subjective and loving (doing) is objective (Hodges [1983]), but they are as inseparable as all aspects of knowing and doing.

Humility and growth

It takes all of one's body to perceive fully. Since that body is finite, perception requires action in space over time. The psychological and theological implications of this for how humans should live are profound (Hodges [1981]).

As we have seen earlier, much of what we know is tacit. Research (Nisbett and Wilson [1977]; Turvey [1974]) indicates that humans are not conscious of most of what they know, do, and feel. Yet some approaches to psychology (e.g., some forms of phenomenology) have restricted psychology to the study of consciousness. Similarly, some theologies have restricted the content of God's revelation and the obedience required of humans to a set of explicit verbal propositions. These psychologies and theologies are dependent on a conception of truth and knowledge that overemphasizes the role of explicit knowledge. The biblical and psychological data suggest the importance of both explicit *and* tacit knowing (see Hodges [1984] for a hypothesis about the relation between tacit and explicit knowing). Indeed, the psychological data suggest the precedence and greater extensiveness of tacit knowledge. The biblical description of the human task also seems more concerned with unselfconscious control of action, embodied tacit knowledge, than with conscious doctrinal definition of that action. Micah summarizes God's requirement for humans: "to do justice, and to love kindness, and to walk humbly with your God" (6:8, rsv).

Knowledge that is tacitly embodied in action requires humility and patience. Scientists and Christians explicitly urge humility on themselves, and with good reason: knowledge of the world and God is intoxicating stuff and it is easy to become drunk with arrogance. As Proverbs reminds us: knowledge is pleasant (2:10), but "a conceited man seeks wisdom, yet finds none" (14:6, NEB). Scientific faith and Christian faith both demand activity, the sweaty seeking of truth. Both require getting our hands dirty in the data of existence: neither vocation allows theorizing unsullied by messy data. Christians and scientists often forget that knowing is a physical business that demands patience. Perseverance is tiresome but crucial. Humans have an almost irresistible urge to escape wearisome mental toil by jumping to conclusions. Research on human inferences (Anderson, Lepper, and Ross [1980]) reveals that people are content to go with the first reasonable hypothesis they can think of rather than gather more data or explore other theoretical perspectives. Waiting for data to accumulate or theory to progress tries the patience of the scientist. Waiting on God to reveal himself demands the patience of Job (whose friends, so quick to prescribe how he should act, in their arrogant haste completely misunderstood God and his plan). Reality—the Creator and his creation—will not be restricted by the narrow confines of human consciousness, theological or otherwise. True rationality and spirituality begin with intellectual and moral humility. "The fear of the LORD is the beginning of knowledge" (Prov. 1:7, RSV). We truly live only if we recognize our dependence on the creation and Creator.

A skill crucial to increased knowledge and increased commitment is what Gibson calls the "education of attention," the "tuning" of bodily activities to environmental information. This educational process is humbling because it requires the organism to admit that it could be a better organism. Learning to know and do requires that we be self-critical. Two activities that are crucial to comprehensive criticism are asking questions and listening. As Bransford (1979) has put it, "Effective learning . . . seems to involve a critical attitude regarding our current level of knowing, which prompts us to ask questions, test ourselves, seek alternate opinions. . . . [Unfortunately,] it is frequently less threatening to hold to one's current ideas than to explore alternatives and hence face being wrong" (pp. 201–02). Learning truth is more a matter of asking the right questions than devising clever answers to the questions handed to us by our cultural, scientific, or religious tradition. Sticking with the old questions may avoid the anxiety associated with new questions which have no ready answers, but in the long run the price of avoiding this anxiety will be petrified knowledge irrelevant to the here and now.

If we ask questions to learn, we must also listen if we are ever to hear the answer. A pride which thinks it has nothing to learn is quick to speak, while humility patiently awaits new information revealed by another's perspective. One value of community (e.g., religious, scientific) is that occasionally we are forced to shut up and listen to what someone else has to say (e.g., a sermon, a review of an article submitted for publication). Listening in the sense used here is more than hearing; it is attending to the environment and not ourselves. Instead of deciding in advance what a person will say, or what the data of a study will show, listening is patient and expectant (rather than expecting).

Learning involves another form of humility: practice. Our clumsy initial attempts to master a new skill and our repeated errors often make us feel stupid. In the end, of course, it is the person too proud to practice who is truly embarrassed. The New Testament letter to the Hebrews rebukes such people: "Though by this time you ought to be teachers, you need someone to teach you the ABC of God's oracles over again; it has come to this, that you need milk instead of solid food. . . . But grown men can take solid food; their perceptions are trained by long use to discriminate between good and evil" (5:12–14, NEB). Being a good Christian, a good scientist, a good perceiver of any kind, requires training to discriminate good from evil. And that is hard work, because, as we know from the biblical metaphors for evil (e.g., the weeds amid the wheat, the leaven of the Pharisees), evil is dispersed and subtle. Extensive training is necessary to perceive good and evil in others or ourselves. Thus, we must make a commitment to long practice if we are to "grow in . . . grace and knowledge" (2 Peter 3:18, RSV) in our lives as Christians, scientists, and human beings.

To make a commitment to a scientific paradigm, a world-view, a spouse, is not to shut one's eyes to reality. Any commitment that is true must change and grow; else it is a dead faith. Knowledge grows or it dies. In this sense truth is not so much something one *has* as it is something one *does*. If I still loved the woman I promised to love eighteen years ago, I would not be still married to her. She is, in important ways, a different woman from the wife of my youth. We each have had to change so that the relationship remains invariant; we have had to take risks in order to maintain stability. Since knowledge grows, commitment is a continuing process. Certainty is not required for this commitment—only humility, hope, and the faith to persevere.

The contextual nature of truth, knowing, and meaning

Our earlier discussions of Gibson's perceptual theory, factual relativity in science, and the dispersed and tacit nature of knowledge, indicated that truth and meaning emerge only in context. Knowing is relative. This does not mean that anything goes, but the reverse, that knowing is *constrained*. Knowing is *ecological:* it depends on and thus is true to the creature, the creation, and the Creator.

The contextual nature of knowledge has important implications: (1) to detect truth, multiple perspectives are necessary; (2) perception and revelation are progressive by nature; and (3) knowledge grows only in community.

1. God has given humans multiple perspectives on the creation-Creator relationship. The structure and complexity of creation, the Jewish and Christian Scriptures written by patriarchs, prophets, poets, and apostles, and Jesus the Messiah are all the revelatory Word of God. The various embodiments of the Word are context-dependent; each functions with greatest clarity and comprehensiveness in the light of the other two. We cannot comprehend the Scriptures apart from knowing something about the world, language, and culture; we cannot know who Jesus is apart from the Scriptures. Even within each single embodiment of God's Word, there are multiple perspectives. For example, in the Scriptures there are multiple authors, literary genres, and historical contexts. The multiplicity of perspectives on God's activity allows humans to discover his invariance (his covenant faithfulness). Only a variety of perspectives can begin to do justice to the complexity and invariance of the one God.

2. Not only is revelation like perception in its multiplicity of perspectives, but revelation is also necessarily progressive. Just as events must unfold for us to perceive them, so must the history of the world unfold for us to perceive God's redemptive purposes. Our knowledge of God, the world, and ourselves must progress if we are to maintain a hold on the truth. Scientific activity and Christian living are events that unfold slowly. Perception, science, and Christian living require risk. A continuing reinterpretation of knowing and doing is necessary to remain in (to conserve) the truth. Human action is always in need of recalibration to current information, and the theory of knowing always needs the corrective of the data of current activity. Data and theory, action and knowledge, cannot exist in the absence of the other. Thus, the Scriptures continuously reinterpret the cosmos for us Christians, but those same Scriptures are also reinterpreted by what we come to know of and do in the world.

3. Since any individual's time and energy are in short supply, how can the multiple perspectives and extended observation necessary to effective knowing and doing be obtained? The answer is obvious but profound: knowing is enhanced by social interaction, a fact which is underemphasized by the ecological theory. Perception, science, and Christian living are really possible only in community. Knowledge is

embodied more in community than in any single perceiver. A scientific community or a church is more likely to know the truth than is any individual scientist or Christian. Not only do communities embody more perspectives than does an individual, but the shared commitment to the particular discipline (be it psychology, physics, or Christianity) increases the possibility that the knowledge will be dispersed throughout the entire community. The prophetic insight of a saint or the pioneering ideas of a scientific genius may come to be understood by most members of the community, but only if the community has attended to the usual disciplines of religious or scientific practice. Without the shared commitment *and* diversity of viewpoints that characterize a true community, growth of knowledge will be greatly retarded.

Perception is relative *and* true. Both individual persons and communities (including science) can discover real relationships between themselves and their world that are meaningful. These meaningful relationships allow effective action that fulfils the purposes and identity of the person or the community. These contextual relationships both constrain (limit) us and free (make it possible for) us to act. Individual and communal action is grounded in the responsibility to take care of the earth, love our neighbors, and serve God. If we are to love earth, neighbor, and God, we must know them. It is only by losing ourselves in knowing them and acting truly toward them that we can discover our own identity.

References

Anderson, C., M. Lepper, and L. Ross (1980). Perseverance of social theories: The role of explanation in the persistence of discredited information. *Journal of Personality and Social Psychology* 39: 1037–49.

Berlin, B., and P. Kay (1969). *Basic color terms: Their universality and evolution.* Berkeley: University of California Press.

Bransford, J. (1979). *Human cognition: Learning, understanding, and remembering.* Belmont, Calif.: Wadsworth.

Coon, D. (1977). *Introduction to psychology: Exploration and application.* St. Paul: West.

Cutting, J., and L. Koslowski (1977). Recognizing friends by their walk: Gait perception without familiarity cues. *Bulletin of the Psychonomic Society* 9: 353–56.

Gibson, J. (1966). *The senses considered as perceptual systems.* Boston: Houghton Mifflin.

_____ (1979). *The ecological approach to visual perception*. Boston: Houghton Mifflin.

Gregory, R. (1972). Seeing as thinking: An active theory of perception. *London Times Literary Supplement*, 23 June 1972, pp. 707–08.

Heider, E. (1972). Universals in color meaning and memory. *Journal of Experimental Psychology* 93: 10–20.

Hodges, B. (1981). Any body can be spiritual. *His* 41: 17–19.

_____ (1983). Love is more than a feeling. *His* 43: 13–15.

_____ (1984). Learning as incarnation: A contextualist approach to learning about learning. In N. DeJong, ed., *Christian approaches to learning theory*. Landham, Md.: University Press of America.

_____ (1985). Human identity and the values of learning: The seven C's. In N. DeJong, ed., *Christian approaches to learning theory*, vol. 2. Washington: University Press of America.

Johansson, G. (1973). Visual perception of biological motion and a model for its analysis. *Perception and Psychophysics* 14: 201–11.

Koslowski, L., and J. Cutting (1977). Recognizing the sex of a walker from a dynamic point-light display. *Perception and Psychophysics* 21: 575–80.

Kuhn, T. (1970). *The structure of scientific revolutions* (2d ed.). Chicago: University of Chicago Press.

Labov, W. (1973). The boundaries of words and their meaning. In C. Bailey and R. Shuy, eds., *New ways of analyzing variation in English*. Washington: Georgetown University.

Lakatos, I. (1968). II—Criticism and the methodology of scientific research programmes. *Proceedings of the Aristotelian Society* 69: 149–86.

Land, E. (1977). The retinex theory of color vision. *Scientific American* 237: 108–28.

Lewis, C. (1946). *An analysis of knowledge and valuation*. LaSalle, Ill.: Open Court.

Maas, J. (1971). *Motion perception I and II*. Syracuse: Syracuse University Films.

Michaels, C., and C. Carello (1981). *Direct perception*. Englewood Cliffs, N.J.: Prentice-Hall.

Nisbett, R., and T. Wilson (1977). Telling more than we know: Verbal reports on mental processes. *Psychological Review* 84: 231–59.

Polanyi, M. (1966). *The tacit dimension*. Garden City, N.Y.: Doubleday.

Pritchard, R. (1961). Stabilized images on the retina. *Scientific American* 204: 72–78.

Rosch, E. (1973). Natural categories. *Cognitive Psychology* 4: 328–50.

_____ (1975). Universals and cultural specifics in human categorization. In R. Brislin, S. Bochner, and W. Lonner, eds., *Cross-cultural perspectives on learning*. New York: Halsted.

————, and C. Mervis (1975). Family resemblances: Studies in internal structure of categories. *Cognitive Psychology* 7: 573–605.

Shaw, R., and M. McIntyre (1974). Algoristic foundations to cognitive psychology. In W. Weimer and D. Palermo, eds., *Cognition and the symbolic processes*. Hillsdale, N.J.: Lawrence Erlbaum Associates.

Shaw R., M. Turvey, and W. Mace (1982). Ecological psychology: The consequence of a commitment to realism. In W. Weimer and D. Palermo, eds., *Cognition and the symbolic processes*, vol. 2. Hillsdale, N.J.: Erlbaum.

Taylor, S., and S. Fiske (1975). Point of view and perception of causality. *Journal of Personality and Social Psychology* 32: 439–45.

Turvey, M. (1974). Constructive theory, perceptual systems, and tacit knowledge. In W. Weimer and D. Palermo, eds., *Cognition and the symbolic processes*. Hillsdale, N.J.: Lawrence Erlbaum Associates.

Weimer, W. (1979). *Notes on the methodology of scientific research*. Hillsdale, N.J.: Lawrence Erlbaum Associates.

———— (1982). Ambiguity and the future of psychology: Meditations Leibniziennes. In W. Weimer and D. Palermo, eds., *Cognition and the symbolic processes*, vol. 2. Hillsdale, N.J.: Lawrence Erlbaum Associates.

Wolterstorff, N. (1976). *Reason within the bounds of religion*. Grand Rapids: Eerdmans.

———— (1980). Theory and praxis. *Christian Scholar's Review* 9: 317–34.

Emotion and the Fruit of the Spirit
Robert C. Roberts

Our emotions are at the core of who we are as human beings. But they are difficult to understand, and we are further muddled by the contradictory clichés we hear about our emotions as we live our day-to-day lives: "You can't help your feelings," "Snap out of it! Don't be so emotional!" "Don't be such an unfeeling computer!" "Live by fact, not by feeling," "Go with your feelings," "You can't trust your feelings," and so forth.

Historically, psychologists and philosophers have struggled to understand the nature of human emotion. As we think critically about the various theories of emotion, we must look for a view that is compatible with Christian belief. This chapter attempts to develop such a view and to interact with contemporary psychological research on emotion. The reader will benefit from comparing the view of emotion which is delineated here with the theories explained in the typical introductory psychology text.

Robert C. Roberts (B.A., M.A., Wichita State University; B.D., Ph.D., Yale University) is professor of psychology and philosophy at Wheaton College. He is a Kierkegaard scholar, a frequent contributor

This chapter is a revision of chapter 2 of Robert C. Roberts, *Spirituality and Human Emotion* (Grand Rapids: Eerdmans, 1983). Reprinted by permission.

to Christianity Today, *and the author of two books exploring the nature of the Christian virtues, namely,* Spirituality and Human Emotion *(Grand Rapids: Eerdmans, 1983) and* The Strengths of a Christian *(Philadelphia: Westminster, 1984). Along with Robert B. Kruschwitz he is editor of the forthcoming* The Virtues: Contemporary Essays on Moral Character *(Belmont, Calif.: Wadsworth). He has also authored numerous articles for professional journals, including* The Philosophical Review *and the* Journal of Psychology and Theology.

Emotion, Reflective Thought, and Spirituality

Among the virtues that constitute the mature Christian life, a number are emotions. Examples are gratitude, hope, peace, joy, contrition, and compassion. Other virtues, such as patience, perseverance, and self-control, are clearly not emotions. I have elsewhere called them "strengths," or the virtues of will power (1984a, 1984b). Still others, such as mercy, forgiveness, humility, gentleness, generosity, and advocacy in behalf of the suffering and oppressed, are neither emotions nor virtues of will power. Since they are all traits which reflect God's character, they could perhaps be called image virtues, or style virtues, or even the holiness virtues. It is on the emotions, however, that I shall focus here. They constitute one group among those Christian personality characteristics which Paul categorizes as the fruit of the Holy Spirit (Gal. 5:22–23).

People who are inclined, as I am, to connect spiritual growth with thoughtful reflection may be put off by the idea of emotions as fruits of the Holy Spirit. There are two reasons for this reaction. First, if these emotions occur simply as a result of God's direct action—when God takes possession of an individual's personality—it seems there is nothing to be done to foster them. They are supernatural, and if we covet them, we just have to wait, knowing that God will act. And second, emotions as such (quite apart from any consideration of the supernatural) may seem to be intellectually disreputable. Instead of being the sort of thing which can be fostered by thinking matters through, they seem to be something which, like superstition or bad logic, disappears from a person's life as one becomes more thoughtful. Let me begin by answering these two objections.

In the New Testament, the working of the Holy Spirit is normally not something which occurs under just any conditions; it occurs typically in connection with the preaching of the Good News about God's redemption of sinners through the life, death, and resurrection of

Jesus of Nazareth. This Good News has two aspects. First, it is the news that God has reconciled the world to himself, that he has accomplished our personal salvation in Christ. Secondly, and at the same time, this Good News is the means by which that reconciliation is worked out in the communities and individuals who give ear to it. The outworking of that reconciliation takes the form of our becoming obedient, grateful, hopeful, at peace with ourselves and God and our neighbor, and filled with joy in the Lord and love for our brothers and sisters. So great is the role of preaching and hearing the gospel in effecting this transformation that we could call these emotions of the mature Christian life "fruits of the gospel." But if we did, they would be no less fruits of the Spirit of God. For the work of reconciliation in which they participate is God's work in his people; the gospel is his instrument in this work.

Now if this is what the fruits of the Holy Spirit are, and this is the way the Holy Spirit bears fruit, then reflection takes on an obvious importance. First, the gospel, being news, is something that can be thought about and meditated on. Indeed, it is hard to see how the gospel can be planted in people so as to bear its fruit if it is not in some sense thought about or meditated on. But beyond a simple and straightforward meditation on the gospel, the individual interested in deepening his spirituality may find it helpful to become clearer about what emotions are and what kind of control we have over them. The emotions which make up the Christian life are not inscrutable psychological phenomena mysteriously caused by God, as inaccessible to our understanding as is the origin of the universe. Thus, reflection about the nature of emotion may lead to a kind of self-knowledge which can be applied, in various ways, to the task of becoming and being a Christian. That, at least, is the hope and project of this essay.

But what about our second objection? Are not emotions, as such, fairly disreputable little items in the spectrum of human traits? Are they not more like warts than like hands and fingers and toes, at best useless and at worst troublesome little accretions?

Certainly, when we describe someone as an emotional type, we do not intend the comment as a compliment. We mean that he is not quite in possession of himself. He is weak, immature, hollow, shallow, flabby. Trivial successes and modest beauties, which would only ruffle a stronger man's hairdo, are to him a gale which blows him away. He cries easily, even on occasions which only by a stretch of the melodramatic imagination might be thought to warrant a tear. He is useless in times of crisis, being thrown into total confusion by circumstances which a man of more firmly drawn personality takes in stride.

This is not a pretty picture, and it has led many to be suspicious of emotions in general, and to conclude that personal maturity is largely a matter of suppressing the emotions. But only a little observing of human nature is needed to see the falseness of this conclusion. The capacity to be affected emotionally is a characteristic not only of weak people but also of very strong ones. Churchill, Socrates, and the apostle Paul were all strong people of deep feeling. As I shall argue in a moment, emotion is founded upon concerns. It is the fact, among other things, that a person is driven by some passion or other—whether it be love of country, concern for intellectual and moral integrity, or the love of God—that makes him or her a strong, integrated person. Such passion is also the basis for a wide repertoire of emotions.

The "emotional" person is weak not because he has emotions, but because he has poor ones, or a limited variety of them. He lacks personal integration and depth not because he feels strongly, but because his feelings are erratic and chaotic, or because he feels strongly about the wrong things, or because he lacks something that ought to be present in addition to his strong feelings, something we might call presence of mind, self-possession, or self-control. Such self-possession may itself be largely a matter of having certain concerns. Most people feel fear when they are endangered, but some fall apart and become unable to act intelligently, while others keep calm. What might the difference be between these types of people? It might well be that some of those who are disconcerted by fear lack a sufficiently strong countervailing concern. Part of Socrates's ability to face death with equanimity was that while he may have feared death, he feared something else (namely the betrayal of his moral self) even more. And a mother may master her fear and go into a burning house because she fears something else more than the danger to herself, that being the death of her children. In such cases the concern for moral integrity or the concern for one's children (which are emotion-dispositions) plays a role in holding the person together.

Emotions and Concerns

Behind every emotion there is a specific concern. An emotion is a construal of one's circumstances (whether that is one's very narrow, immediate circumstances or the general situation of the whole universe) in relation to a particular concern. Perhaps this point can be clarified with a simple illustration. Consider Hank the gardener and his response to the weather bureau's prediction of hail. He is apprehensive. Why is Hank apprehensive? Well, because he has sown new tomato plants. But of course this is an incomplete answer, for Hank's having sown tomato plants would not explain his apprehensiveness if he did not care about the welfare of those plants. If he were not a conscientious gardener and did his job just because he is paid for it, perhaps he would not care what happens to the plants. In that case Hank would not be apprehensive about the approaching storm—at least not on account of the tomatoes. So his apprehensiveness is grounded in his concern for his plants. If the storm passes, his apprehensiveness will pass too—most likely into a quietly joyful sense of relief. And this emotion is grounded in the same concern as the other, namely, Hank's concern for his tomato plants.

Hank's concern for his plants is what I call an emotion-disposition. It is not itself an emotion, but instead a disposition to a variety of emotions. What, then, determines which emotion arises in Hank's heart? It is how Hank construes or sees the circumstances which impinge on his concern. If the weather bureau predicts hail, Hank will see his tomato plants as possibly threatened, and his emotion will be apprehensiveness, fear, anxiety, or some such thing. If the storm passes, then he will construe his plants as safe after all, and he will have a sense of relief; his heart will be glad. If he thinks his plants are being deliberately damaged by a responsible agent (if, say, the teenager next door tears across the tomato patch on his motorbike), his emotion will be anger. If he wakes up on a frosty morning and finds that during the night his neighbor, realizing the danger to Hank's plants, has covered them while Hank slumbered, Hank's emotion will be gratitude. And so forth. So an emotion is a way of seeing things which is grounded in a concern. (I shall for convenience employ the language of vision when I talk about construals, ways of "seeing" things, but of course not all construals are visual. I can construe a person's spoken words as an insult or a compliment; I can construe the smell of smoke in the house as harmless, etc.)

The application of these ruminations is briefly this. Just as Hank would have no emotional response at all to the news of the approaching storm if he did not care about anything upon which that news impinges, so the candidate for being a Christian will not respond to the news of the gospel with joy, peace, gratitude, and hope, if he or she does not have the concerns upon which this news impinges. Now the gospel message provides people with facts which distinctively impinge on basic human concerns:

> The maker of the universe is your personal loving Father and has redeemed you from sin and death through the life and death and resurrection of his Son Jesus. You are a child of God, destined along with many brothers and sisters to remain under his protection forever and to be transformed into something unspeakably lovely. Because these others are also his children, you are expected to treat them gently, to help them

when they are in need, and in general to respect and love them as fellow heirs of your Father's kingdom.

So there are two necessary conditions for experiencing the Christian emotions: (1) a hunger for righteousness and eternal life, and (2) an informal theology. If a person does not feel a hunger for the righteousness and eternal life which are proclaimed and promised in the Christian message, the gospel falls on deaf ears. And if a person does not know and take seriously a minimal amount of informal theology— roughly, the picture of the world sketched above—then the person does not have enough knowledge to construe and respond to his or her circumstances with the Christian emotions.

Emotions and Passions

A few pages ago, in connection with Socrates, Churchill, and Paul, I spoke of how a certain kind of concern, which I called a passion, can integrate and focus the personality and give a person character. A passion, then, is a kind of concern, but not every concern is a passion. The word *passion* has a variety of uses in modern English, and I am trading on only one of these. We sometimes speak of a person as "flying into a passion" if he is overcome by a strong emotion, especially anger. We sometimes say, too, that a person "has a lot of passion," meaning that she is an intense individual—that whatever she does she does with gusto. But I am not using the word in either of these two senses. I use it to refer not to emotions, nor to a general spiritedness of personality, but to one's special interests, concerns, preoccupations. In this sense of the word, a person can have a passion for antique automobiles, for justice, for historical scholarship, for the well-being of poor people, for photography, biking, intellectual honesty, or any number of things.

Now we would not want to say that Hank the gardener has a passion for those tomato plants of his. He might have a passion for gardening, and even for tomato plants in general, but it would be strange if he had a passion for those particular plants. He is concerned about them, but his concern is not a passion. Why not? The reason, it seems to me, is that his concern for them does not dominate long stretches of his life. He cannot be concerned year in and year out about those plants in the way that he can be about his children, or biking, or intellectual honesty. That is, concern for those particular tomato plants may characterize Hank for a few weeks, but it does not characterize him as a person. It is not a character trait.

On the other hand, Socrates's concern for intellectual integrity, the caring for honesty and virtue which led him daily into the marketplace to converse with others and try to get them to care more for virtue than for getting money and fame and preserving their lives—this concern was surely a passion. It formed the deepest regions of his personality. It determined how he daily saw the world and conducted himself, but more than that it gave him a kind of consistency and equanimity in the face of events which would bring others to despair. This points up an ambiguity in our use of the word *character*. In one sense very many people have a particular character by virtue of their being dominated by certain passions. Thus a woman's long and steady devotion to moneymaking constitutes her character. But when we say that a woman "has character," we mean to praise her as being a relatively rare kind of person, to say that she is not easily undone by circumstances—by the disapproval of her colleagues and friends and enemies, by the prospect of losing her position or possessions because of the stands she takes on issues. It was Socrates's passion, in part, which made him a "man of character" in this sense. His passion enabled him to remain consistent in his unwillingness both to speak any word which he believed untrue and to adopt any course of action which would save his life but fit ill with his lifelong insistence on integrity. One must not draw a false conclusion here. One might think that only moral passions give a person character in this sense, but such is not the case. One has only to read G. Gordon Liddy's autobiography *Will* to see that a person whose dominant passion is a yearning for power can also be a man of character in this sense.

It is common to encounter people whose lives are shaped by deep and abiding concerns. One is possessed by a concern to become famous, another to become rich, yet another to alleviate the sufferings of the poor and hungry. Of course, concerns are often mixed. A woman who deeply desires to become rich may also be interested in fame, and may even have some abiding concern for the hungry. No one, I suppose, has only one single passion. Even a saint may not be entirely unconcerned about his reputation, or even his fame. And so it is the order of our cares, as Socrates points out, which determines our character: "I tried to persuade each one of you to take care for himself first, and how he could become most good and most wise, before he took care for any of his interests . . . : that . . . this was the proper order of his care" (Plato *Apology* 36c). A person with the order of passions that Socrates recommends has ethical character. One who has some concern for ethical goodness, but whose concern for it is usually overridden by considerations of fame and pleasure and wealth and safety, does not have (or has little) ethical character.

And so we have here another criterion for distinguishing passions from lesser concerns, though it is not a very precise one. In general, passions are those concerns which, in any given personality, rank higher in the order of the individual's cares. Thus the saint I mentioned above has a passion for the kingdom of God; that is his overriding concern, which, if necessary, suppresses and eradicates competing ones. Even though he still has a concern for fame, he looks upon it with regret or even horror if it goes contrary to his life before God; by virtue of his passion for the kingdom he construes himself as something of a failure or even as a monstrosity when his concern for fame interferes with his serving God. A person who is not a saint will not experience these emotions when contemplating his concern for fame.

Let me summarize. Whatever is of concern to us is an emotion-disposition, and concerns of a special type which can be called passions constitute our character, our inmost self. Passions differ from other concerns in determining a person's actions and emotions over relatively long stretches of his life; in rough terms, they are higher in the order of his cares. If an individual's passions are moral, they give him ethical character. If they are Christian, they give him Christian character. All passions are emotion-dispositions and issue in a specific emotion when the individual construes his circumstances as imping-ing upon the object of his passion.

Emotions as Construals

I have said that emotions are construals of our circumstances in relation to a particular concern, but after reflection on my examples one might think I should have called them beliefs or judgments. After all, were not all the different emotions that Hank might have experi-enced out of concern for his plants beliefs about what was happening or likely to happen to them? He believed that a storm was threatening their safety (and later that the danger had passed), or that a neighbor had rescued them, or that the teenager was purposefully damaging them. Of course, one could say that he construed them as threatened, rescued, or damaged; but would not "believed" be a more precise term?

I think not. But before I can show this, we ought to reflect a bit on what a construal, in my sense of the word, is. Jastrow's (1900, p. 295) illustration of the duck-rabbit will be useful here (Figure 1). It can be seen as a picture of a duck's head or as a picture of a rabbit's head. When we first glance at it, we may see it only as a duck's head. But upon being told that it can also be seen as a rabbit's, and perhaps looking at it again, searching the figure a bit, maybe turning it on its side, then the rabbit's head appears as well. That is, the experience of the duck-rabbit as a rabbit's head comes to or over us; the rabbit's head emerges

FIGURE 1. **The duck-rabbit.**

in the figure, much as our view of somebody as offensive or pitiful or generous or conniving sometimes comes over us all of a sudden. After we have managed to see the figure both ways, with a little practice, we can see it as one or the other at will. There is, of course, a sense in which, having seen the figure in these different ways, we will see it only as a duck-rabbit. What we see in this sense is not subject to our will. That is, if our eyes are open and functioning normally and if the figure is well lit, we will see the figure of the duck-rabbit. We have no choice about it. But after we have learned the trick, we do have a choice about how we construe the duck-rabbit, and which of the two very different experiences of the figure we have depends on this choice. That is, though we may first have construed the duck-rabbit figure as a duck, once we have learned to see the figure as a rabbit also, we can choose to experience the figure as either a duck or a rabbit.

Now one aspect of having an emotion is very much like seeing the duck in the duck-rabbit. (Obviously, this experience is not an emotion. The ingredient that is missing is concern: the sight of the duck in the duck-rabbit does not impinge on any concern of the construer.) To be indignant is to see myself or someone whose welfare is of concern to me as intentionally injured by someone. To be in despair is to see my life, which I deeply desire to be meaningful, as holding nothing of importance for me. To be envious is to see myself as losing against some rival in a competition upon which I am staking my self-esteem. To feel guilty is to see myself as having offended against a moral or quasi-moral standard to which I subscribe.

In the case of the Christian emotions, it is necessary to have at least some knowledge of the Christian story. To experience peace with God is to see God as a reconciled enemy and to care deeply about that reconciliation. To experience hope is to see one's own future as having a share in the eternity and righteousness of God's kingdom. To be Christianly grateful is to see various precious gifts, such as existence, sustenance, and redemption, as bestowed by God. There is a necessary connection between the Christian emotions and the Christian story, because emotions are construals, and construals always require some knowledge, and the knowledge required by the Christian emotions is provided by the Christian story. So people who do not want to think of the spiritual life in terms of emotions and feelings because they believe that emotions are subjective and cut off from doctrine and thinking, can lay their fears to rest. Emotions are no less tied to concepts than arguments and beliefs are.

Perhaps the reader feels that my claim that emotions are construals is not true to emotions as we feel them. After all, are not emotions in some sense to be *contrasted* with thoughts? What about the old distinction between the mind and the heart, between the cognitive and the emotive? Have I not committed the philosopher's arrogant mistake of subsuming the heart under the mind, thus really denying the heart altogether? In defining emotions as construals, as ways of seeing a particular situation, have I not made them just a species of thought?

I admit to making emotions a species of thought, in some broad sense of that word, but not to denying the heart. As the reader will remember, emotions are not just any kind of construal; they are concern-based construals. But this answer may not quite satisfy. A further argument against my position might go as follows: Concern-based construals are capable of being declared right or wrong by the kind of standards we use to declare our judgments right or wrong. Suppose I make the judgment that the people in the car behind me are following me with some sinister intent. I may be right or I may be wrong; the basis on which I have made my judgment may be rational or irrational. Now this judgment may also be the basis of my construal of the situation, which could be fear or indignation; if so, then the emotion itself is either right or wrong, either rational or irrational. But, the argument continues, emotions are not either right or wrong, either rational or irrational; being feelings, they are not subject to this kind of evaluation. Therefore, my view that emotions are construals must be wrong.

In response, I say that people who think emotions are not subject to rational adjudication are usually confusing emotions with either sensations or moods. If one has a bodily sensation, such as an itch on the back or a fluttery feeling in the diaphragm, it of course makes no sense to ask whether the itch or flutter is true or false, or based on good evidence or valid reasoning. An emotion differs from a bodily sensation precisely in that, among other things, it can, like an opinion, be well- or ill-founded, and things like itches and flutters are not. Hope, anger, envy, embarrassment, grief, and gratitude can obviously be rational or irrational; it follows that they cannot be bodily sensations. Some emotions, especially those we share with the lower animals, such as fear and anger, are associated with typical bodily sensations, such as dryness in the mouth, heat at the back of the neck, erection of the hair, an odd sensation in the abdominal or chest region, and trembling of the extremities. But these cannot be more than *accompaniments* of emotion, for the reason given above.

Emotions are also sometimes confused with moods. This is a more forgivable confusion, because of the close connection between emotions and moods. Moods, like sensations, are not subject to rational adjudication. Of course, they may be pleasant or unpleasant, and so may be good or bad; and a person is undoubtedly irrational if he knowingly does something (like take a drug) which will put him in an unpleasant mood. But the mood itself is neither correct nor incorrect, nor is it based on either good or bad reasoning. Moods are such states as being elated and cheerful, depressed and blue, or grumpy and irritable. If asked, "Why do you have that itch?" one will answer not with an evaluation of the reasonableness of the itch, but with its cause: "Because I wash my clothes in hard water." Similarly, the child who asks "Why is Daddy grumpy?" is not asking for an adjudication of the correctness of his mood, but for the cause of his state: "He hasn't had his dinner yet." Just as itches have various causes, so we are put in moods by various causes. Lack of sleep over a period of time can cause depression; caffeine causes irritability in some people and mild elation in others; deeply repressed factors in one's psychiatric history inevitably have their influence on his or her moods and susceptibility to them; different kinds of music seem to put people in tranquil, excited, or aggressive moods; cacophonous noises—one baby screaming, another banging on pots and pans, and someone else using a vacuum cleaner— make some people feel irritable; jogging long distances makes some people feel "high"; and of course narcotic drugs are notorious mood-changers.

Another important cause of moods is emotions. If a woman wins the lottery, she will very likely not only feel the emotions of joy and hope in seeing her financial situation changed for the better; very likely the cheerfulness of her emotion will spill over into other contexts. For a few hours, or days, or even weeks, she will have a brighter outlook on everything; her mind will be pervaded by a general optimism. Similarly, grief at the death of a loved one can color one's entire outlook on life for a period; grief, which is clearly an emotion, begets a general depression, which is not an emotion but a mood. Here we can see an important source of our temptation to think that moods are emotions. For sometimes when we are asked, "Why is Daddy so grumpy?" our answer makes indirect reference to an emotion: "Because he lost money on the farm sale." What we actually mean is that the financial setback is the rational basis for his disappointment (an emotion), which in turn has caused him to sink into his grumpy state (a mood). Moods are not emotions, but since they are sometimes caused by emotions, we are inclined to think they are. If we are careful to keep the distinction in mind, we will see that emotions, unlike moods, can be evaluated as right or wrong, correct or incorrect, rational or irrational. On this basis we are justified in defining emotions as construals.

The Debate over the Role of Cognition in Emotions

In the continuing struggle to understand the nature of emotion, a debate is currently raging among some psychologists, led on one hand by R. B. Zajonc and by R. S. Lazarus on the other, as to whether "cognitions" are a necessary precondition for emotions. Zajonc argues (1980, 1984) that it is possible to have "affect" that is not preceded by any "cognition," while Lazarus (1982, 1984) argues that emotions are always "cognitive" in that they are always preceded by "cognitions."

As I have suggested by putting scare-quotes around the words *affect* and *cognition*, it seems to me that this debate is shot through with vagueness and confusion. Most of the time, for example, Zajonc does not even seem to be speaking to the issue of whether *emotions* (such things as anger, indignation, hope, fear, shame, embarrassment, remorse, envy, resentment, jealousy) must be preceded by cognitions. Instead, he addresses a different question from what Lazarus addresses (though he seems not to notice that he is doing so): he addresses the question whether *affects* must be preceded by cognitions. But what is an "affect"? Zajonc seems to assume that the word denotes a specific kind of psychological phenomenon, but he himself uses the term in a rather amazing variety of ways. Sometimes he means by it the very general phenomenon of reactiveness to environmental stimuli. Thus he says (1980, p. 156), "Affect is the first link in the evolution of complex adaptive functions that eventually differentiated animals from plants." And he gives as an example of affect the way in which a rabbit reacts by running away when the form of a snake stimulates the rabbit's visual receptors. Because the rabbit reacts this way without going through any process of reasoning (e.g., "Snakes are dangerous to rabbits; I am a rabbit; that is a snake; therefore I'd better jump"), Zajonc concludes that it is possible to have affect without cognition! At other times in the same paper Zajonc uses the word *affect* to denote not reactiveness, but mood. Thus he says that affective judgments "cannot be focused as easily as perceptual and cognitive processes. They are much more influenced by the context of the surround, and they are generally holistic" (1980, p. 168). But most of his article is about yet another phenomenon, that of liking or preferring such things as melodies and polygons. Not only is this a rather confusing array of things all gathered together under the epithet *affect;* none of it seems to have any relevance to Lazarus's claim that *emotions* are always preceded by cognitions because neither bare reactiveness, nor bare mood, nor bare preference, comes even close to being emotion.

On his side of the debate, Lazarus at least seems to be talking about emotions. And he is clear, in his 1982 response to Zajonc (p. 1019), that emotions might be cognitive without being caused by something that is inferential, deliberate, rational, or conscious. There are plenty of cognitions that are none of these things. For example, many construals are none of these things (we are assuming here that the idea of cognition is broad enough to include construals). But Lazarus himself remains vague as to what kind of cognition necessarily precedes emotions.

To help Lazarus out a bit, let me offer two arguments to the effect that it is better to associate emotions with construals than to associate emotions with judgments. (I have elsewhere [1984c] argued this in more detail.) Judgments are truth-asserting, whereas construals are not. Thus, if I judge a person to have insulted me, then I am committed to regarding as a true statement the claim that he has insulted me. But if I merely *see* him *as* having insulted me, all I am committed to is that it appears to me that he has insulted me. It is possible for it to appear to me that he has insulted me (he just has that look about him) at the same time that I believe that he has not insulted me. For example, many parents react negatively (as if they have been insulted) when their little darling one-year-old suddenly sticks out her tongue at Mom and Dad. They might rationally recognize that the child has not as yet come to identify this gesture as an insult, but they still feel insulted. Many irrational emotions have precisely this structure: I feel anger even though I know there is no basis for it; I feel guilt even though I know there is no sense in it. That many of our emotions are without rational basis is one argument that the cognitions behind emotions are not judgments, but construals.

The second argument has to do with the degree of control that we have over our emotions. I can often decide whether I am going to be angry with someone. But a reasonable person cannot just decide whether to believe or judge that someone has offended him. This is not a matter of his decision, but of his assessment of the evidence. On the other hand, construals, like emotions, are (sometimes) subject to the voluntary control of reasonable people. This fact makes it probable that construals, rather than judgments, are the cognitions relevant to emotions.

Throughout their debate both Lazarus and Zajonc assume that the question about the relation between cognition and emotion (or affect in Zajonc's case) is about whether emotions are *caused* by cognitions. The picture they draw for us is of two different kinds of mental events, cognitions on the one hand and emotions on the other. If Lazarus is right it is just a law of nature that the one kind of event (emotion) never occurs unless it is preceded by the other (cognition). Now it is self-evident that when one event causes another, there have to be two distinct events; no event is its own cause. So if the construal theory of emotion is correct, Lazarus has misunderstood the relation between the construal and the emotion. It is a matter of logical, rather than causal, necessity that we experience anger when we construe someone as having offended. (This thesis has been powerfully argued by philosophers for many years now; see Kenny [1963] and Thalberg [1964].) It is not as though the construal first occurs, and then the emotion follows; rather, the construal, if it is based in a concern, *is* the emotion. Those readers who wonder whether this is correct should ask themselves what is left over to be the emotion if the concern-based construal is removed. The answer is that there may be some physical symptoms (faster heartbeat, sweating, muscle tension, erection of hairs, trembling of extremities, etc.), and there may be a mood (perhaps a general depressed feeling, or a feeling of exhaustion). But neither the physical symptoms nor the mood which is left over is the emotion, so the fact that these events are caused by the construal does not imply that the emotion is caused by the construal.

How We Can Control Our Emotions

It is important to us as Christians that emotions are partially within our control, that they can be commanded. Jesus says that everyone who is angry with his brother shall be liable to judgment (Matt. 5:22). Paul tells the Romans to rejoice with those who rejoice and weep with those who weep (12:15), and he tells the Philippians to rejoice in the Lord always (4:4). When he says that love is not jealous, or irritable, or resentful (1 Cor. 13:5), he seems to assume that this feeling is largely within the control of his readers. Being resentful is not like being five foot six or having congenitally bad teeth.

The fact that emotions are construals goes a long way toward explaining how it is that we can exercise some control over them, and also why we sometimes fail to control them when we try. (I am talking about a genuine control of emotion, and not just a suppression of the behavior which threatens to result from an emotion.) I can bring myself into a certain emotional state by coming to see my situation in certain terms. I can dispel an emotion by somehow getting myself to stop seeing the situation in one set of terms and to begin seeing it in another. But this process is a little bit like imagining. Sometimes my mother's face appears to my imagination uninvited, sometimes I can imagine it if asked to do so, and sometimes I cannot imagine it, no matter how hard I try. It is the same with figures like the duck-rabbit, though most construals are more complicated than visualizing the duck-rabbit. And it is the same with emotions. Sometimes I am hopeful without trying, sometimes I can make myself hopeful by trying to see promise in my situation, and sometimes I cannot make myself hopeful no matter how hard I try. So the first way we can control our emotions is to work to construe our situations in the right terms. But we can also control our emotions by controlling our behavior.

In *The Principles of Psychology*, William James (1950), whose theory of emotion is very different from the one I am proposing, makes the following sensible observation about how emotions can be controlled through behavior:

> Everyone knows how panic is increased by flight, and how the giving way to the symptoms of grief or anger increases those passions them-selves. . . . In rage, it is notorious how we "work ourselves up" to a climax by repeated outbreaks of expression. . . . Whistling to keep up courage is no mere figure of speech. On the other hand, sit all day in a moping posture, sigh, and reply to everything with a dismal voice, and your melancholy lingers. [vol. 2, pp. 462–63]

In other words, if we want to encourage an emotion, we should act in conformity with it, even if we are not initially inclined to act that way; and if we want to discourage an emotion, we should refuse to act in conformity with it, or better yet, we should act in conformity with a contrary emotion. This of course does not always work, but very often it does, and undoubtedly it would work even more often if we practiced the principle more assiduously and self-consciously.

My suggestion that emotions are construals will help us to understand why this way of controlling our emotions sometimes works (and also why it sometimes does not). The key is this: when I act angry, it is natural to construe the situation as one to which anger is the appropriate response; when I act in a compassionate manner, it becomes easier to construe the situation as one to which compassion is the appropriate response. Let us say that I have explained a point to a student a number of times, and he has now come to my office complaining that he still does not understand. By this time I am inclined to see him as obnoxious, and as imposing unnecessarily on my time and energy. But

I sit down with him and explain the point once more by making a diagram on a piece of scratch paper. He still does not (or will not) understand, and there is something in his voice which seems to accuse me of making things too complicated. I am inclined to rebuke him sharply and send him out of my office summarily. But instead, applying James's principle, I lay my hand on his shoulder in a fatherly way and speak some gentle words of encouragement to him. And the anger which was threatening to come over me is dispelled.

The reason this strategy is often effective is that becoming angry with someone necessarily involves construing him as obnoxious, offensive, or some such thing. And it is much more difficult to see someone as obnoxious if I have my hand resting affectionately on his shoulder and I am speaking gentle words of encouragement to him than if I am yelling at him and throwing him out of my office. The reason it is not always effective is that it is not impossible to construe someone as obnoxious while assuming the opposite posture toward him. Sometimes that initial construal seems so right, and so superior to every alternative construal, that no amount of dissonant behavior will change it. But our emotions are intractable less often than we imagine.

C. S. Lewis, I think, somewhere advises this: If you want to become a Christian, but find it presently impossible to believe the things Christians believe, you might begin by *acting* like a Christian. No need to start out with anything as heavy as belief. Just sing praises to God along with the Christians, imitate them in their posture toward suffering, join with them in their life of compassion and sacrifice. You will begin to construe the world as a Christian does, to experience Christianity from within. And who knows? That way of looking at things may eventually come to seem so superior to every other way that you may find, one day, that you believe. When that happens, your disposition to the Christian emotions will have become firm.

Finally, let me suggest that Christian spirituality is not merely a matter of right belief, but is also a matter of seeing or construing the world rightly, and thus having the emotional fruits of the Spirit as well as the other fruits. I have argued that emotions are not judgments; there is a further argument that emotions are not beliefs. Typically, beliefs are permanent (though often unconscious) fixtures in the mind, whereas emotions are temporary occurrences in consciousness. A Christian's belief that eternal life awaits him is not something that occurs at various times of the day. He does not cease to believe it when he concentrates his mind on a mathematical puzzle or when he falls asleep. He may believe it and yet, if he is not very faithfully practicing his Christianity, go for days or weeks without thinking about it. Now if he is not at all attending to eternity, then he cannot be experiencing Christian hope as an emotion. For Christian hope is a way of looking at things, especially eternity. He may, of course, be a person who is disposed to be hopeful; that is, he may be the sort of person who would experience hope if something stimulated him to do so. But hope itself, like the other Christian emotions, involves setting one's mind on the things of the Spirit. This is why belief is not enough for spirituality. Christians must not only believe, but also must learn to *attend to* the things of God. For only in doing so will they begin to bear all the fruits of God's Spirit.

References

James, W. (1950). *The principles of psychology*. New York: Dover (original work published 1890).

Jastrow, J. (1900). *Fact and fable in psychology*. Boston: Houghton Mifflin.

Kenny, A. (1963). *Action, emotion, and will*. London: Routledge and Kegan Paul.

Lazarus, R. (1982). Thoughts on the relations between emotion and cognition. *American Psychologist* 37: 1019–24.

―――― (1984). On the primacy of cognition. *American Psychologist* 39: 124–29.

Roberts, R. (1984a). Will power and the virtues. *The Philosophical Review* 93: 227–47.

―――― (1984b). *The strengths of a Christian*. Philadelphia: Westminster.

―――― (1984c). Solomon on the control of emotions. *Philosophy and Phenomenological Research* 44: 395–403.

Thalberg, I. (1964). Emotion and thought. *American Philosophical Quarterly* 1: 45–55.

Zajonc, R. (1980). Feeling and thinking: Preferences need no inferences. *American Psychologist* 35: 151–75.

―――― (1984). On the primacy of affect. *American Psychologist* 39: 117–23.

5

Developmental Psychology and Spiritual Development
Les Steele

Over time, perceptive individuals begin to take note of and ask questions about the differences between people at different stages of life, including different stages of spiritual development. How do we account for the different ways in which new Christians and mature Christians experience their faith? What are the differences between a person who commits his or her life to God at age thirteen and one who does so at forty-seven? Is there a regular pattern to how people's faith changes over the course of their lives? Should the church minister differently to people of different ages?

This chapter does not answer all these questions, but it does give us a framework for beginning to address such questions. By relating spiritual development to other aspects of human development, this chapter helps us begin to make sense out of religious experience. It also shows us some of the possible ways in which we as Christians can critique developmental theories.

Les Steele (B.A., M.A., Azusa Pacific University; Ph.D., Claremont Graduate School) is assistant professor of religion at Seattle Pacific University. Trained in adolescent and adult development, he specializes in the area of spiritual maturation as it relates to the field of Christian education.

95

T his chapter will discuss some critical concepts in developmental psychology and the contributions they can make to understanding spiritual development. The first part of the chapter will briefly introduce key developmental theories; the second part will utilize the concepts and implications of these theories to describe spiritual development across the life span.

Developmental psychology is the subfield of psychology that addresses the question of change across the life span. Developmental psychology used to be seen as synonymous with child psychology since many in the field assumed that major developmental changes occur almost exclusively in childhood. Over time, however, developmental psychology has come to study human change and growth across the entire span of life. It will be assumed here that the study of human development is central to an understanding of spiritual development, in that our spiritual journey always interacts with our overall growth as persons. Further, as we become more aware of the inclusiveness of the spiritual, we realize that the spiritual has an impact on all parts of our development. Thus, we must study how other areas of development affect the spiritual and how the spiritual development of the person affects the other areas.

Basic Assumptions

As with all areas of inquiry, developmental psychology begins with certain basic presuppositions (see the discussion of control beliefs on pages 22–23). It is not enough to state a particular theory or follow a particular approach to research and assume that everyone will agree. One must look past the particular theory or methodology to the underlying assumptions that inform the theory or guide the methodology.

Within developmental psychology, two major sets of assumptions seem to dominate: the *mechanistic* and the *organismic*. The central distinctive feature of the mechanistic model is that it considers persons to be passive reactors to the environment. By contrast, the organismic model sees persons as active or interactive in the process of development. Briefly, the mechanistic model views the development of a person as the result of changes external to him or her, while the organismic model places the locus of development within the individual (for more explanation of these models, see Looft [1973]).

An acquaintance with these two models is important for anyone intending to critique from a Christian perspective the various theories of human development. If a person is only reactive to the environment, as the mechanistic model would have us believe, then humans are not responsible for their behavior. The mechanistic model not only takes away the responsible self, but it actually eliminates any discussion of the self. Thus B. F. Skinner classifies his autobiography as the biography of a nonperson.

By contrast, the organismic model sees persons as creative and interactive with their environments. For example, the Swiss scientist Jean Piaget describes what he calls the adaptation tendency in persons, our innate desire or drive to adapt to or make sense out of our world. This along with other key notions of the organismic model preserves the self as responsible.

Other major sets of assumptions which must be examined involve the concept of stages of development. This is a difficult issue in that there are different definitions of what a stage is. When the various uses of the term *stage* are analyzed, however, most fit one of two categories: the *structural* or the *functional*. Structural-stage theories of human development focus primarily on the structure of thinking or how thinking is done, and not on the content or what is thought about or grappled with. The first structural-stage theory was conceptualized by Jean Piaget. Piaget's work on cognitive development led him to be concerned with how people think about ideas and problems and not so much with what they think.

Lawrence Kohlberg's theory of moral development is also a good example of a structural theory. For Kohlberg the moral choice that a person makes (the content) is not as important as the stage of moral reasoning a person has achieved. What matters is how the individual makes that choice (the thinking structure or process). The "Heinz dilemma" is a typical experiment of Kohlberg. Briefly, a research subject is told that Mr. Heinz's wife is dying of cancer and circumstances are such that he must decide whether or not to steal a drug that could save her life. The subject is asked what Mr. Heinz should do and why. A person who responds, "He should steal the drug," might well be scored at the same developmental level or stage as someone who responds, "No, he shouldn't steal the drug." What is of interest to Kohlberg is the way the subjects arrive at their decision, with the decision itself being of secondary importance. The strength of the structural-stage approach is that it allows for universalizing across cultures. No matter what the particular issues are in various cultures, comparable structural stages can be found.

Functional-stage theories of human development focus more on the content of thought (the what) than on the structure (the how). Erik Erikson's theory is the best example. Erikson's focus is on the changing self, including personal, interpersonal, and social roles. Development is seen as a progression through various tasks or issues. The level at

TABLE 1   **The Major Developmental Stages: Four Theories**

	Piaget's Cognitive Stages	Kohlberg's Moral-Reasoning Stages	Erikson's Psychosocial Stages	Fowler's Faith-Development Stages
Infancy (0–2)	Sensorimotor thinking		Basic trust vs. basic mistrust	
Early Childhood (2–7)	Preoperational thinking	Preconventional	Autonomy vs. doubt and shame Initiative vs. guilt	Intuitive-projective
Middle Childhood (7–12)	Concrete operations		Industry vs. inferiority	Mythic-literal
Adolescence	Formal operations	Conventional	Identity vs. identity confusion	Synthetic-conventional
Adulthood		Postconventional	Intimacy vs. isolation	Individuating-reflective
			Generativity vs. stagnation and self-absorption	Conjunctive
			Integrity vs. despair	Universalizing

which the person is scored is determined by the issues he or she is grappling with. What the person is grappling with (the content) is more significant than how it is dealt with (the process).

It is important to note here that neither type of theory claims to be totally exhaustive in its understanding of human development. The major advocates of each have stated that they are looking at different sides of the same phenomena. There is an interaction between the two major types of theories that provides a more complete picture of human development.

An Outline of Developmental Theories

Both the structural and functional theories assist us in understanding spiritual development. Therefore, I will briefly describe in general terms the theories of Jean Piaget, Lawrence Kohlberg, James Fowler, and Erik Erikson. Then the implications of these theories for spiritual development at the various stages of the life span will be explored. Table 1 summarizes the basic proposals of the four theories.

Jean Piaget is best known for his work in the area of cognitive development. Piaget combined his training in biology, philosophy, and psychology to pioneer the field which he called genetic epistemology, studies in the development of the process of knowing. Piaget's basic assumption was that all persons seek to adapt to their environment by the simultaneous operations of assimilation and accommodation. In essence humans try to make sense out of their world, confronting various stimuli and constructing schemas or mental images of those stimuli. If we can explain a particular type of experience, we assimilate that experience into our existing mental structure whenever we encounter it. But if an experience does not fit our mental structure, like a square peg in a round hole, then the process of accommodation creates a new schema or image (like a square hole). Following this initial assumption, Piaget proceeded to describe four stages of cognitive development: the sensorimotor stage, the preoperational stage, the stage of concrete operations, and the stage of formal operations. These stages, which differ in the manner in which mental images are formed, are adequately described in the typical introductory psychology text.

Beginning with the structural assumptions of Piaget, who had principally examined problem solving, Lawrence Kohlberg investigated the ways in which people think about moral situations. From his research he postulated three levels of moral reasoning, with each level containing two stages. The three levels of reasoning are the preconventional, conventional, and postconventional. His theory, which is based on the philosophical assumption that justice is a universal principle (he regards justice as the determinant in postconventional reasoning), focuses on how people make moral choices, and claims to be unconcerned with the actual decisions that are made.

Continuing in the structural approach of Piaget and Kohlberg, James Fowler has proposed a theory of faith development. Fowler defines faith as a way of knowing. What this means is that faith is not necessarily a particular set of beliefs, but a basic attitude which shapes the person's life. Faith is much more a philosophy of life than a particular set of beliefs. Faith, therefore, may include a religious dimension but it need not. Fowler's theory is structural because it focuses not so much on what we believe as on how we believe. In developing his theory, he utilized an interview method of research from which he claims to have found six stages of faith development. These stages, just like Kohlberg's, are considered to be hierarchical and sequential. This means that later stages incorporate previous stages and that a person must pass through the earlier stages before reaching the higher stages.

Erikson is the primary theorist in the area of a functional approach to developmental psychology. He studied with Freud for many years and has built his own theory on psychoanalytic assumptions. Although this was his starting point he has moved beyond many of Freud's basic ideas. Erikson's theory is much more positive and optimistic than that of Freud, and it gives greater consideration to the social and cultural influences on the developing person. Also, where Freud stops at adolescence, Erikson moves beyond that period to postulate a theory of psychosocial development across the entire life-span. He delineates eight functional stages of growth. Each stage centers around a particular issue, a psychosocial crisis, which rises to prominence at a particular age. A positive resolution to these crises needs to occur for optimal development to proceed. Positive resolutions lead to ego strengths in the personality; inadequate resolutions produce weaknesses which will influence further personality development in a negative way. Erikson is helpful in that he places before us a developmental pattern which has implications for healthy spiritual maturation.

Spiritual Development Across the Life Span

Having given these brief descriptions of key structural- and functional-stage theories of human development, we will now examine how these theories assist us in the understanding of spiritual development at various periods of life. The life span will be divided into infancy, early childhood, middle childhood, adolescence, and adulthood. It should be noted that while the various stages of development are presented in connection with certain chronological ages, it is nevertheless the case that individuals enter the various stages at different times. The age of a child (or an adult) is not an infallible indication of his or her particular stage of development.

Infancy

Infancy is defined as the period from birth to about two years of age. Piaget considers this period to be an active one in terms of cognitive development, one which is crucial to the further development of the ability to adapt to the environment. He calls this period the period of *sensorimotor thinking*. The child comes into the world with a few innate responses such as sucking and grasping, and uses these responses to meet basic biological needs; as time passes, these responses become more intentional and generalized. The infant begins to place things in her or his mouth to see what they are all about. The infant also begins to coordinate several of these responses with newfound abilities and thus deliberately creates novel situations which elicit particular reactions, such as dropping a spoon to hear the sound that it makes. This simple act incorporates many sensorimotor actions, the intention to perform them, and a recognition of their probable result.

Soon these manipulations of objects become even more sophisticated as the infant tries new ways of eliciting responses, such as dropping the spoon from different heights. Throughout this period, continual differentiation and integration of responses occur, producing more novel situations. This form of intelligence appears before the use of language. As Piaget (1967) states, "It is an entirely practical intelligence based on the manipulation of objects" (p. 11). The significance of this practical intelligence is that it is the necessary precursor to the development of language as well as to the manipulation of ideas and concepts.

From a functional perspective, the psychosocial focus (or "crisis" as Erikson calls it) of infancy, the particular issue grappled with, is *basic trust versus basic mistrust* (Erikson [1980], p. 57). The task of the infant in relationship to the mother is to develop a sense of trust and confidence that someone will take care of him or her. Erikson is careful to say a "sense" of trust due to Piaget's findings that the infant is not really aware that he or she is separate from the maternal figure. The issue is whether or not the mother and the environment can be trusted to provide for the infant's needs. For trust to develop, there must be continuity and sameness in maternal care. According to Erikson (1980, p. 58), trust is the cornerstone of a healthy personality. The opposite of trust is mistrust or a sense that the maternal person and the environment cannot be counted on to provide for and sustain the child. There is no sense of sameness and continuity in the care provided. It must be realized that Erikson does not advocate a resolution of this crisis (or of any of the others) totally to the positive side. He speaks of a ratio weighted toward trust; some mistrust must be included to preserve the infant from a totally naive complacency in a world that is not thoroughly trustworthy.

Out of a healthy resolution of this crisis comes an ego strength, the virtue of hope. "Hope is the enduring belief in the attainability of fervent wishes" (Erikson [1964], p. 118). The ego strength of hope will be a foundation for further development of a healthy personality. Erikson goes on to say, "Hope is the ontogenetic basis of faith" (p. 118). He is very clear that a healthy religious life in the future depends on a positive resolution of this stage. Fowler (1981) agrees: "The quality of mutuality and the strength of trust, autonomy, hope, and courage (or their opposites) developed in this phase underlie (or threaten to undermine) all that comes later in faith development" (p. 121).

What is clear is that even if spiritual development is not evident at this age in the understanding and acceptance of specific religious doctrines, the psychosocial needs of the infant must be met to foster healthy spiritual growth in the child in the future. A sense of childlike trust is central to commitment to God. If we cannot trust those who are our first authority figures, then we will most likely have a difficult time trusting God when we can cognitively understand who he is. This hypothesis seems borne out in practical experience in that many (not all) who struggle to trust in God report not having had a sense of trust in parental figures early in life.

It is important that we help new parents deal with the experience. They must come to understand that the primary relationship of the infant to its parents needs to be trust-filled. A sense of trust and hope will give the child a foundation which in turn will facilitate healthy spiritual development.

Early childhood

Early childhood includes the years from two to seven. In this period physical, intellectual, and psychological growth occurs by leaps and bounds. The typical child will by age two have a vocabulary of about three hundred words; in just one year it will expand to three thousand words. Piaget describes this age as that of *preoperational thinking*. The term *preoperational* implies that children at this age are unable to use logical arguments in their attempts to make sense out of the world. It is a stage where intuition is at its best. Piaget (1967) states, "One quality stands out in the thinking of the young child: he constantly makes assertions without trying to support them with facts" (p. 29). This is both a limitation and a blessing. Unable to reason objectively, a child may misinterpret the causes of events, as when parents divorce and the child places the blame on himself. On the other hand, this is truly the stage of imagination; for creativity and imagination to be a part of later thinking abilities, the fantasy-type of thinking in the young child needs to be nurtured.

Functionally, this age period incorporates two of Erikson's stages. First comes the psychosocial crisis of *autonomy versus doubt and shame*. The world of young children begins to expand not only mentally but also physically as they move about freely by themselves. The issue to be resolved is that of autonomy, self-control, and the need to do things by oneself. The dangers of this stage are that the child may be restricted and thus never develop an adequate sense of autonomy, or that overexertion of autonomy may result in failure and a feeling of shame at not being able to do things on one's own. If the issue is resolved in a favorable ratio between the two extremes (i.e., a ratio emphasizing but not overemphasizing autonomy), then strength of will begins to emerge as a part of the child's developing personality, and the child will be enabled to exercise properly both freedom of choice and self-restraint.

The next functional stage of this age is that of *initiative versus guilt*. Initiative implies the ability to step out and begin action and relationships; it adds a new dimension to the stage of autonomy. Erikson (1950) states, "Initiative adds to autonomy the quality of undertaking, planning and 'attacking' a task for the sake of being active" (p. 255). Taken to negative extremes, this stage can result in guilt for the child: Have I gone too far? Have I hurt others in my attempt at relationships or action? Am I really a bad child who cannot control or direct myself? The virtue resulting from a positive resolution to this stage is purpose. This implies aim-directed action or the courage to pursue valued goals.

In relation to spiritual development, Fowler calls this age period the stage of *intuitive-projective faith*. Here faith depends generally on the beliefs of the parents for its specific content, which usually takes the form of images of a magical world. The child's preoperational perceptions, which emphasize myth and fantasy, make for some very interesting conversations about religion. His or her thinking is, as Fowler (1981) states, "unrestrained and uninhibited by logical thought" (p. 133). Early in this stage children conceive of God as a fantasy character like Santa Claus or Superman. Later in this period, somewhere between the ages of three and six, when children are asked to draw a picture of God, they usually draw him as a king or as a father figure (Elkind [1971], p. 672). What appears to be occurring is a change to a more humanlike perception of God. With this change may come questions like, Where does God live? and What does he look like? Also, an awareness of death begins to appear. Due to limitations in preoperational cognition, children do not completely sense human finiteness nor the meaning of death, but they do begin to understand that life is not exactly what they previously assumed. At this stage they may be able to parrot complex answers to doctrinal questions, but their thinking and understanding lag behind the ability to regurgitate religious formulas they have heard.

A sense of morality begins to come into focus in this period also. With the psychosocial crises of autonomy and initiative comes the awareness that one's will or desire can conflict with others and that there is a code or set of rules which exists to determine whether or not one's behavior is acceptable. Kohlberg calls this level of morality *preconventional* because children are more concerned about protecting or enhancing their own interests in a situation than they are about the interests of others. "Will I get punished if I go too far?" and "What will I get if I control my desires?" are the questions children consider in making a decision. Similar thinking seems to go into their images of God in that they tend to view God as someone who will punish or reward them for their behavior.

This is a period of great potential for children to explore their environment and to take initiative. It is a period of wonderful fantasy and imagination that should be nurtured so that they will be creative as they grow older. Children need a religious community that allows free-flowing thought and a chance to stretch their boundaries so that they come to realize that God is not limited to punishing and shaming and restraining.

Middle childhood

Children in middle childhood (ages seven to twelve) in our society are immersed in the process of schooling. The sphere of influence has enlarged from parents and a few playmates to teachers and a multitude of potential friends and role models. New forms of thinking and new potentials for the personality arise that make possible greater spiritual development than in the previous periods.

Children are now at the stage of cognitive development that Piaget calls *concrete operations*. The previous two stages of sensorimotor and preoperational cognition did not include the ability to carry on mental operations. An operation for Piaget is some kind of organizing action whose root is either physical reality or intuition. It is a grouping of objects or events that follows rules. Prior to this stage children do not group events or intuitions.

When children reach the stage of concrete operations, they develop several other abilities as well. They begin to appreciate the concepts of time, space, and volume, as when the child comes to understand that when a clay ball is flattened only the shape and not the volume of the clay is changed. Another gain that accompanies concrete operations is an increase in the capacity to see beyond one's own needs. Prior to this stage, children are quite egocentric, believing that the world revolves around them. They previously interpreted events from their own perspective and had no idea that others also have a perspective. But now that changes as the child's world continues to expand. Real discussions are now possible. True cooperation can take place because children now realize that others may have a different perspective.

The major limitation of this stage is that the operations that are performed are limited to concrete objects and experiences. The stage is very reality-centered in that children cannot think in terms of hypothetical situations, nor can they think abstractly. This manifests itself in the way they reason about moral situations. According to Kohlberg, children of this age are still at the level of preconventional morality. They are still concerned primarily about consequences, and do not as yet think in terms of intention in assessing moral responsibility, although their cognitive development allows them to take into consideration quantity of damage. If a child breaks one drinking glass in trying to get a cookie that he or she was told not to get, the child feels less guilty than if he or she breaks three glasses while washing the dishes. To sum up: in middle childhood the individual makes great strides in cognitive abilities, with thinking becoming more organized and logical; there is the limitation, however, that that logic is restricted to concrete objects and events.

The functional crisis of *industry versus inferiority* occurs at this period in the psychosocial development of children. The sphere of those with influence expands beyond the immediate family to include the broader community. Children begin to be aware that the role of school is to prepare them to make a contribution to society and that they need to be developing some skills and abilities to offer to society (the attribute of industry). The danger at this stage is that the child may come to believe that he or she cannot make a contribution or does not have the ability to produce something significant. Erikson calls this a sense of inferiority. If a positive resolution is reached, however, the virtue of a sense of competency is added to the developing personality.

Erikson discusses the way people interact with others at each of the eight stages. At the stage of industry versus inferiority children are either engaging in relationships which contribute to the development of competence and the feeling that they can make contributions to society, or they are engaging in relationships which result in a sense of inferiority, the feeling that they have nothing to contribute. An important relationship is that of the student and the teacher in the school setting. The play of childhood has turned into homework, and the teacher either encourages particular abilities in the student or communicates a sense of inferiority. A danger here is that the child may misunderstand and begin to think that all work and no play is what makes a competent person and that a sense of self-worth is derived only through work.

Fowler (1981) identifies middle childhood as the *mythic-literal* stage of spiritual development. He states that this "is the stage in which the person begins to take on for him- or herself the stories, beliefs and observances that symbolize belonging to his or her community. Beliefs are appropriated with literal interpretations" (p. 149). An example is a boy of about seven who decided to become a Christian in a vacation Bible school. When asked, "Where is Jesus now?" his response was, "In my heart." This seems to be a profound statement, but when he was further questioned, "How do you know that?" he answered, "I know because I saw him come in through my arms and up my nose and through my ears!" Such a response is a result of concrete thinking. In middle childhood the metaphor of "in one's heart" can be understood only in concrete terms.

The tendency at this age to be rigid and formalized in one's thinking and conscience can lead to a rigid works-righteousness, an attempt to please or appease God with good deeds. Add to that the concrete, quantitative structure of thinking at this stage, and the result may well be an unhealthy faith. This should raise questions about evangelical Christianity which has a strong revivalistic approach. Do we really need to convict children of sin by scaring them with a view of God that may affirm an already fearful, legalistic conception?

For children at this age the ideal community of faith affirms the idea of a loving God who does not seek to repress us and punish us but to free us and lead us to an abundant life. It appreciates the freshness of their concrete interpretations and affirms their spontaneous responses to the Christian message. As children experience the warm love of the faith community, they will gain an image of God as one who cares for and loves them. Another result may well be a new approach to religious instruction which is not so concerned with their knowing the right answers as it is with their being in loving relationships with others. This will lead to an understanding of faith as a relationship with God.

Adolescence

There are three distinct groups of adolescents: young adolescents, middle adolescents, and late adolescents. For lack of space we will combine these groups. Needless to say, many changes occur in this stage, which, depending on one's perspective, is either the last stage of childhood or the first stage of adulthood. It is noteworthy that this is the age at which religious conversions have most often occurred.

Structurally, the individual's thinking now moves from concrete to *formal operations*. Piaget (1967) states, "Formal operations provide thinking with an entirely new ability that detaches and liberates thinking from concrete reality. . . . With the advent of formal intelligence, thinking takes wings" (pp. 63–64). The adolescent can now think about thinking. Keating (1980) lists new abilities present by virtue of formal operational thinking: thinking about possibilities, thinking through hypotheses, thinking ahead, thinking about thoughts, and thinking beyond old limits.

With formal operations come some interesting, occasionally humorous, and at times depressing effects. Elkind (1981) describes four such effects beginning with what he calls pseudostupidity. Adolescents think that their newly acquired formal operations must be applied in all situations, even in the most concrete, simple task. For example, a mother complained that her son, whom she had asked to take out the trash, had spent twenty minutes trying to map out the shortest way to collect all the household trash and get it outside! By using his formal thinking in a concrete situation, he appeared to be stupid. The second effect that Elkind speaks of is the imaginary audience. Adolescents learn to think about other people's perspective. This can result in extreme self-consciousness, for they imagine everyone is watching them. Third, Elkind speaks of the personal fable, the belief that the individual is not subject to the natural laws which pertain to others. For example, the young adolescent believes that accidents, pregnancy, and other sad realities can happen only to someone else. Finally, Elkind speaks of the "apparent hypocrisy" of the idealistic adolescent who fails to link beliefs with behavior. As an adolescent, I participated in a walk to raise funds for cleaning up the environment. After the thirty-mile walk I drove back along the route and was astounded by the incredible amounts of trash that we had strewn on the road. We had not thought of our actions as hypocritical.

The development of formal operations influences moral reasoning, resulting in what Kohlberg calls the *conventional* level of moral reasoning. The adolescent perceives that "right is playing a good (nice) role, . . . and being motivated to follow rules and expectations" (Kohlberg [1981], p. 410). The onset of formal thought, however, also brings with it the ability to take another's perspective on issues. It also leads to the realization that many moral situations are not clear-cut but demand that we abstract from principles. The individual realizes that others have perspectives, and that the right choice in some situations is to do what pleases them. In the case of young adolescents, however, concern with rules and regulations in group life seems to stem more from a desire to please authority figures than from a real commitment to principles. In summary, formal operations influence the way an adolescent perceives self, others, and moral situations. It is, indeed, the stage of thinking set free.

The psychosocial crisis of adolescence is that of *identity versus identity confusion*. Erikson is best known for his description of this stage. Identity implies a sense of continuity and selfsameness. This means that we have a sense of being the same person across a variety of situations and that others perceive us as we perceive ourselves. Existentially, a sense of identity is accompanied by a feeling of being at home or knowing where one is going. The primary task is to answer the question, "Who am I?"

Erikson (1980) emphasizes that identity formation is not a product of adolescence alone but is a lifelong and ongoing process that is a special emphasis of this stage. The individual continues to develop chronologically and make very pragmatic identity decisions. Of these decisions, vocational, ideological, and relational choices are most important in the identity-formation process.

Vocationally, the adolescent must ask the question, "What will I be when I grow up?" Included in this question is, "What will I spend my life and energy on, and will I contribute to society?"

The adolescent also develops a set of values or beliefs, an ideology, that gives a sense of coherence or wholeness to life. An ideology motivates the young person in her or his participation in sports, music, or politics. It yields a consistent pattern of behavior. Followers of a particular ideology will act in much the same way. Consider, for example, the crowds at football games, the "groupies" following a band, or young people who dress and act like a charismatic figure. An ideology can make positive contributions to identity formation: (1) it can give one a perspective on the future; (2) it can help to coordinate actual behavior with internal beliefs; and (3) it can provide an authority figure in the adolescent's life. Negatively, ideology can degenerate into "totalism." Erikson (1982) defines totalism as "fanatic participation in militant ritualisms" (p. 74). A young person may become totally consumed with a narrow world-view or cause and summarily reject all other perspectives. Totalism can be seen most readily in religious cults that force young people to repudiate their parents and any other part of their life that does not align with the group.

Relationally, the adolescent now begins to be more selective in making friends and realizes that association with some former friends is no longer possible. Decisions about sexuality must also be made by the adolescent as he or she attempts to figure out what it means to be male or female.

A danger at this stage is the possibility of identity confusion or role diffusion. As Biff says in *Death of a Salesman*, "I just can't take hold." The decisions about vocation, ideology, and relationships become too much to be dealt with. The young person is bewildered. Further danger comes when the adolescent who is unable to come to basic decisions about personal identity assumes a negative identity. This is "an identity which he has been warned not to become" (Erikson [1958], p. 102). The adolescent may respond to an untrusting parent, "If you say I'm bad and not to be trusted, then I will be bad and untrustworthy."

The ego strength or virtue that arises out of a favorable resolution at this stage is fidelity. Erikson (1964) defines fidelity as "disciplined devotion" or "the ability to sustain loyalties freely pledged" (p. 125). He further defines it as a renewal on a higher level of trust and the ability to be trustworthy and to commit oneself to a cause (1982, p. 60). If a favorable resolution is achieved, then the adolescent will go on in the process of identity formation with some sense of direction, commitment to self and others, and a set of beliefs or values to guide further choices.

Structural and functional theories both give much that informs us on spiritual development in adolescence. Fowler calls this the period of *synthetic-conventional faith*. Faith is synthetic in that the person attempts to make sense out of the various and undoubtedly conflicting authorities in his or her life. Given the ability to reflect on self as well as others' opinions, the adolescent must somehow bring these together to synthesize them. This is done either by "compartmentalization," which means that the adolescent believes whatever is believed by the group she or he is presently with, or by "hierarchization," which means that the young person evaluates beliefs and values according to the level of importance which the particular people who hold them have in his or her life. This stage of spiritual development is also called conventional in that the young person becomes temporarily or permanently dependent upon authority figures for the construction and maintenance of identity and faith. What is problematic about this is that adolescents judge the validity of a leader by his or her personal qualities and not by objective criteria. Faith decisions may be made on the basis of the charisma or loving-kindness of a leader, not on the basis of the truth of her or his claims. This seems to be characteristic of the faith of many (though not all) young persons.

The distinction between a sense of identity built on the Bible and one built on contemporary theories is that the former is grounded in otherness or God, and the latter in self. Jesus says in several ways that true life or identity is found in denying self and losing self for his sake. Paul says that he no longer lives, but Christ lives in him (Gal. 2:20). The phrase "in Christ" brings to mind a sense of belonging which is at the core of identity. This is quite different from the philosophy of those who deny having any need to be grounded in otherness or to seek the welfare of others before self.

It can now be seen why adolescence is the most common age period for religious conversion. The person is both cognitively and psychosocially ready to find something or someone to live for. As Virgil Gillespie (1979) states, "Through religious conversion's experience an all-embracing goal is obtained and focused around which the experiences of life will be grounded and interpreted" (p. 171).

Christian faith gives the young person an ideology to live by and for. We must be careful not to think of all ideologies as of equal worth in this process. Secular ideologies and faith in Christ are not the same. An ideology can function in such a way as to leave the person unconcerned about and unrelated to the transcendent God. It is essential to find one's sense of identity in the living God and not merely in a secular world-view.

From a Christian perspective vocational identity also takes on a radically different dimension. Brueggemann says that to be in relationship with God "transposes all identity questions into vocational questions," and that vocation is finding "a purpose for being in the world that is related to the purposes of God" (quoted in Fowler [1984], p. 93). Christian adolescents must not only ask, "Who am I?" but must also be clear regarding to whom they belong and how this identity will be concretely translated into the vocation to which they have committed their lives.

When adolescents place themselves in Christ, their identity is solidly grounded in the reality of a living faith. That faith must then be critically reflected upon with all the formal operational ability the young person has so as to come to a faith that is well thought out. In this process the young person will also find guidelines for relational and vocational decisions.

Adulthood

Piaget thinks that the shift to formal operational thought in adolescence or beyond is the final major structural development in cognitive maturation. Several others have speculated about additional stages, but the evidence is inconclusive. This is not to say that in adulthood there is no change in the cognitive process. What happens is that the formal operations are generalized to other content areas of a person's thinking. When formal operations begin, they are usually confined to the area of thinking that the person uses most. Generalization means that formal thought now begins to be used in areas other than the individual's primary interests. One other shift which may occur is the move from problem solving to problem posing. This implies that the person is becoming so competent with formal thought that he or she can see issues behind the obvious.

Kohlberg believes that in adulthood it is possible for the individual to attain a final level of moral development, though passage into this *postconventional* stage of moral reasoning is by no means automatic. In this stage, the individual is committed, not to specific rules of right and wrong, but rather to higher, more transcendent principles of morality; the foremost of these universals Kohlberg considers to be justice. Adults who are at the highest stage of moral thought make personal commitments to the principles of the good because that is what they value, not because they fear the consequences if they do not behave.

Kohlberg's work has been criticized for his use of a confusing and almost unreplicable methodology. The theory has also been criticized on philosophical grounds for its Western, male, rationalistic biases (Kurtines and Greif [1974]). It is also generally viewed as a flaw that Kohlberg does not link moral reasoning to behavior, as if the actual decisions people make were unimportant. Can structure (how the decisions are reached) truly be divorced from content? Kohlberg's theory also falls short in that, unlike the Christian view, he neglects relationships and their impact on moral reasoning. Carol Gilligan (1982), an associate of Kohlberg's, argues that a theory of moral reasoning or knowing must include the "Biblical conception of knowing as a process of human relationship" (p. 173).

Theologically, "one of the critical problems with Kohlberg's theory of moral development stems from the fact that he does not take human sinfulness seriously" (Dykstra [1983], p. 153). Kohlberg seems to think that all persons can achieve the highest level of morality. By contrast, the Christian view argues that our reason must be transformed before higher moral reasoning can occur. It also argues that actual behavior necessarily results from moral reasoning. From a Christian perspective, there are also problems with his definition of and focus on justice. He seems to see justice only in terms of rewarding right and punishing wrong. The biblical sense of justice, on the other hand, inherently includes grace and mercy.

Further, it is argued that Kohlberg's theory is based on a view of ethics which focuses on the rightness or wrongness of particular acts. The Christian ethic, however, also necessarily includes a vision of what it is to be a good person. The Bible presents us with a vision of what the moral life is like, an ethics of character which asks us to do as Jesus did: to feed the hungry, clothe the naked, and help the oppressed (Matt. 25:31–46). Beyond doing specific good acts, we are told to develop a certain kind of character as Christians (see, e.g., Phil. 2:1–13). The morality exhibited by Jesus goes far beyond any mere reasoning about the rightness or wrongness of specific acts to a character ethics that demands we exhibit a love like his.

The primary developments which occur in adulthood are functional changes. Erikson (1982) says that the psychosocial crisis of young adulthood is *intimacy versus isolation*. Intimacy is described as "the capacity to commit oneself to concrete affiliations which may call for significant sacrifices and compromises" (p. 70). The task is to be willing to share oneself with others in marriage, in work, in friendship. The opposite of intimacy is isolation, inability to share oneself in deep relationships.

Given a favorable resolution, the ego strength of love emerges. Erikson (1982) defines love as "mutuality of mature devotion that promises to resolve the antagonisms inherent in divided function" (p. 71). It is important that a young adult find a group of friends who are held together by common patterns of thought and action. The danger here is that they may form a group which excludes anyone whose thoughts and actions differ from theirs.

The psychosocial crisis of middle adulthood is *generativity versus stagnation and self-absorption*. Generativity includes procreativity, productivity, and creativity. We need to give ourselves in some way to the new generation. This can be accomplished by bearing and nurturing children or creating products and ideas that contribute to the welfare of the upcoming generation. Stagnation and self-absorption suggest inability and lack of desire to give beyond oneself. There is no desire to see that life is better for others. The ego strength which emerges from a positive resolution is concern: a commitment to take care of and to care for the next generation. Persons in middle adulthood must understand their position as role models and act appropriately. The danger at this stage is an abusive, uncaring use of authority which discourages and defeats the upcoming generation.

The final psychosocial crisis defined by Erikson is that of *integrity versus despair*. Older adults attempt to come to some sense of integrity as they reflect on the totality of their life cycle with its successes and failures. A negative resolution results in despair, the feeling that all of one's life has been a failure. The virtue which emerges from a positive resolution is wisdom. Wisdom is an informed and detached concern with life. It implies a peaceful acceptance of death and a willingness to support others. The role of the older person as the holder of wisdom is to give purpose and hope to the culture. The danger is older persons who become so sure that their way is right that they have no openness to new thoughts.

Fowler has several useful insights concerning spiritual development in adulthood. Before discussing them, however, some criticisms must be presented. First, a question must be raised about Fowler's definition of faith. He says that faith is a human universal that may or may not include a religious component. Is this the way that faith is understood biblically? It is helpful to know that people think about faith in different ways, but this definition neglects the fact that faith leads to salvation and gives us hope regarding things unseen. Could faith as it is defined by Fowler have been what empowered Abraham and Moses? Surely not! Secondly, a question needs to be raised over any developmental theory that is more concerned with stages than with the process of development. Do people pass through nice neat stages as they mature in faith, or do they develop by sometimes going backward, sometimes forward, sometimes moving by inches, sometimes by leaps and bounds? It seems that a good developmental theory would concentrate on the processes involved more than on temporary plateaus. Also, a question must be raised concerning the descriptions of the higher stages of faith. Fowler's final stage (stage 6) is that of "universalizing faith." Those persons who have attained it "have generated faith compositions in which their felt sense of an ultimate environment is inclusive of all being" (Fowler [1981], p. 193). This ambiguous and ethereal description raises questions as to whether such a stage really exists. Further, it should be pointed out that any evaluation of different types of faith as more or less mature is colored by the world-view and faith commitments of the researchers. This is necessarily the case, since there are no purely objective bases for judging whether, for example, a literalistic understanding of miracles is more or less mature.

Fowler (1981) further describes persons who have reached the final stage of faith as "ready for fellowship with persons at any of the other stages and from any other faith or cultural tradition" (p. 193). But this is the description of a classic nineteenth-century liberal theologian. Goldberg (1982) suggests that Fowler should examine the lives of saints like Augustine to see how the theory holds up. Augustine as well as others whom we esteem as exemplars of faith tended to narrow their vision of faith instead of making it all-inclusive. Did Paul's or Peter's faith gradually broaden or did it continue to be Christocentric? Goldberg also criticizes Fowler's exclusive concern with the map rather than with the destination. Given these problems, some suggest that Fowler's (1984) description of conjunctive faith (stage 5) should be seen as the end point of the model (pp. 72–73).

It may be that Fowler's view is not a good developmental theory (people do not progress naturally through the stages); nevertheless, it is still a good way of describing different types of religious faith. Of course, in doing so one must constantly be aware of the presuppositions with which a theorist like Fowler is working. These presuppositions must be reflected on from the perspectives of both social science and theology.

Let us now examine the third, fourth, and fifth of Fowler's stages of spiritual development. We omit stage six due to a lack of clear evidence and conceptualization. The third stage, which we have already described in the section on adolescence, is synthetic-conventional faith. It is characterized by conformity and deference to authority. Young adults, faced with both the need to have right answers from an authoritative source and the psychosocial task of intimacy, may develop a faith that is overly dogmatic and exclusive. They may trust only a few theological authorities to give the right answers. Also they will affiliate only with those who think the same as they.

The fourth stage—*individuating-reflective faith*—can be defined as individualized theological certainty. People now begin to have a faith that is their own. They move beyond dependency on authority figures to finding answers for themselves. Fowler sees two prerequisites to this type of faith. First, the person must begin to ground his sense of self in himself and not others. Secondly, the person must be able to objectify and think critically about his beliefs. At this point one moves beyond simple belief to a type of faith that is constructed and appropriated individually. This stage of faith is limited by its need for right answers. Although the individual wants a personally constructed faith, he or she is unable to live with paradox; there must be one right answer!

The fifth stage is *conjunctive faith*. The primary difference from the fourth stage is a newly developed ability to live with paradox and tension. The person sees that apparent contradictions are a part of life; and instead of being blinded to them, he or she chooses to address them and live with the tension. These persons exhibit a "second naiveté" in that they move beyond a critical approach and a need for right answers to faith. Due to their willingness to live with doubt, they will most likely be unacceptable to the adherents of rigid conservative theology.

How the adult psychosocial crises are resolved is the key to the type of faith people have. It has already been said that a negative resolution of intimacy versus isolation may yield an exclusive, narrow type of faith, but what about the psychosocial crisis of generativity versus stagnation and self-absorption? Positively, people who are generative and caring model a concern for the future generation which communicates a loving, gracious type of faith. Negatively, if people become self-absorbed and model a life of authoritarianism, they will exhibit a repressive, legalistic type of faith, a faith which is narrow and exclusive.

Illustrative of the self-absorbed adult are those who take refuge in the notion of a midlife crisis. Many have found in Daniel Levinson (1978) and the others who have popularized the midlife crisis an explanation for events in their lives, and this is good. The problem comes when we uncritically accept his developmental periods as inevitable occurrences at specific ages and use them as excuses for irresponsible behavior. Levinson's view that change in adulthood is acceptable is to be applauded; its advocacy of a selfish stance in life, however, must be rejected.

Levinson's theory stands in stark contrast to the Christian view of adulthood, which holds us responsible for our actions. In describing the Christian idea of adulthood William Bouwsma (1978) states, "The goal of human development is total conformity to the manhood of Christ" (p. 85), which is not a model of separation and self-centered achievement, but of self-denial and commitment to others. Bouwsma continues, "Since this [Christ-likeness] is a transcendent goal, the practical emphasis in Christian adulthood is on the process rather than its end" (p. 85). In this regard Levinson is valuable in that he helps us see that adulthood is not a static end-point, but a dynamic and changing process which continually renews our lives in faith.

The ways we structure faith cognitively and resolve psychosocial crises converge to shape the Christian adult. Adulthood is the dynamic accumulation and formation of past events into new ways of living. In adulthood we have the added potential, through grace, of ever infusing our lives with higher purpose and more mature faith.

This chapter has attempted to describe the contribution developmental psychology makes toward an understanding of spiritual development across the life span. It is important to take structural and functional theory together because one without the other can lead to a lopsided understanding of human development. Structural theory helps us to understand that faith assumes a different nature at various points along the life span. This awareness is useful in that, for example, it relaxes us when a child's image of God is a magical, mythical figure. It is also useful in that it points up one of the possible reasons why the contemporary church often seems to be immature: there is not enough intellectual stimulation to further one's view of God beyond that of a child. Functional theory assists us to appreciate the crises that a person must deal with, the decisions one must make, at particular points along the life span. It is a relief to realize that adolescents' doubting their faith is a normal part of a healthy resolution of the identity crisis. To help young persons realize this will enhance their spiritual and personal development.

Finally, it is hoped that this chapter has made it clear that one must be constantly aware that all developmental psychologists begin with particular presuppositions that color the work they are doing. They have specific views on the moral nature of humans and on the roles of nature and nurture in the developing person. All of these must be detected and evaluated by the serious student. It is necessary that both social-scientific and theological reflection be brought to bear on this task. To achieve honest integration of Christian faith with developmental psychology, one must critique every theory, including its basic assumptions, on both psychological and theological grounds.

References

Bouwsma, W. (1978). Christian adulthood. In E. Erikson, ed., *Adulthood*. New York: Norton.

Dykstra, C. (1983). What are people like? An alternative to Kohlberg's view. In D. Joy, ed., *Moral development foundations*. Nashville: Abingdon.

Elkind, D. (1971). The development of religious understanding in children and adolescents. In M. Strommen, ed., *Research on religious development*. New York: Hawthorn.

_____ (1981). Understanding the young adolescent. In L. Steinberg, ed., *The life cycle*. New York: Columbia University Press.

Erikson, E. (1950). *Childhood and society*. New York: Norton.

_____ (1958). *Young man Luther*. New York: Norton.

_____ (1964). *Insight and responsibility*. New York: Norton.

_____ (1980). *Identity and the life cycle*. New York: Norton.

_____ (1982). *The life cycle completed*. New York: Norton.

Fowler, J. (1981). *Stages of faith: The psychology of human development and the quest for meaning*. San Francisco: Harper & Row.

_____ (1984). *Becoming adult, becoming Christian*. New York: Harper & Row.

Gillespie, V. (1979). *Religious conversion and personal identity*. Birmingham, Ala.: Religious Education.

Gilligan, C. (1982). *In a different voice*. Cambridge, Mass.: Harvard University Press.

Goldberg, M. (1982). *Theology and narrative: A critical introduction*. Nashville: Abingdon.

Keating, D. (1980). Thinking processes in adolescence. In J. Adelson, ed., *Handbook of adolescent psychology*. New York: Wiley.

Kohlberg, L. (1973). Continuities in childhood and adult moral development revisited. In P. Baltes and W. Schaie, eds., *Life-span developmental psychology*. New York: Academic Press.

_____ (1981). *The philosophy of moral development*. Essays on moral development, vol. 1. New York: Harper & Row.

Kurtines, W., and E. Greif (1974). The development of moral thought: Review and evaluation of Kohlberg's approach. *Psychological Bulletin* 81: 453–70.

Levinson, D., et al. (1978). *The seasons of a man's life*. New York: Knopf.

Looft, W. (1973). Socialization and personality throughout the life-span. In P. Baltes and W. Schaie, eds., *Life-span developmental psychology*. New York: Academic Press.

Piaget, J. (1967). *Six psychological studies*. New York: Random House.

Biblical Teaching on Personality
H. D. McDonald

In the first chapter, it was pointed out that a significant number of Christians who work in the field of psychology see the primary task of integration as having our Christian commitment determine the fundamental presuppositions we bring to the social-scientific task. To accomplish this, we must know what the faith has to say about human nature. Every Christian in psychology, regardless of his or her views of integration, would agree that it is imperative for Christians to be informed about what the Bible and Christian theology have to say concerning the nature of human existence.

And yet it is very difficult to find a balanced, thoughtful presentation of what the Bible and Christian theology have to say about humanity. Many naive personality-theories have been proposed in religious books, each promoted as the Christian personality-theory. This chapter summarizes the essence of biblical and theological teachings about anthropology, the doctine of humanity. The balanced and scholarly conclusions will challenge the reader to think deeply about the interface between Christian belief and psychological theory.

H. D. McDonald (B.A., B.D., Ph.D., D.D., University of London) was formerly the head of the Department of Philosophy and Historical Theology and the vice-principal of London Bible College. He has been a visiting professor of theology at many American seminaries and colleges. He is the author of a number of books, including The Christian View of Man *(Westchester, Ill.: Good News,*

1981) and The Atonement of the Death of Christ *(Grand Rapids: Baker, 1985).*

The question, "What is man?" is, according to Immanuel Kant, the last of the four basic issues which have to be faced in the pursuit of knowledge. And indeed, this question has been the last in the order of historical discussion. The immediate past and the present age have, in parallel with a growing interest in the conditions of the human person, witnessed the establishment of psychology as a credible scientific methodology. Much of what we know today about man, about the psychological and sociological laws that govern his life, about his actions and his reactions, was unknown in past ages. Yet in spite of the abundance of material at the disposal of the modern researcher, the judgment of Martin Heidegger is essentially true: No age has known so much, and so many things about man, as does ours, and yet no age has known less than ours what man is.

The reason why this is so is not difficult to discern. We now live in what has come to be designated a post-Christian age, so that explanations of man's existence and nature are presently sought without reference to God. It is, in fact, characteristic of our times that the reality of a divine Creator and providential Ruler is either denied outright or politely ignored. The theistic view of the world is given short shrift by the makers of modern thought, with the result that accounts of man's presence and purpose in the world are elaborated solely in the context of the mundane and the natural. Earlier certainties about man, based on biblical data, are summarily dismissed as the antiquated notions of a prescientific age. And gone with them is that security man had in regarding himself as God's creature in God's world.

Yet in the final analysis it is the biblico-religious account of persons which accords best with our convictions about ourselves. We know that we carry deep within ourselves, as a property of our essential natures, a moral and spiritual sensitivity which gives us a special value and significance. In contrast with the many contemporary theories of personality, the dramatists and poets of former times better understood people for who and what they are because they more readily acknowledged the biblical view of persons which they saw validated in real life.

Taken as a methodology, a scientific psychological perspective on man may be authentic enough as far as it goes, or can go. But if taken as a final statement of all that belongs to human personhood, then its conclusions must be regarded as incomplete and misleading. The root meaning of the term *psychology* is "the science of the soul," but many psychological theorists deny to man the presence of soul. To regard psychology merely as the science of behavior is to leave unknown and unreached that existential selfhood behind and present in observable behavior patterns. For "however important the body may be, it can never be regarded as the whole self or even the most essential part of the self" (Stout [1920], p. 661). The truth of the matter is that these realities about human beings—the person, the soul, the consciousness, and the self—are beyond the range of psychological probing and, indeed, of philosophical proving. As the ultimate constituents of personal human life they have their source and secret in the mystery of life itself.

The presence of life is an impenetrable mystery. Life just is; there is no scientific explanation of its source or its existence. Science can and does explain many things about *living*, but *life* itself it does not understand. It is not enough to say that life results from the activity of living phenomena, for living phenomena themselves presuppose life. In addition to the physical and the psychical or self-conscious, which are in their measure accessible to science, there is a life-principle which cannot be caught in any scientist's net, and which in union with or, better perhaps, in its action upon the physical and the psychical, gives an individual uniqueness and purpose as a person. Clearly, answers to the questions of the "whence?" and the "what?" of life are not to be sought within any actions or processes of the inorganic. Only by taking seriously the theistic view of creation can an entirely worthy and a completely acceptable explanation of the origin of life be laid bare. It is God, the living God, who "gives to all men life and breath and everything" (Acts 17:25, RSV). By means of the union of God's breath and dust from the ground, man became a living being (Gen. 2:7). Thus the life-principle which makes man man has its source in God.

Man as a Divine Creation

The world of inanimate things and animals was brought into being by God's declared word. "God said . . . and it was so." God's *speech* was his creative act. Now God was more intimately involved in his creation of man than in his creation of the inanimate world and animals. At the same time he maintained a distance. Here there was the union of God's otherness from man—"the LORD God formed man of dust from the ground" (Gen. 2:7, RSV)—and his likeness to man—"So God created man in his own image, in the image of God he created him" (Gen. 1:27, RSV). Thus man is at once of nature and of God, a combination of dust and deity. "As the Creator's creation, man reflects his Maker in mind and conscience and is both a part of nature yet distinct from it" (Henry [1976], p. 248).

In creating man, the living God spoke and acted. And in his speech and acts there is man's life. By imparting breath to the man he formed, man lives (Gen. 2:7; cf. Rev. 11:11); and if God "should take back his spirit to himself, / and gather to himself his breath, / all flesh would perish together, / and man would return to dust" (Job 34:14–15, RSV; cf. Pss. 90:3; 104:29–30; Eccles. 12:7).

Such is man's dependence on the living God for his existence and his being that man's breath and spirit can be declared one with God's breath and spirit (Job 27:3; cf. 33:4; Gen. 6:3; Isa. 42:5). Man's life is maintained by everything that proceeds out of the mouth of the Lord (Matt. 4:4). Man's being is from God and his very life continues because of him. So throughout the Old Testament revelation, God makes appeals to man on the grounds of being his Creator (e.g., Deut. 4:32; Isa. 40:28; 43:15). Furthermore, because of man's creation in the image and likeness of God, there is a kinship between the human spirit and the divine which constitutes the grounds for the appeal of the gospel.

Essential Characteristics of Human Beings

The image of God

Human beings are unique. This fact is affirmed in their creation by a special resolve and distinct act of God; this sets them apart from the rest of the created order. Men and women are beings capable of fellowship with God himself, for they are created in his image.

The declaration of Genesis 1:27 is specific: "God created man in his own image, in the image of God he created him; male and female he created them" (RSV; cf. 5:2; 9:6). Man not only has his life from God, he has a fundamental likeness to God. Genesis declares both man and woman to be the bearers of the divine image; consequently, they are equally the objects of his concern and care. But what precisely is to be understood by the expression "the image of God"? This question has given rise to a large literature in which various answers have been given. These answers include assertions that the "image of God" refers to our bodily form, our existence as spirits, our lordship over nature, our existence as male and female, and our rational and moral personality (McDonald [1981]).

We suggest that all these views can be subsumed under the one concept of "sonship." Each of them is but one aspect of the deeper and more fundamental truth that we are all God's sons and daughters. All of the views we have mentioned coalesce in this idea. Herein lies the essence of the image in which man was created. Human beings were created for sonship; such was our original state before God. This does not mean that we may appeal to a natural and continuing kinship with God to assure every individual a ready acceptance with God, for the human race has rejected and sinned away this sonship. Nevertheless, the personal appeal of the gospel rests on the sonship which belongs to every person. The explanation of this fact is that the image of God itself, although defaced by sin, has not been totally destroyed. James Orr (1897) points out: "As made by God, and as standing in his normal relation to Him, man is without doubt a son. . . . The fact that the title "son of God" should belong to *any*, already implies a natural kinship between God and man, else the higher relationship would not be possible. If there were not already a God-related element in the human spirit, no subsequent act of grace could confer on man this spiritual dignity" (pp. 119–20; cf. Acts 17:28).

Sometimes in the history of Christian doctrine one aspect of the God-man relationship has been given exclusive emphasis to the denial of its opposite. In deism, God was so separated from man that the divine and human were thrown into absolute opposition. German speculative theology, on the other hand, under the influence of Georg Hegel, so accentuated the kinship between God and man as to present man as but an aspect of deity. Both these antitheses are false if taken by themselves. The truth is that there is between God and man an actual inner relationship, a connection between the divine spirit and the human spirit which makes man capable of receiving from God his living image.

The incarnation of God the Son is the supreme demonstration of this truth. For in the one person of the Word made flesh there is a union of the human and divine so close and intimate as to constitute Christ the perfect image of God (Col. 1:15; cf. Rom. 8:29; 2 Cor. 4:4; Col. 3:10). In this regard Christ is the personification of the biblical doctrine of man. To get a knowledge of the true essence of anything, as Aristotle has taught us, we should look at its best specimens, and not at its ruder and cruder forms. Christ is the best of humanity. For not only is he the organ of the divine revelation to humanity, he is our only example of full humanity. In him is embodied in perfect form the divine idea of what man was meant to be. All human beings are measured by this man. In him we have some idea of what kinship to God means. His eternal sonship in relation to the Father provided the pattern, the original image, in which man was created. All persons were created for sonship in the image of Christ's sonship. In this sense he was the archetypal man. By becoming man the uncreated Son revealed the ideal according to which human nature was originally planned. And having become man, he is now the head of a new humanity renewed to sonship "after the image of its creator" (Col. 3:10, rsv; cf. 1 Cor. 11:7; 2 Cor. 3:18).

Man's permanent dignity derives, then, from the reality of the *imago Dei* (the image of God) in which he was created. It is this relationship to God which gives him his unique worth in comparison to the rest of creation. Man was divinely fashioned for a high role in God's world. He was crowned with glory and honor (Ps. 8:5). A crown is a sign of a special status and standing. "As God's imagebearer, man was to hear God's word addressed to him and to respond in the joy of adoring obedience" (Henry [1979], p. 215). Alas, however, for man as he now is, the crown has become somewhat tarnished, and slipped sideway on, if not altogether fallen off, his head. For no longer does the human race bear the image in its full splendor. No longer does man live before God as a son, and no longer does he act as a brother toward his fellows. How are the mighty fallen! Man soiled and spoiled his status with God. This is vividly evident in Genesis 5:3, for instead of reading that man was created in God's image (cf. Gen. 1:27), we are told that Adam "became the father of a son in his own likeness, after his image" (rsv).

Personhood

From the biblical declaration of man's creation in the image of God it follows that each member of the human family is to be regarded as a unique personhood. The Christian doctrine of God as personal carries with it this same certainty about man. The one conviction is indeed the guarantee of the other; both stand or fall together. Yet while Scripture uniformly presents both God and man as personal, it does not give any formal definition of the personhood of either party. Here, as is often the case, lack of exact definitions in the Bible results in our being unable to extract from it the precise nomenclature required by scientific psychology. Biblical revelation is less concerned with scientific psychology than with a presentation of man in terms of his relationship to God, to his fellow man, and to natural phenomena. Throughout the biblical account there is a constant awareness of the unique existence and personal identity of the individual, of a distinctive essence in each man by virtue of which he can be characterized as a selfhood. This requires that he speak as an "I" and be spoken to as a "you."

Person and personality. The term *personality* is generally held to be derived from the Latin *persona*, the mask worn by ancient actors. "Personality," then, literally refers to an individual's outward appearance or the role one plays. It may be viewed as the general impression a person makes. As a result of this impression, one individual may be described as having a pleasing disposition, another as being morose, and so forth. All such words are really adjectives which indicate the nature of an individual's behavior. Many psychologists, however, deliberately identify the two concepts, person and personality, and contend that a person is what his personality displays. There is, they say, nothing else behind the mask. Thus both terms are given the same definition: "person" and "personality" are defined as the sum of behavior traits bound together (or in the process of being bound together) into a particular unity to constitute a human selfhood. A variety of personality theories have been formulated in attempts to synthesize the manifold data of psychology into a coherent holistic view of human nature. But in the end, of course, each personality theory is built on assumptions about man and the essential characteristics of his being.

It is beyond our purposes to discuss the psychology of personality or to adjudicate between the hundreds of definitions of personality which are available. It is enough to observe here that two of the major personality theories are altogether conditioned by their initial approach. The classic behavioral view puts the emphasis on the external influences affecting the individual, the classic Freudian view on his internal structure. We will briefly explore these differing perspectives to highlight their implications for human personhood.

Behaviorism, as a body of psychological doctrine, had its birth in the wide acceptance of philosophical materialism, an understanding of the universe in terms of matter in motion. John B. Watson's (1913) article "Psychology as the Behaviorist Views It" provided the blueprint for this new psychological realism. Supported by experiments on animals which suggested that behavior results from reactions to stimuli, Watson set about establishing human psychology on an objective basis of external observable actions. Eliminating all conscious elements from psychological data, he sought to present a picture of the human organism as a sort of physical machine. Man is simply what he does. And so Watson states, "I believe we can write a psychology . . . and . . . never use the terms consciousness, mental states, mind, content, will, introspectively verifiable imagery, and the like" (p. 167). Accordingly, the classical behaviorist presents man as a curious sort of empty shell without mind or soul. There is nothing in the individual beyond his overt bodily actions in response to stimuli. Classic behaviorism leaves no place for moral action. It makes a mockery of all ethical judgments based on anything other than physical phenomena, and so denies the existence of a divine moral absolute which calls for man's willed response. The behaviorist denies the existence of "willed" events distinct from physical ones. By declaring all acts to be bodily functions, all man's behavior becomes, at least in theory, entirely predictable.

The consistent behaviorist must accept that if human actions are purely the result of irresistible universal laws (i.e., are mechanically determined), then all life itself has no reason. And "if there is no rational grounds for anything, it is useless to ask the behaviorist why he writes books apparently aimed at inducing his reader on rational grounds to change his opinions" (Hodgson [1930], p. 29). For if the basic behaviorist premise is correct, then the doctrines of behaviorism are nothing other than the physical activity of a number of like-bodied psychologists. Opposing theories could claim to be equally true, since they are also the reflexive reactions prevailing in the bodies of rival psychologists. Both philosophical materialism and its offspring psychological behaviorism suffer "from one great defect": they take "from man his significance in the cosmic scheme of things" and deny "reality to his mind" (MacMurray [1957], p. 123). Because consciousness is denied, the person disappears from behavioristic psychology, a result which is unacceptable to the Christian. Classic behaviorism, then, though it may have its uses, cannot be judged to have an adequate view of the whole person.

Is classic Freudian psychology any more acceptable? According to J. C. Flugel (1945), Freud's "outstanding achievement" was "to have opened up a vast region (the unconscious psychic) which before him had been suspected to exist, but never entered by a scientist" (p. 293). It was on the basis of his hypothesized psychological structure of the human person that Freud developed his analytic method as a means to explore and explode man's inner stresses. This method led the way to the healing of psychological wounds and can be used by the Christian pastor as a helpful handmaid in applying the gospel to human needs. But we are concerned here with the propositions about religion and the nature of personhood which Freud believed to follow from his basic hypotheses and findings.

Freud regarded man as the product of his environment. In his efforts to relate to the environment, he develops a psychological neurosis. This fundamental neurosis, this unconscious reservoir of instinctual urges, is the cause of all man's woes. It gets its start from conflicts set up in early childhood and colors the person's outlook throughout life. From this perspective, Freud makes his theological pronouncements. Religion, he declares, "is comparable to a childhood neurosis" (1934, p. 92); and God is an illusion produced by the instinctual desire for protection, the outworking of the innate father-complex (1940, p. 237). Morality and conscience likewise have their origin in the conflict between the unconscious factors and the conscious in the developing individual.

Two implications of Freud's analysis of the structure of the human individual bring his view of man into conflict with that of Scripture. The first is *determinism*. Freud held that the origins and causes of all conscious action are to be found in the unconscious, which lies outside of the control of the individual. Conscious action is clearly a by-product of unconscious processes, and is thus determined by those processes. The conscience is also seen as a product of unconscious forces. The conscience, which Freud called the superego, is created by the incorporation into the self of the moral standards of society. Conscience, for Freud, is little more than society's way of imposing its collective demands on the individual. In the end, asserted Freud, all human action is determined by the interaction between the unconscious and the superego, neither of which is under the person's control.

It follows that the individual does not have responsibility for his or her deeds, a conclusion which undermines the traditional basis of general ethics (Smethurst [1955]). Such a fatalistic attitude regarding human nature affects moral conduct in two ways. First, there is a tendency (openly affirmed by many psychiatrists) to say that people cannot be blamed for their unethical ways since they are the victims of forces beyond their control. Second, Freud's thesis has weakened the desire to strive for right living in contemporary society, for it leads to the conclusion that one need not feel a sense of guilt for failure to do so.

The other implication which clashes with Scripture is that of *irrationality*. According to Freud, reason is the tool of the unconscious instincts. It is the instincts which determine and control the operations of the conscious mind. The sole function of reason is discovering means for the satisfaction of those instincts which employ it. For Freud the instincts are the real movers of human activity. "Reason, in other words, is a mechanism; it is the engine of the personality, and instinct is the steam that sets it going. And, since reason can operate only when driven by the impulsive force of instinct, it can proceed only along the path which instinct indicates to the goal which instinct dictates" (Joad [1948], p. 263). This means that the reason is no longer to be regarded as free, and that all reasoning is but rationalization. But this is surely not a right view of the nature and function of reason in man, who was created for fellowship with God.

Maybe earlier ages gave to the reason too high a place in the catalogue of those properties which distinguish man from the rest of created beings. But to virtually denude man of reason altogether by declaring it the tool of the instincts is to make man no different from the animal kingdom and to deny him that otherness from the rest of creation on which the biblical account insists. Man's thoughts are not indeed God's thoughts, but man can have thoughts and can know truth. In fact, God would have man "reason together" with him (Isa. 1:18; cf. 1 Sam. 12:7; Job 13:3), and instructs him, "Be not like a horse or a mule, without understanding, / which must be curbed with bit and bridle, / else it will not keep with you" (Ps. 32:9, RSV). It is with rational beings God would have communion. Thus throughout Scripture we are called both to think and to understand.

In the Freudian view, people have neither true rationality nor true freedom. The effects on modern thought have been dramatic: the belief that we can know truth, the position that we are responsible moral beings, and our motivation to exercise moral restraint have all been undermined. Of course, psychoanalytic theory has also afforded many benefits. It has helped us to recognize that certain distresses and mental illnesses are beyond relief by mere physical antidotes. It has rightly contended that the area of conscious life is not of the same order as the physical. This is a profound insight with the potential for much good, for all mental disorders had previously been attributed to physical causes. But with the good has come the bad. Owing their allegiance to biological reductionism, the major spokespersons of psychoanalysis expanded mechanical determinism from physical causation to all of the sequences of man's mental life. Psychoanalysts, anxious to secure for themselves the status of scientists, denied that the psychic in man can ever generate free action.

The truth is, however, that while our actions are in some respects predictable, we are nevertheless free beings. Thus, while "on the level of psychological analysis . . . freedom seems impossible . . . on the level of moral personality, freedom is essential" (Robinson [1911], p. 292). The being of man cannot be absolutely determined. Man exists in the union of soul and body. The existence of human beings may "be thought of as material in so far as their behaviour is a passive functioning in accordance with forces acting on or through them, and spiritual in so far as it is the expression of their having made up their minds to do this or that. We use the word freedom to describe this ability of the spiritual being to act on purpose as contrasted with the inability of the material thing to do more than respond willy nilly to stimuli" (Hodgson [1956], p. 171).

At the beginning of this section, reference was made to the distinction often drawn between person and personality. Personality, it was stated, is the role played by the person. It is with the personality that psychoanalysis is concerned. On the fundamental reality of personhood, the self, the soul, it has nothing to say, for into this ultimate citadel its techniques cannot penetrate. The psychoanalyst is, as it were, on the stage with the actor. He gives directions and makes corrections to assure that the mask is rightly adjusted so that the actor might the better play his role in the community drama. Yet while the psychologist may make the mask easier for the actor to wear, he cannot get behind it; nor is he allowed into the actor's private dressing-room where he may take off the mask to disclose his true selfhood. There the individual is with himself alone, beyond the reach of any probing intruder. Only the God who knows what is in us (John 2:25) can uncover what lies within the inner sanctuary of our soul. It is there the Spirit of God enters to bear witness with our human spirit that we are children of God.

Persons and things. By standing over against the world of natural phenomena, man becomes aware of his otherness. In relation to them he has a feeling of aliveness and a realization of selfhood. By confrontation with things, man knows that he is not a thing and so learns the use of "I" and "me." The reaction called for by the world of things is in marked contrast with that called for by the world of persons. Things are neutral in relation to human individuality. Things are there to be used by persons, not the other way around.

Martin Buber (1937), in his small but influential volume *I and Thou*, has made the fruitful distinction between our relations to the world of persons ("I-thou") and our relations to the world of things ("I-it"). His main contribution to our understanding of man is his deepening of our awareness of the other person, who is viewed not as an "it," but as a distinctive subject, "thou." Too often in the modern world of commerce, social science, and medicine, the person has been used as an "it" to increase production and advance knowledge. Humans have wrongly been reduced to mere means toward a specific end. From the Christian point of view, we also see the world transgressing the divine charge to love one's neighbor as oneself. It is essential to move in the world of persons and treat them as equals. For, as Paul Tournier (1957) has said, either "we move in the world of things, phenomena, personages, and God himself becomes just an abstract idea; or else we enter the world of persons; God becomes personal; we meet persons everywhere" (p. 190).

Most scientific disciplines study human beings as things. Anatomy and physiology study humans as somatic machines; psychology studies the mind as a brain mechanism; economics sees people as instruments of production and consumption; and to the sociologist, individuals are mere fractional elements in society. Each one of these disciplines has frequently presented its reductionist account of man as the full story about him. But not one of them has the full story; indeed, while each one of them has certainly laid hold of an aspect of what it is to be a man, all of them together fail to give the complete picture. In truth, they have all missed out on what is absolute about man, his fundamental personhood. Personhood, not "thinghood," is essential to being human.

Our interests turn readily to things; we seek in things satisfaction and fullness of life. But the more we become absorbed in things, the less truly personal we ourselves become. We become slaves of things, victims of their tyranny. "Everything with which we come in contact takes on the tone-quality of thing or of person, according as to whether we are ourselves a thing or a person, in respect to it" (Tournier [1957], p. 183). In relating to others as persons, we reaffirm our own personhood.

The reality of personhood. To be a person is to be a self, a responsible moral agent with at least limited freedom. But it is presently questioned by psychologists and philosophers whether indeed man is a self in any sense which gives him the right to maintain that he has what in religious language is called a soul. Some dogmatic psychologists disregard the idea of soul; some empirical philosophers strongly deny the idea of self. Such repudiation of the ideas of soul and self is for the Christian believer a serious matter. Why?

First, if there is no soul, what then becomes of the possibility of life beyond the grave? For if all we are is a conglomeration of behavior patterns, their disintegration at death leaves nothing to endure beyond. But Christians are certain that there is in man a soul, a higher and inner nature which is related to, yet distinguished from, the body. Christians believe that the spiritual substance of the soul can live a life of its own after separation from the physical body, which is subject to corruption.

Second, if there is no self, that is, no seat of man's thinking, willing, and doing, what then can be said about man's freedom and moral responsibility? They simply do not exist! But the reality of moral responsibility is recognized everywhere. This recognition requires a picture of man as the possessor "of a sort of inner man or self, who is essentially mysterious and unpredictable: the person's 'soul' or his 'will.' This inner man is inviolable, and not acted upon by causes" (Wilson [1961], p. 20).

Many have attempted to repudiate these notions, but it is our conviction that the idea of self is given to us by and assured for us in our own self-awareness. We know ourselves to be our self, and that is, as Hywel Lewis (1961) contends, "as direct a way as any" (p. 210). The self is known intimately, personally, and existentially, in just being one's self. True, while we know that we are a selfhood, we do not fully understand the self that we are. For we "are just as mysterious to ourselves as we are familiar" (Trethowan [1954], p. 172). Yet we can most surely affirm that, from a psychological point of view, self-consciousness of subsistent being constitutes man's uniqueness and subjectivity, just as does, from a theological point of view, his being created in the image of God. We begin with the "I am."

It may appear from the foregoing that the terms *self* and *soul* have been used synonymously. And from one point of view this is perfectly legitimate. If, however, differentiation is necessary, we will take the term *self* as the more general to specify the conscious subject of experience or, as stated by Leonard Hodgson (1930), "the spiritually alive subject of consciousness" (p. 10). The self is the experience of self-consciousness. To define what is meant by the soul is, however, more difficult. Soul cannot be identified with mind (for a man still possesses a soul if he should lose his mind). Nor, of course, is the soul to be identified with body. Later in this chapter (p. 135), we will see that soul is best defined as the inner aspect of a person's being.

Immortality

From the distinction affirmed here between the soul and the body, the spiritual and material elements of man's nature, there follows the idea of the person's immortality. There are powerful philosophical considerations which can be urged to corroborate the biblical presentation of the soul of man as fitted for eternity. There are also the facts of man's instinctive belief in his own continued existence and his persistent high estimate of his own value.

From his first appearance, man seems to have thought of himself as something special. He has felt himself to be distinct from the rest of the created order and to be other than a creature of passing time. He senses eternity in his heart (Eccles. 3:11), and he also believes that even death cannot finally annihilate his essential life. The idea that man possesses something immortal is one of humanity's strongest convictions. It is not a conclusion to which he has come as a result of hard thinking, but rather as a result of a strong feeling that his person possesses qualities which are imperishable, qualities which need eternal scope for their fulfilment. Unless we can be sure of immortality, energy and zest will necessarily be drained out of living. And that will mean loss of dignity, mockery of the self's hidden wealth, and negation of all things that are worthwhile.

While it must be allowed that the idea that immortality is an instinctive belief has its source in Platonic philosophy, the value of the human person as a premise for the everlastingness of the soul has a specific Christian origin. It is through Christ that the recognition that men and women have enduring value in their own right first found expression in human history. Christ gave his authority to the view that man possesses an immortal nature. Christ saw man as a spiritual being with a Godward inclination. For all his regard for man's body, Christ's supreme concern was for man's eternal welfare. He taught that true wealth is that of the soul. It profits nothing to gain the whole world and lose one's essential selfhood (Matt. 16:26), for life is more than food and the body than clothing (Matt. 6:25). In the pagan world of Christ's time, as in the pagan world since, however polluted or polished that world may be, the human person has always been regarded as having no lasting worth. Celsus, that early opponent of Christianity, even while proclaiming his disdain for the gospel, is a witness to one of its supreme blessings to human society. "The root of Christianity," he declares, "is its excessive valuation of the human soul, and the absurd idea that God takes an interest in man." The biblical view of man suggests that he is destined for some other port than any on these earthly shores. What man is in mind, heart, and spirit, in the range of his interests and the lift of his soul, can be explained only on the supposition that he is preparing, and being prepared, for another and vaster life hereafter.

Morality

It is the uniform teaching of Scripture that man in his very essence is a moral being. In a profound sense, to be human is to be morally capable and vice versa. To act according to moral principles is a human obligation. There must, then, be "something common to men in virtue of which they can be moral agents and can be treated as such" (Paton [1955], p. 301). Paul tells us there is an inherent awareness in all men of the reality of a natural moral law to which they ought to subscribe (Rom. 2:14–15). So man is in himself a moral being with moral obligations and responsibilities. Moral neutrality in a being otherwise so evidently the possessor of rationality and freedom is impossible. Man "as created was like God in that he was good. He was not created morally neutral—indeed the whole notion of a morally neutral person is a monstrosity—but his nature was positively directed to right as opposed to wrong. Goodness was not something that came after he was created, but something that was stamped upon him from the beginning" (Machen [1965], p. 147).

Consequently, the "good" deeds of a man need not be designated "virtuous sins." All of a man's acts are, indeed, the acts of a sinner; but not all his acts are sinful acts. A man decides to open his door and go for a walk. It is certainly a sinner who goes through these activities, but these acts cannot, on that account, be designated "sinful." Similarly, a woman's decision to be generous to others in want, in spite of the many pressures to act otherwise, cannot be accounted "sinful," although, again, it is the act of a sinner.

Humans have an ability for morality and a capacity for religion. The key word of morality is "duty," and the key word of religion is "grace." As regards duty a person can act freely, while as regards grace he can but receive humbly. Thus morality is concerned with activities freely performed in which there is the possibility of doing otherwise and for which the agent is credited with either praise or blame. Religion, on the other hand, is a grace relationship with One whose mercy we desire and salvation we need. The presuppositions of each are consequently different. Responsibility is the essential note of morality, while responsiveness is the requisite attitude of religion.

The apostle Paul took the universality of conscience in man as attestation of his moral nature, and the universality of the sense of guilt arising out of its judgments as evidence of man's innate moral awareness (see Acts 23:1; Rom. 2:15; 9:1; 13:5). Paul taught that conscience is a natural property of man; it is not an addition to his being but a reality of his essential selfhood as rational and free. Conscience can stir man to nobler deeds as it can awaken in him a sense of need of God's forgiveness. Conscience, then, reveals man "to belong to the moral order" (Denney [1918], p. 215).

The ideas of the soul's immortality and man's morality interrelate. It is, of course, true that a denial of man's immortality does not foreclose the possibility of a good life. There are those who, while believing that death ends existence, still find goodness to be good. They would do well to consider the question, But why be good? What is the good of goodness anyway?

The shortening of the soul's career to the span of this life alone necessarily brings about an impoverishment of our interests and a narrowing of our initiatives. It is the hope of life immortal that gives life its purpose and its poise. If there is, indeed, an eternal dimension to which our present experiences may be oriented, then a sense of worthwhileness is brought into the business of living. But if all come to the same end, why bother to be good? Why should one follow, or be required to follow, the harder way of righteousness at cost and loss to oneself? If the good and the bad alike consist only of dust, then the call to virtuous living is a hollow mockery, and the maxims of justice, patience, goodwill, brotherhood, and every other ethical virtue are so many empty words. Clearly, then, morality is intimately interrelated with immortality.

Man's Constituent Elements

The Bible is *not* a textbook of psychology, and thus it does not give us a precise scientific delineation of the elements of man's makeup. There are certain realities of our being, however, which Scripture presents as contrasting truths that yet interrelate in the structure of the human person. In seeking to relate these opposing truths we will gain a clearer view of what it is to be human; in clarifying these realities, we will begin to develop a more formal doctrinal statement of the Christian view of man.

Unity and duality

Although the Genesis account specifies two constituents in the creation of man, the dust of the ground and the divine breath of life, the emphasis falls upon the resulting unity. Man becomes an animated being through the unity of these two diverse elements. It is the synthesis of these two factors which constitutes man as person. It is therefore characteristic of the biblical presentation "to assert the solidarity of man's constitution,—that human individuality is of one piece, and is not composed of separate or independent parts. This assertion is essential to the theology of the whole Bible—to its discovery of human sin and of divine salvation" (Laidlaw [1895], p. 55).

This unity of man's nature is basic to all of God's dealing with man as the Lord of man's creation and the God of man's redemption. It is the uniform teaching of the Bible that man exists, now and forever, in the oneness of his complex nature. The passages concerning man's relationships with God, his fellow man, and the natural order all presuppose the unity of his nature. The biblical assurance of the final resurrection of the body and the resulting eternal state of living as an embodied soul is the final proof of the unity of man's nature. Historic Christian faith has consequently "proclaimed, against experience, against intelligence, that for the achievement of man's unity the body of his knowledge is to be raised . . . the body is to be the same, the very body of the very soul that are both names of a single man" (Williams [1973], p. 31). Thus in the days of his earthly ministry Jesus dealt with man, not just as spirit only or body only, but as the living unity of both in one person. And for the apostle Paul, too, while man is part of the created order he is also the possessor of a spiritual element which constitutes him "a living being" (1 Cor. 15:45).

Along with this stress on the unity of man's nature, there is also throughout Scripture the suggestion of a duality in the makeup of his being. But this duality does not leave man as a loose conjunction of conflicting opposites or antagonistic principles. There is certainly an antithesis of the physical and the spiritual, of the earthly and the heavenly, but these are *not* presented as two distinct and separable elements. There is the suggestion of a dualism of aspects, but as uniting in a single harmonious whole. It is this unity of two aspects which accounts for the imprecise use of terms, especially in the Old Testament. The terms *soul, heart,* and *spirit* are frequently used to designate our higher natures, sometimes used to designate the lower element, and at still other times used to designate the whole person. Occasionally two terms will be used in conjunction to point out that man's unity is a duality; for example, "flesh" and "life" (Job 13:14, RSV), "flesh" and "soul" (Job 14:22, KJV), "mind" and "flesh" (Prov. 14:30, RSV), "mind" and "body" (Eccles. 2:3; 11:10, RSV), "heart" and "flesh" (Ezek. 44:7, 9, RSV).

Body and soul

In the Old Testament there is no sharp distinction between the body (Heb., g^ewiyah, etc.) and the contrasting terms *soul (nephesh)* and *spirit (ruah)*. The term *body* is thus occasionally used to designate the whole man. The New Testament word for body (Gr., *sōma*) follows closely the Old Testament usage and so lends no support to the Greek philosophical view which sharply distinguished between body and soul to make the former the source of sin and the soul's prison house. In harmony with the whole tenor of the Old Testament the apostle Paul presents man as a unity, yet as seemingly dichotomous in nature. This unity of the two elements is so close as to make them mutually dependent. Johann Gerhard (*Loci Theologici* 17. 149) states: "For the soul does nothing whatever outside the body, nor does the body do anything independently of the soul." Although Paul sees the body as influenced by sin and subject to death, he does not regard sin and death as inherent in it. Neither sin nor death belongs to the body as such; they are aliens come to occupy a foreign territory. Distinctive of the fuller revelation of the New Testament is the concept of a resurrection body. In the resurrection the believer receives an incorruptible, or spiritual, body because of his new relationship with the living Christ (1 Cor. 15:42–43; 2 Cor. 5:1–5; cf. Rom. 8:11; Phil. 3:21; Col. 3:4).

The Hebrew word for soul *(nephesh)*, which occurs more than seven hundred times in the Old Testament, has the general meaning "possessing life." In this connection it can be used of animals (e.g., Gen. 1:20). Most of its many uses in the Psalms carry the connotation of "life-principle." It has a distinctively physical reference in numerous passages (e.g., Job 33:20) and a psychological reference (moral action) in others (e.g., Job 7:15). It is sometimes used to specify the individual person (e.g., Lev. 7:21) or the self (e.g., Judg. 16:16; Ps. 120:6). The Greek word *psychē* has in the New Testament the same general meaning as *nephesh* in the Old. Its occurrences in the epistles of Paul are variously translated in the Revised Standard Version: "human being" (Rom. 2:9); "person" (Rom. 13:1); "living being" (1 Cor. 15:45); "self"

(1 Thess. 2:8); "life" (Rom. 11:3; 16:4; Phil. 2:30); "mind" (Phil. 1:27); and "heart" (Eph. 6:6). This diversity of usage conditions its general meaning. As the vital principle of individual life, the "soul" may refer to the concrete individual (Rom. 2:9) or to specific psychical elements which make up the person.

Although the terms *body* and *soul* can often overlap to indicate an individual as such, the fact that the person can be approached, now from the one perspective and now from the other, leaves the impression of a duality of elements. And this impression of a dichotomy leads us to characterize the body as the outer and the soul as the inner aspect of man's being (see 2 Cor. 1:23; 12:15). Other New Testament writers seem to give to *psychē* this heightened significance (see, e.g., Heb. 4:12; 3 John 2). The Epistle of James (1:21) and the Epistle to the Hebrews (10:39; cf. 1 Peter 1:9) speak of the Word of God and faith as the way of the soul's salvation.

Flesh and spirit

The Hebrew word for flesh *(basar)* occurs over 250 times in the Old Testament. It can refer to human nature generally (e.g., Gen. 6:3; Job 34:15), to the substance of a living body (e.g., Gen. 2:21), or to the corporeal aspect of man (e.g., Job 19:26; Ps. 63:1). On some few occasions the term *basar* has the additional idea of man's frailty in relation to God (Pss. 56:4; 78:39). The parallel term in the New Testament *(sarx)* carries the same idea, but it has a deeper dimension with regard to the concept of human frailty in contrast with God's strength: because of our sin there is something more seriously wrong with the human condition than merely our physical weakness. Thus, what is in the Old Testament a relatively rare connotation of the word *flesh* becomes of first importance in the biblical gospel of salvation.

Of the more than ninety occurrences of the term *sarx* in the letters of Paul, the majority have merely a physical connotation (e.g., Rom. 1:3; 2:28; 4:1). In the rest of its New Testament usages, however, more is involved. References to the passions (Rom. 7:5), the filthiness (2 Cor. 7:1, KJV; cf. 1 Peter 3:21), the desires (Gal. 5:16; Eph. 2:3; 2 Peter 2:18), and the sins (Col. 2:11) of the flesh speak of man's whole personality as absorbed in earthly pursuits in organized opposition to what is good and of God. The mind set on the flesh is hostile to God and cannot please him (Rom. 8:6, 8). In the flesh there dwells no good thing (Rom. 7:18). A more precise understanding therefore of what Paul means by the term *flesh* in its religious significance relates it to human nature as affected by the fall. "Flesh" specifies man's fallen state inherited from the sinful race of which he is in essence and character an individual member. "What, indeed, does flesh mean," asks Karl Barth (1933), "but the complete inadequacy of the creature when he stands before the Creator? What does it mean, but everything that is unrighteous before God?" (p. 89). Or, as simply stated by James Stewart (1941), flesh "is man apart from God" (p. 104).

The basic idea of the Old Testament word for spirit *(ruah)* is "wind" (e.g., Gen. 8:1) or "breath" (e.g., Ps. 18:15). Imaging God's inbreathing by which man became a living being, the term *spirit* came to signify the principle of life in man and so to express his nature as incorporeal and the source and seat of his psychical activities. Spirit connotes, then, what is proper to man's essential being. In reference to the human individual, spirit characterizes what is the most distinctive element of personhood. Psychologically, the term focuses on "the innermost of the inner life, the higher aspect of the self or personality" (Laidlaw [1895], p. 91). As a native reality of man's personality, and the distinguishing mark of his being, spirit is the ultimate constituent of human nature.

In contrast with the term *flesh*, which relates man to fallen human nature, the term *spirit* relates him to the world of the imperishable. Thus spirit is that element of man's being which, as derived from God, "is kindred to God, and bears within it the potency of an endless life" (Stevens [1941], p. 104). It is the spirit in man which provides the point of contact for the regenerative action of God's Spirit in the inner being of man. "It is precisely because man possesses pneuma that he is capable of being related to God" (Ladd [1975], p. 463).

Although we have given emphasis to the terms *spirit* and *soul* as significant for man's makeup, they are not to be regarded as separate faculties of the person. By "spirit" is to be understood man's direct dependence on God for life. By "soul" is to be understood that life, isolated and in itself, which we have from God by our very nature. Thus spirit represents the principle of divine life in man, while soul represents the actualization of that life in man. Put otherwise, the soul is man's life in its special and individual aspect, while the spirit is that living power which forms, and informs, its special character.

Individuality and community

From all that has been said throughout these pages about the reality and value of the human person, it follows that a certain individualism is compatible with the biblical understanding of man. From the perspective of Scripture, all humans, being created in the image of God, are important. This individualism of the Bible, however, contrasts strongly with humanistic individualism, which is nothing other than the rationalization of fallen man's native pride and egoism. Biblical individualism, on the other hand, assures to each person the right of direct approach to God. It is an individualism in grace under the sovereignty of Christ. Christ found the single man in the social mass, and in finding him brought him under his lordship. It is not quite accurate to assert, however, as is often done, that the Reformation made religion individual; the truth is rather that it made the gospel personal. This distinction preserves the concept of the individual as a social being as well.

Man was created for fellowship with God, and in his human condition he was provided with fellowship in the form of the woman as bone of his bone and flesh of his flesh (Gen. 2:18–25). But because of their sin all such fellowship has become distorted, and we all seek to do what we deem right in our own eyes. Only when we are restored to fellowship with God by faith in the redemption of Christ is our social nature renewed in the family of the redeemed (of which a local church is the visible expression). Being born anew into the believing community, the church, the renewed individual will find a sphere for the exercise of his God-given gifts and for the fulfilment of his redeemed social nature.

No person is truly alone and in self-isolation. We exist in and for relationships. Thus man, while himself essentially personal, is at the same time "bound up with the activities and relationships of life" (Wingren [1961], p. 176). No man is an island apart, an isolated unit who neither touches nor is touched by others. There is no such thing as an absolute human being who can exist of himself alone. "All are members of a society in which they live, move and have their being morally, and in all they do of right or wrong, they both affect and are affected by the body to which they belong" (Denney [1918], p. 91).

The individualism of the Bible is, then, a moral and spiritual individualism which has its authentication in dependence on God and its fulfilment in the recognition of, and in sensitivity towards, other persons. Thus does the individualism of the Bible stand in the sharpest contrast with the Buddhist doctrine of salvation with its rejection of all individuality. Biblical individualism affirms the value of individual persons and of our communal natures.

The natural ("old") man and the spiritual ("new") man

Although the issues opened up for discussion under the heading of the natural and the spiritual man go beyond the requirements of our subject, a few remarks are necessary to complete the picture of the biblical teaching on personality. The apostle Paul specifically uses concepts like "the natural man" (1 Cor. 2:14, KJV; cf. Eph. 2:3) and the "old man" (Rom. 6:6; Eph. 4:22; Col. 3:9, KJV) in contrast with terms like "spiritual" man (1 Cor. 14:37; cf. 3:1; Rom. 8:6; Gal. 6:1) and the "new man" (Eph. 4:24, KJV; cf. 2 Cor. 5:17; Gal. 6:15). The former terms characterize man in his state by nature, and the latter terms in his position by grace. Paul speaks also of the "outer nature" of man which perishes and his "inner nature" which abides and is daily being renewed in Christ (2 Cor. 4:16, RSV; cf. Eph. 3:16).

Although Paul contrasts body and soul, flesh and spirit, it is not his teaching that the source and cause of sin lies in the physical body or flesh as such. He does, indeed, speak of "the body of sin" (Rom. 6:6, KJV; cf. 8:10, 13), and of the evil "works of the flesh" (Gal. 5:16–21; cf. 2 Cor. 10:2–3; Eph. 2:3). But the fact that the body can be sanctified to become a temple of the Holy Spirit and be presented to God in an act of spiritual worship (Rom. 6:13; 12:1; 1 Cor. 6:13–20; 2 Cor. 7:1) clearly argues against the heretical Gnostic view of the inherent evil of physical existence. Far from locating sin in the material of the body, Paul's introduction of a contrast between soul and spirit and his description of the "soulish" *(psychikos)* man as "unspiritual" (1 Cor. 2:14, NEB, RSV) or "natural" (KJV) indicate that man is a sinner in his total inwardness, and not just in his body. The "pneumatic" or "spiritual" man *(pneumatikos)*, on the other hand, is the one with whom the Holy Spirit makes contact, bringing God's redemption through Christ to the whole person. The psychical or soulish man is then in Paul's account man as nature has constituted him and as sin has affected him. As such, his wisdom is "earthly, unspiritual, devilish" (James 3:15, RSV). He is "worldly . . . , devoid of the Spirit" (Jude 19). The pneumatic or spiritual man, by contrast, is man reconstituted by divine grace and indwelt by the Spirit of God. In the process of his salvation his natural or psychical selfhood, which he shares with fallen humanity, is transformed and fashioned anew into the image of Jesus Christ, into God's "proper man," to borrow Luther's phrase. For as the first head of the race was made a living *psychē*, the second Adam is a life-giving *Pneuma* for as many as receive him (1 Cor. 15:44–47). By nature all people have their pedigree and their place in "the book of the generations of Adam" (Gen. 5:1, KJV). By grace some also have a position in "the book of the generation of Jesus Christ" (Matt. 1:1, KJV).

In this concluding remark we wish to affirm that there is no purely psychological theory of personality which can give effective account of the ethical and religious concerns of the human individual or of the sinful state of his natural life. Every proffered personality theory must be judged by the Christian scholar in the light of the biblical view of man, especially with regard to his dependence upon God and his relation to objective moral law. It is on these counts that the views of many psychological theorists fall short due to their necessarily naturalistic approach, even though they are in certain respects sensitive to man's religious needs. No personality theory, conditioned as it must be by its scientific approach, can give full and final account of personhood since there is that in man beyond its province and power to investigate.

This appraisal does not permit the decrying of the value and use of psychology as a method. Indeed, every personality theory has contributions to make as well as drawbacks. As E. Mansell Pattison (1973) reminds us, "all personality theories have scientific assets and liabilities with no necessary Christian or anti-Christian basis." He goes on to warn, however, that "it is fatuous to assume that we can emerge with some definitive 'spiritual psychology,' for personality theory must remain at the level of scientific hypothesis. As such, every personality theory is temporary, expedient, and subject to new experimental and clinical data. We should be alert to any theology that attempts to 'Christianize' a particular personality theory" (p. 502). For psychology is limited to man's psychical nature. Into the inner depths of that more fundamental reality of man, his substantial selfhood, scientific psychology cannot enter; for his more fundamental need it has no answer. In the innermost of man's being there is that sinful self which not even the best-equipped psychological oarsman can reach. Beyond the physical and the psychical, man, as Carl Jung (1936) says, "suffers in spirit" (p. 277). And into that sphere, that ultimate citadel of man's warped nature, only the Spirit of God can come to make the redemptive healing of the gospel of Christ effective for the whole person. Thus we must declare, with P. T. Forsyth (1909), that our supreme need "is not the education of our conscience, not the absorption of our sins, nor even our reconciliation alone, but our redemption. It is not cheer that we need but salvation, not help but rescue, not stimulus but a change, not tonics but life. Our one need of God is a moral need in the strictest, holiest sense. The best of nature can never meet it. It involves a new nature, a new world, a new creation. It is the moral need, not to be transformed, but to be saved" (p. 62).

References

Barth, K. (1933). *The Epistle to the Romans*. Translated by E. Hoskyns. London: Oxford University Press.

Buber, M. (1937). *I and thou*. Edinburgh: T. and T. Clark.

Denney, J. (1918). *The Christian doctrine of reconciliation*. New York: Doran.

Flugel, J. (1945). *A hundred years of psychology* (5th ed.). London: Duckworth.

Forsyth, P. T. (1909). *Positive preaching and the modern mind*. London: Hodder and Stoughton.

Freud, S. (1934). *The future of an illusion.* Translated by W. Robson-Scott. London: Hogarth.

————— (1940). *Totem and taboo.* Translated by A. Brill. London: Kegan Paul.

Henry, C. (1976). *God, revelation, and authority,* vol. 2. Waco, Tex.: Word.

————— (1979). *God, revelation, and authority,* vol. 4. Waco, Tex.: Word.

Hodgson, L. (1930). *Essays in Christian philosophy.* London: Longmans, Green.

————— (1956). *For faith and freedom,* vol. 1. Oxford: Basil Blackwell.

Joad, C. (1948). *Guide to modern thought* (rev. ed.). London: Faber and Faber.

Jung, C. (1936). *Modern man in search of a soul.* London: Kegan Paul.

Ladd, G. E. (1975). *A theology of the New Testament.* London: Lutterworth.

Laidlaw, J. (1895). *The Bible doctrine of man.* Edinburgh: T. and T. Clark.

Lewis, H. (1961). God and mystery. In I. Ramsey, ed., *Prospect for metaphysics.* London: Allen and Unwin.

McDonald, H. D. (1981). *The Christian view of man.* Westchester, Ill.: Good News.

Machen, J. G. (1965). *The Christian view of man.* London: Banner of Truth.

MacMurray, J. (1957). *The self as agent.* London: Faber and Faber.

Orr, J. (1897). *The Christian view of God and the world* (3d ed.). London: Morrison and Gibb.

Paton, H. (1955). *The modern predicament.* London: Allen and Unwin.

Pattison, E. M. (1973). Person and Personality. In C. Henry, ed., *Baker's dictionary of Christian ethics.* Grand Rapids: Baker.

Robinson, H. W. (1911). *The Christian doctrine of man* (2d ed.). Edinburgh: T. and T. Clark.

Smethurst, A. (1955). *Modern science and Christian beliefs.* London: Nisbet.

Stevens, G. (1941). *The theology of the New Testament* (5th ed.). Edinburgh: T. and T. Clark.

Stewart, J. (1941). *A man in Christ* (5th ed.). London: Hodder and Stoughton.

Stout, G. (1920). *Manual of psychology* (3d ed.). London: W. B. Clive.

Tournier, P. (1957). *The meaning of persons.* London: SCM.

Trethowan, I. (1954). *An essay in Christian philosophy.* London: Longmans, Green.

Watson, J. (1913). Psychology as the behaviorist views it. *Psychological Review* 20: 158–77.

Williams, C. (1973). *Descent into hell.* Grand Rapids: Eerdmans.

Wilson, J. (1961). *Philosophy of religion.* London: Oxford University Press.

Wingren, G. (1961). *Creation and law.* Edinburgh: Oliver and Boyd.

The Self in Contemporary Psychology
C. Stephen Evans

The student of psychology may soon get the impression that psychologists conceive of human beings as either "very bright, complex rats or very dumb, slow computers." This impression seems to result from the psychologists' use of mechanistic forms of analysis in their research. The student is often unaware that there are other traditions in the history of psychology and on the contemporary scene as well, traditions wherein the human person as a responsible agent, rather than as a mechanism, is the focus of study.

In this chapter, C. Stephen Evans develops his argument as to why Christians should avail themselves of a diversity of methods in the study of the person rather than adhering narrowly to the traditional laboratory methods. This argument is based on his view of persons as selves. The present chapter will enable the reader to begin to grapple with what it means to be a self and whether his or her definition of what it means to be a self is necessarily in tension with mechanistic explanations. In chapter 2 Donald M. MacKay addresses these issues very differently.

Evans (B.A., Wheaton College; Ph.D., Yale University) was formerly professor of philosophy and psychology at Wheaton College, and is now associate professor of philosophy and curator of the Howard and Edna Hong Kierkegaard Library at St. Olaf College. He

*has published widely in Kierkegaard studies as well as in the area of
Christian faith and the social sciences. Among psychologists, he is
best known for his book* Preserving the Person *(Grand Rapids:
Baker, 1982).*

What Is a Self?

A self is essentially a *substantial subject,* a being with a *continued
identity* through time who is the bearer of distinctive psychological
predicates. A self is an *agent;* selves are not simply links in a rigid
causal chain of events, but *originators of actions.* A self is *self-conscious,*
capable of reflection on both environment and itself as it confronts its
environment. A self is a *relational being;* both its actions and its self-
awareness are mediated through its relations with others. Many other
significant features are essential to human selfhood. Among these
might be listed the capacity to make rational inferences, the capacity
for emotions, both fleeting and enduring, and the power of imagination.

The concepts of moral freedom and responsibility are closely linked
to the concept of selfhood. No one holds inanimate objects or the lower
animals morally responsible for events they have a role in causing. For
example, termites may cause a floor to collapse, but are not seen as
morally responsible for their acts. However, human beings are often
held to be responsible for their actions, even for actions which were
performed in the past, as the continuing efforts to apprehend Nazi war
criminals clearly show. We normally hold people responsible for their
actions because we believe that these actions are usually free. Human
actions are not regarded as the inevitable outcomes of causes over
which the person has no control, but are seen as the outcomes of the
self's free choices. We normally hold people responsible for their past
actions because we regard the individual who performed the past
actions as in some way the same self as the person whom we now
confront. Praise, rewards, blame, and punishment are thus logically
tied to the concept of selfhood insofar as they are tied to the person
deserving the praise or blame; rewards and punishment are not regarded simply as mechanisms for influencing future behavior.

The Importance of the Self for Christians:
Moral Responsibility, Freedom, and Self-Identity

Since the concept of the self is linked to the concepts of moral
responsibility and rewards and punishments, its significance to Chris-

tianity is not hard to discern. The Bible portrays God as holding people responsible for their actions and administering both rewards and punishments. The central Christian doctrine of salvation by grace does not undermine this truth, since God's unmerited favor (his grace) is given in a context in which the notion of desert is clearly fundamental. Sinners do not deserve God's love, but his wrath. His love is nevertheless offered to them; if it is spurned, however, they call down on themselves the wrath they actually deserve.

Although some Christians have difficulty in reconciling a strong doctrine of divine sovereignty with their conviction that humans are responsible agents, almost no one is thereby moved to deny human responsibility. To deny that sin is due to free human choice, and to claim that humans are created by God in such a way that sin is inevitable, would make God the author of sin, an unthinkable consequence for Christians.

The concept of selves as possessing a continuing identity is just as crucial for Christians, since it would be immoral for God to reward or punish a person for things done in the past, unless that person is the same person who performed the actions. Under normal circumstances an individual is not punished for doing what some other individual has done.

Some have argued that the freedom required for moral responsibility is compatible with a deterministic view of human behavior that sees all human actions as the inevitable result of preexisting causes. According to this "compatibilist" view (often called soft determinism) freedom is defined as lack of coercion, the ability of the self to act in accordance with its own internal desires or volitions. Those desires or volitions are, however, causally determined. Thus my actions can be causally determined and yet free in the sense that they reflect my own desires and are performed without any external compulsion. For example, my writing this chapter should be seen as the inevitable result of the causes that shape my desires (and hence behavior), and yet also as a free action in that no one is forcing me to write this chapter by threats or other means.

There are independent philosophical reasons for doubting the adequacy of this analysis (Campbell [1967]), but it seems especially dubious from a Christian perspective. If determinism is compatible with freedom, then it is very difficult to understand why God did not make humans free and responsible and at the same time determine them to refrain from sin. In such a view God appears to be at least the indirect author of sin, if not the direct author, since he ultimately is responsible for the desires or volitions which cause "free" human actions.

The same problem is also present for a new kind of compatibilist view which has been developed by Donald M. MacKay (1974). MacKay does not claim that determinism is true, but he does claim that if true it would not undermine human freedom. Now assuming for the moment that determinism is true, and thus that an agent's behavior is shaped by the brain understood as a mechanistic system, we might reasonably conclude that an all-knowing observer could infallibly predict the agent's behavior through his absolute knowledge of the agent's brain. MacKay acknowledges that a detached all-knowing observer could in fact infallibly predict the agent's behavior, but he also contends that this does not mean the agent is unfree. The reason, he argues, is that the prediction is predicated on the observer's knowledge of the agent's brain, the condition of which is partly correlated with the beliefs of the agent about his actions. This means, says MacKay, that "no completely detailed description of the present or immediately future state of [the agent's] brain could be equally accurate whether or not [the agent] believed it" (1974, p. 79). One cannot say that a description of an agent's brain, including a prediction about what he will do, ought to be believed by a truth-seeking agent prior to the agent's accepting it, because if the agent does accept it, the agent's brain will be somewhat altered, and the prediction rendered out of date and no longer unconditionally valid. On the other hand, if the prediction takes into account the agent's believing it to be true, then if the agent were not to believe it, the agent's brain would once more be altered and the prediction out of date. In neither case is the agent obligated to believe what the observer (correctly) believes. The prediction is not a truth which commands universal assent, because it has no unconditional claim on the agent himself.

This implies, says MacKay, that a person's future is not inevitable for that person, however predictable by an observer, because it is "logically indeterminate." The observer's prediction, even if infallible, is not inevitable for the agent, because if the agent knows it, the prediction will not be correct unless and until the agent decides to accept it and act in accordance with it. (See p. 44 of this volume for MacKay's own presentation of this argument.)

MacKay's argument does show that even if an infallible specification of the present and immediately future state of a person's brain mechanism could be made, he or she would not be obligated to accept it. Furthermore, if he or she did come to accept it, the description would no longer be totally correct. This does not show, however, that the person is genuinely free. Rather, it shows simply that the person is not under any obligation to believe the all-knowing observer's infallible description and predictions. Ignorance may be bliss, but it is hardly freedom.

In any case, from a Christian perspective MacKay's view has the same problem we noted with the older compatibilism: there seems to be no reason why God could not determine people to always do what is right and never sin. One cannot say that sin is due to freedom and that God necessarily had to allow the possibility of sin to give humans true freedom, since God could have (from this compatibilist standpoint) set up the universe in such a way that humans would infallibly have chosen the good, yet still have been "free" in MacKay's sense.

For Christians it seems necessary therefore to claim that humans are sometimes free in a strong "incompatibilist" sense. That is, a free act is not inevitable, even given the individual's complete prior history. In some cases what an individual does is truly up to him or her; prior to the individual's free choice, there are no causal conditions sufficient to guarantee the act will be done.

This strong sense of freedom requires a belief that humans are selves—beings who do not simply figure as links in rigid causal chains, but are originating centers of activity who bring forth genuinely new things into the world. As originating centers of action, human selves must be regarded as substantial beings, continuants, since they have the power to bind their future through commitments and are responsible for their pasts. This self-identity over time is very basic for Christians, since they believe that a person will live after death in a new, radically transformed body and still be the same person. Self-identity, then, is not rooted in physical continuity, nor is it merely something which we attribute to persons for the purpose of and in the process of describing their functions. Rather, it is a basic aspect of being human.

The Flight from the Self

Reasons why the self has been avoided in psychology

Psychology has from the moment of its birth as an autonomous, empirical discipline been suspicious of, and in many cases downright hostile toward, the self. There are many reasons for this, some respectable, some not so respectable. None of these reasons is decisive, however, when subjected to critical examination.

One good reason psychologists have avoided the concept of the self is that it "makes everything too easy." It is tempting to explain some or all aspects of a person's behavior by simply referring them to the desires, choices, or volitions of the self. A self that explains everything explains nothing, however.

Another good reason for avoiding the concept of the self is that the self has sometimes been seen as a homunculus, a little person inside the person, that is supposed to serve as an explanation for the person's behavior, but whose behavior is never itself explained. This merely postpones the problems.

A third reasonable fear of the concept of the self rises from its association with the introspective method of psychology. To the extent that introspection falls short of objectivity by failing to provide for inter-subjective testing, it seems less than a desirable method for psychology.

A less respectable reason for avoiding the self is the reductionism that has been so pervasive in psychology, fueled by two philosophical assumptions: empiricism and naturalistic mechanism. As empiricists, psychologists have tended to shy away from concepts that cannot be directly observed. Such movements as operationism, associationism, and behaviorism all pushed strongly in the direction of limiting psychology to discovering patterns of events. The self is suspect both because it is not directly observable nor definable in an operational way, and because as a continuant it is neither an event nor a sequence or pattern of events.

The assumption of naturalistic mechanism is, if anything, even less hospitable to the concept of the self. The mechanist assumes that science requires us to view the whole of nature as a machinelike process, thus making the job of scientist to be that of discovering the mechanistic laws. Allowing free selves into such a tidy universe seems to the mechanist like inserting the proverbial bull in the china shop. Many psychologists believe wholeheartedly that determinism is an essential assumption for scientific psychology.

It is hardly surprising then that psychologists of all types have shied away from the self. The most extreme examples are the radical behaviorists and the stimulus-response theorists who look on the human being as an empty organism. The self also plays little or no role in trait psychology and in various psychometric perspectives. Freudian theory, with its talk of an ego, might seem to be an exception to the rule, but the Freudian ego is far from a true self. Orthodox Freudian theory describes the ego in objective terms as a derivative part of a warring three-part system which functions in an essentially mechanical way.

The inadequacy of these reasons

The good reasons for avoiding the concept of self turn out on reflection not to be reasons for avoiding the concept altogether, but reasons for avoiding certain forms of the concept. Theorists who wish to employ the concept of the self must be wary of making it into a dumping ground for all unexplained phenomena, or an easy answer to every question. They must also be clear that the self is not a little person inside the person, but it is the person himself. Further, they must realize that accepting the concept of the self does not compel adoption of introspection as the prime method in psychology. (Ideally, it seems to me, psychology should neither rule out nor limit itself to introspection.) For there is no reason why we must restrict our knowledge of selfhood to our own cases. People observe other people as selves every day and draw many reliable conclusions from their observations. Psychologists are presumably not inferior when it comes to such skills. Rather, their disciplined methods should give them an advantage in these pursuits.

The reductionistic reasons for avoiding the concept of the self actually give us cause for reexamining reductionism. Positivistic empiricism and mechanistic naturalism do not have much going for them, and they are especially unappealing from a Christian perspective.

The empiricist dogma that all scientific knowledge must by definition be expressible in experiential terms is woefully inadequate, especially when judged against the successes of a hard science like theoretical physics; in this field many concepts get their meaning from their role in a comprehensive theory, with the individual concepts making contact with experience only at certain limited points. Correspondingly, Christians who believe in God and sense the power of the indwelling Spirit of God certainly need not reject these realities simply because they cannot be directly observed.

The empiricist equation of science with a search for observable patterns of events also seems inadequate. Natural scientists do not merely record empirical sequences; they seek to understand the observable patterns of events by grounding them in the underlying structure of the physical world. In a similar way psychologists should not be content merely to know about empirical regularities. These regularities may be useful for prediction (to the extent that they can be generalized), but they do not necessarily produce understanding. The genuinely scientific attitude is one which seeks explanations which increase our understanding of the nature of what is studied. This usually requires probing beneath surface regularities.

The deterministic assumption of the mechanist does not fare much better. First, the indeterminism of quantum physics, while providing no positive support for human freedom, does undermine the claim that science must always assume determinism. Secondly, it is not true that psychologists must affirm universal determinism to carry on their business. One does not have to assume all behavior is causally determined in order to look for the determining causes which actually do exist. The rejection of philosophical determinism leaves open the empirical question of the degree to which human behavior is actually determined. It could well be that much, but by no means all, of human behavior is causally determined. Keep in mind that the actual regularities which psychologists do discover are always probabilistic and statistical in character. Such regularities do not require universal determinism nor do they support it, but are at best only consistent with it.

The hypnotic effect of mechanistic determinism has blinded psychologists to the attractiveness of alternative, nonmechanistic modes of explanation and understanding. In the philosophy of action, in phenomenology, and in hermeneutics a variety of modes of explanation have been proposed which focus on human behavior as purposive and on causes which cannot be understood simply as links in a mechanistic system (Evans [1984]).

Many philosophical arguments can of course be given for and against the existence of human freedom. But at a practical level, we all must make decisions and choices, and it is hard to see how a person can rationally deliberate about choices and decisions without presupposing that the choices are real possibilities. Thus freedom seems to be an unavoidable assumption for humans as practical beings. It is hard to see, then, how science could deny freedom without undermining itself, since science is itself a human activity (Evans [1982]).

How the Self Has Crept Back into Psychology

Despite the bias of psychology against the self, the concept has never been completely banished from psychology. Many of the concerns about the self were relegated to the "softer" areas of psychology such as personality theory and social psychology. Personality theorists usually avoided an explicit concept of selfhood, but often helped themselves implicitly to related notions such as the notion of identity.

In many ways personality theory was an unhappy place for concerns about the self to light, since it is clearly possible for a self to alter its personality quite drastically and still remain the same self. The self is not identical with its character nor the person with the personality (Campbell [1957]; Bertocci [1970]). Nevertheless in personality theory those questions in psychology which were not congenial to empiricism and mechanism at least found a temporary home.

Allport's attempt

A noteworthy attempt to resuscitate something like a conception of the self was made by Gordon Allport (1955). Allport developed the concept of the *proprium*, the region of personality which includes what is "peculiarly one's own," and which engages in many of the traditional actions of a self, including rational agency. Allport could not, however, bring himself to acknowledge the *proprium* as a true self. He was open to the possibility that the self may be necessary for theological and philosophical purposes, but resisted the concept as necessary for psychology. What Allport failed to see is that without the concept of the self psychology necessarily limits itself to a truncated understanding of human life. A psychology which ignores the self is less than complete. However, despite his final failure of nerve, Allport deserves much credit for venturing as far as he did in the positivistic era of the mid-fifties.

Psychoanalysis

The self has gradually crept back into many areas of psychology. Psychoanalysis, always officially marginal to American psychology but unofficially influential, is an excellent example. As previously noted, Freud's concept of the ego was far from a true self, as the ego was simply derivative of the id, and a weak part of a warring system. However, the situation changed under the pressure of clinical experience; in fact, the history of psychoanalysis is in many ways the history of ego psychology. Not only did Freud's defectors, Carl Jung and Alfred Adler, strengthen the concept of the ego considerably, but so did Anna Freud and other orthodox psychoanalysts.

The curiously named object-relations theory in psychoanalysis, pioneered by W. R. D. Fairbairn and popularized by Harry Guntrip (1971), views the ego as a truly responsible self. Though object-relations theorists do recognize the importance of unconscious conflicts, they tend to see the unconscious not in biological terms, but as something formed by the self. The person is not a bundle of instincts out of which emerges a self, but a conscious self, which, as it develops, hides and disguises from itself its own deepest longings and fears. Such a view does not see the ego as merely a part of a warring system, but as a responsible self.

Behaviorism and cognitive psychology

It is not surprising that the self managed to stay on the fringes of personality theory. By contrast the reemergence of the self in the psychoanalytic tradition is somewhat unexpected. More surprising than either of these developments is the way in which the self has pushed its way back into the mainstream of American academic psychology, where radical behaviorism once held the center stage. Probably the main impetus to the dethronement of radical behaviorism has been the growth of cognitive psychology.

It is true that much of cognitive psychology is rooted in models drawn from artificial intelligence, in which the self is seen in machine-like terms. Still, the change from regarding the human being as an empty organism whose behavior is a direct function of the environment is striking and represents a profound shift in view of the empiricist assumptions which were so unfavorable for development of the concept of the self. Indeed, psychologists who still officially think of the human being in machinelike terms (e.g., the "central processor") have begun to endow the person with selflike characteristics.

Albert Bandura (1978) is an excellent example. Bandura rejects a simple environmental determinism. The environment works on the individual through "self-variables," which represent the way the person selectively perceives and interprets, among other things, the environment and his or her own history. But even when the self-variables are considered along with the environment, the organism cannot be viewed as determined. What is left out, says Bandura, is the behavior of the organism itself. Through our actions we alter both the environment and our self-variables. Humans are not simply passive products but active shapers of their environments and their selves.

Bandura will not admit it, but he is implicitly regarding the person as a responsible self. For what is it that engages in the behavior which Bandura stresses so much? And how is it that one's behavior is not simply a product of other factors but acquires a certain autonomy? Once more the self seems to be pushing its way in. In all these movements we have reality pressuring psychology. If God made human beings responsible selves, then sooner or later this truth will make itself felt.

Proper Functions of the Concept of Self

How should Christian psychologists respond to these developments? They should strive to push these developments to their logical conclusion by elaborating psychological theories which explicitly build on the notion that human beings are selves—responsible agents with continuing identities. One should of course not think that the concept of selfhood by itself will lead to new and provocative discoveries or insights. In this respect the concept of selfhood may be analogous to the concept of matter in physics. The concept of matter by itself led to no specific discoveries. Nevertheless the concept was of foundational importance to the development of physics and continues to be significant. The importance of the concept of matter lies in delimiting the field, giving physicists a rough idea as to what they are studying, and putting some constraints on the kinds of explanations to be sought.

In a similar way the concept of selfhood may help to shape a new science of psychology, by giving psychologists a rough idea of the type of beings they are attempting to study, and the kinds of explanations that may be appropriate. Note that we say rough idea, for there is room here for interpretation and development of the concept, as has been the case with the concept of matter in physics. One could call concepts like matter in physics and self in psychology "limiting concepts," since, being basic and ultimate, they delimit their field of study. The concept of selfhood delimits psychology in two ways, one negative and one positive.

The negative function of the concept of self: Delimiting mechanistic approaches

A good deal of contemporary psychology is mechanistic in character. It attempts to describe and explain human behavior in terms which are not essentially different from those used to describe the behavior of organisms such as pigeons and rats. Some more contemporary theories, inspired by the digital computer, attempt to explain human behavior in terms also used to explain the operation of machines. Obviously, terms used to describe the activities of rats and computers are not very personalistic, and it would seem that those theories which employ such terms do not need the concept of a self who is a free, responsible agent. Does this mean that the concept of selfhood has no importance for these regions of psychology, or on the other hand that persons who recognize the importance of the self in psychology must abandon the mechanistic mode of explanation?

The answer to both questions, surprisingly, is an emphatic no. A psychological theory fundamentally oriented around the concept of the self retains at least two positive uses of mechanistic approaches. These uses can be retained without the danger of reductionism because the concept of the self allows us to see that mechanistic explanations are necessarily limited and that in some cases they are simply not appropriate. Recognizing these limitations on mechanistic explanations by stressing the concept of self helps us to see more clearly the positive uses of mechanistic approaches.

The first positive use of mechanistic explanations occurs in the area of elucidating how humans are able to carry out their personal activities. It is evident that a large amount of the powers of humans depends on systems which are at least partially mechanistic in their functioning. The key here is not to suppose that an explanation of how it is that I am able to talk, think, and operate in my environment as a person is itself an account of personhood. Take, for example, the matter of thought. It is empirically obvious that persons cannot think (at least in this life) without brains, and it is empirically obvious that brains function (at least in large part) according to the causal laws of neurophysiology. Thus an understanding of the neurophysiology of the brain is essential to an understanding of how persons are able to think. However, that does not mean that one can understand what it is to think simply by understanding a brain process. In other words, we must understand the brain to understand how humans think, but understanding the human brain is not the same as understanding human thought.

The second positive use of a "delimited" mechanistic approach in psychology is to explain human behavior when humans are not truly functioning as selves. Humans are always selves, but they do not always function as responsible selves. It may well be that for infants and young children, and for some kinds of mentally disturbed people, a mechanistic explanation will prove to be superior to one that presupposes a self.

Besides these cases there may be other situations in which it is helpful to look at human behavior in a mechanistic way. For example, the effects of peer-group pressure on the conformist may be illuminated by viewing the conformist as if he or she were simply a product of the group pressures, even though in reality the person may still bear some degree of responsibility for his or her behavior. There are degrees of freedom and degrees of responsibility. In extreme cases where no genuine freedom is present, mechanistic explanations may be most appropriate. In other cases where a degree of freedom is present, a mechanistic perspective may be illuminating without being the whole truth.

The positive function of the concept of self: Developing and uniting alternative types of psychological investigation

Basic modes of investigating and explaining human behavior in terms of the self do not have to be invented; they are already existent. However, they could be much more fully developed than at present, and the concept of selfhood could help alternative perspectives get a clearer picture of their underlying unity. The hallmark of a psychology which takes the self seriously is an emphasis on understanding the person's beliefs, desires, reflective processes, and choices. The person is seen as a subject not merely in the sense of being an object of study, but also in the sense of having a rich inner life. We will now briefly review some of the methodologies which do take the self seriously.

Cognitive psychology. We have already noted that the combination of an interest in cognition with the principles of behavioral psychology in social-learning theory (Bandura) has helped push selfhood back into the mainstream of psychology. This same phenomenon can be seen more generally in cognitive psychology and in the various areas it influences, such as cognitive-behavior therapy. As a rule it is hard to ignore a person's inner life when cognition is at the center of the stage. A psychology of the self would therefore generally see cognitive psychology as a plus. Two qualifications are in order here, however. The first is that the computer models which have been popular in cognitive psychology must be seen as models of how the self carries out some of its functions, not as models of the self. Secondly, it must be emphasized that there are conscious processes, interpretation and volition, for example, which do not lend themselves to computational treatment. The basic concept of understanding, contrary to the beliefs of many partisans of artificial intelligence, cannot be properly attributed or likened to the operation of machines, except in a metaphorical way (Searle [1980]).

Existential and phenomenological psychology. Existential psychology is a paradigm of an approach which takes seriously the choices and responsibility of the human agent. Phenomenological psychology is a paradigm of an approach that takes seriously the inner life of the agent by trying to describe the world as it appears to the agent. Both of these naturally complementary approaches are capable of much fuller development. There is no reason why their insights cannot be employed for ongoing research to a greater extent than is currently the case.

A danger here is that it is easy to entangle legitimate insights with dubious philosophical commitments to such anti-Christian perspectives as relativism and selfism. Christians who work in this area must be clear that the individual chooses what to value but does not create what is truly valuable—and that while the individual's unique perspective is essential to an understanding of his or her behavior, this does not mean that every individual's perspective is equally true or valid. It must also be emphasized that though selfhood entails the ability to withstand the crowd, one becomes a true self through relations with other selves.

Clinical experience. Clinical and counseling psychologists are on the firing line, constantly dealing with selves. Beginning with Freud, a great deal about human selves has been learned in the clinical setting. The case study, often scorned by experimentalists, can be a legitimate vehicle for investigation of persons as selves. A case study, after all, is essentially a history, and a self is a historical being, a being with a past, present, and future. To understand a self is to understand a history. A psychology of the self will therefore make free use of the resources of clinical psychologists and will perhaps extend their methods to include all people.

The goal of therapy is generally to help the person become more of a self, to gain the ability to behave in a freer, more responsible manner. A psychology which recognizes that persons are selves will allow clinicians to better work towards those goals. It will also make the therapeutic process more sensible and effective, since the best therapists of various traditions agree that the one who is being treated must not be seen as an object to be manipulated, but must be respected as a responsible coworker in his own treatment, with the power to help or to hinder the process.

Self-report and participant observation. Psychologists have discovered the value and power of such procedures as self-report and participant observation. These practices implicitly recognize that the behavior of every individual is unique and that the people who are being studied are, like the ones doing the studying, responsible selves. They have the power of reflection, which can be viewed not simply as an obstacle to be foiled, but as a resource for the investigator.

Selfhood: Minimal and Maximal Concepts

A good deal of confusion has been caused by the fact that the concept of self has different, even though related, senses. One important help to a psychology of the self would be to distinguish selfhood as a substantial category from selfhood as a normative category. The substantial category of selfhood is that which all humans belong to by definition, what I like to call the minimal sense of selfhood. Here a self is what a human being is, and all humans must be understood as selves in this sense. The normative category of selfhood is that toward which we ought to be striving. In this, the maximal sense, a self is what a person should become. Here it is possible to speak of degrees of selfhood, and of failure to function as a true or genuine self. This normative sense is especially perilous since there are different views on what it is to be a true self. Is a true self someone who always is assertive, and demands and gets what he or she allegedly has a right to? Or is a true self someone who is willing to relinquish his or her rights for the sake of serving others? It is crucial that a Christian psychology of the self dissociate itself from egoism and narcissism.

There is a link between the substantial and normative senses of selfhood. God has created us as selves. That is what we are. But one of the characteristics of a self as a substantial entity is that it is created with possibilities. Its future is to some extent in its own hand. It may exercise its power of choice responsibly, or it may choose defiantly or irresponsibly, either flagrantly going against its own good or lazily failing to earnestly seek what it should. Tragically, the human race has failed in this way, and one of the consequences of failing to exercise the powers of selfhood is that selfhood has become distorted and misshaped. Thus, although humans are and remain selves, agents who are responsible for their choices, they continually fail to be selves, agents who in fact choose responsibly. They are already and yet need to become selves. The concept of selfhood, understood in both the minimal and maximal sense, offers fertile ground for integrating the Christian doctrines of creation, sin, and redemption with psychological research and investigation.

References

Allport, G. (1955). *Becoming*. New Haven, Conn.: Yale University Press.

Bandura, A. (1978). The self-system in reciprocal determinism. *American Psychologist* 33: 344–58.

Bertocci, P. (1970). *The person God is*. New York: Humanities.

Campbell, C. A. (1957). *On selfhood and godhood*. London: Allen and Unwin.

————— (1967). *In defense of free will*. New York: Humanities.

Evans, C. S. (1982). *Preserving the person*. Grand Rapids: Baker (originally published 1977).

————— (1984). Must psychoanalysis embrace determinism? or, can a psychoanalyst be a libertarian? *Psychoanalysis and Contemporary Thought* 7: 339–65.

Guntrip, H. (1971). *Psychoanalytic theory, therapy, and the self*. New York: Basic Books.

MacKay, D. (1974). *The clockwork image: A Christian perspective on science*. Downers Grove, Ill.: Inter-Varsity.

Searle, J. (1980). Minds, brains, and programs. *Behavioral and Brain Sciences* 3: 417–57.

Psychotherapy and Christian Faith

David G. Benner and Stuart L. Palmer

There are two major categories of questions which Christians raise about psychotherapy. The first type of question has to do with whether the views of the person which are part of the major theories of psychotherapy are compatible with the Christian view. The second category of question has to do with the particular responsibilities of the Christian, such as evangelism, and how these responsibilities relate to the psychotherapeutic task. This chapter deals with the former type of question and chapter 9 deals with the latter.

Some Christians are singularly uncritical of and superficial in their evaluation of psychotherapy theories. For example, they may reason, "Rogers says people need love in order to grow, and the Bible says that God is love; so Rogers's theory must be all right!" On the other hand, there are Christians who hunt for any hint of incompatibility between a theory of psychotherapy and biblical revelation, and then summarily dismiss the theory totally. This chapter is a model of a thoughtful evaluation of clinical theories. It closes with a discussion of what constitutes a Christian psychotherapy, a question which is dealt with in different terms in the following chapter.

David G. Benner (B.A., McMaster University; Ph.D., York University) is professor of psychology at Wheaton College. He is on

156

the board of the Christian Association for Psychological Studies, and edited the Baker Encyclopedia of Psychology *(1985). Stuart L. Palmer (B.A., M.Div., Asbury College and Theological Seminary) is a candidate for the master of arts degree in the Department of Psychology, Wheaton College.*

Psychotherapy has been variously regarded both as an enemy and as a major ally of Christianity. Both do not seem likely to be true. Furthermore, even if one is true, of which approach to psychotherapy is it true? A recent study found over 250 current psychotherapies. This diversity extends to Christian writers who are claiming one approach or another to be the biblical one. How is the Christian to even begin to evaluate so many approaches? Does the Christian faith provide us with a standard to evaluate various therapies? If so, is there a uniquely Christian approach to therapy?

These are some of the questions we will examine in this chapter. We will first consider what it means to speak of a world-view. Then, having examined six representative psychotherapies to attempt to identify their implicit world-views, and having sketched the Christian world-view, we will compare and evaluate the six secular therapies in the light of biblical theology. Finally, we will consider what it might mean to speak of a therapy as Christian therapy.

"World-View" Defined

The Christian evaluation of psychotherapies begins where all the therapies themselves begin, with their world-view. For the Christian to think intelligently about the various therapies he or she must first identify his or her own world-view and that of the system being evaluated. It is our contention that the most Christian or non-Christian part of any approach to psychotherapy is its world-view and only quite secondarily its particular techniques. The techniques therapists employ are, for the most part, neutral and often relatively independent of their theoretical base. To see this point one has only to note that numerous theoretical orientations to psychotherapy lay claim to the same techniques. But, one may ask, if a therapy's world-view is the criterion of its Christianness, what is a world-view? And how do we recognize and evaluate our own and that of those from whom we are trying to learn?

A world-view is essentially a set of assumptions which we hold about the basic makeup of our world. It is the basic beliefs we have about things. Specifically these assumptions deal with the fundamental nature of reality and persons. With regard to reality, they answer questions like, What actually exists? Is there a two-story or a one-story structure to reality? That is, are there both a divine realm and a natural realm, or does just a natural realm constitute reality? Another way of phrasing the question is to ask, Are there a God and a material world, or is there just a material world? With regard to persons, a world-view answers questions like, what are the origin, nature, and destiny of humans? Are persons moral agents created by God, are they highly evolved animals, or are they merely complex electrochemical machines? Concisely defined, then, a world-view is the set of basic beliefs we hold about reality and persons.

Few people have a carefully constructed philosophy, theology, or psychology, but everyone has basic beliefs about reality and persons. In most cases these beliefs are largely unconscious and unarticulated, but they exert a profound influence in our lives. To illustrate how a world-view impacts our lives we will introduce three simple metaphors. In one way a world-view is like a compass, in another it is like a pair of eyeglasses, and in yet another it is like a filing cabinet.

As a compass orients the explorer in a strange environment, so a world-view orients and guides us. It gives us a sense of what is forward and backward, and what is right and wrong amid the confusing experiences that confront us. We need to be oriented and guided in the living of life; we cannot survive without a creed or a guiding perspective.

A world-view is also like a pair of eyeglasses. As a pair of glasses enables one to focus on details or to see the larger context in a clear manner, so a world-view helps us to focus on specific events and phenomena and also to see them in the larger context. We need both to see detail and also to be able to place the detail in perspective. Without proper perspective the detail has no meaning for us.

Finally, a world-view is like a filing cabinet. Just as an office manager establishes a system to order the diverse data of a business, so a world-view provides compartments in which to place and situate what we think, feel, and experience. It helps us order our world so that we can manage the enormous amount of incoming data.

Simply put, a world-view plays the roles of a compass, a pair of eyeglasses, and a filing cabinet. Both Christians and non-Christians have basic beliefs about reality and persons which enable them to orient, focus, and order their lives in relation to their world. The distinction between a Christian and non-Christian world-view is the result of their arising from different sources. The non-Christian's assumptions are derived from the givens of our present world. That is, non-Christians draw their basic beliefs concerning reality and persons from their own experiences and reflections. They gain their assumptions from their earthbound, limited, temporal perspective. The Christian, on the other hand, has a unique world-view in that it is gained from a twofold perspective. The Christian world-view is built on the givens of the present world, but also on the givens of God as presented in the Scriptures. As Christians we confess the Scriptures have the authority of God, and that perspective brings correction to the assumptions that are skewed because they are earthbound and limited. As Christians, our world-view must be continually shaped and tested by Scripture, or we will soon find ourselves viewing reality and persons in a way which is essentially no different from that of the non-Christian (see Sire [1976], Wolters [1985], or Pepper [1966] for further discussion of the Christian world-view).

Representative Psychotherapies

Christians can learn a good deal about helping people if they will start by evaluating various systems of psychotherapy according to their world-views. To illustrate this we will look at the world-views of several contemporary approaches to therapy. These diverse therapies can be broadly classified in terms of the three major forces in psychology. The first force is psychoanalysis, and as a representative of this tradition we will consider the work of Sigmund Freud. The second force is behaviorism, and here we will consider the work of B. F. Skinner. Closely allied with behavioral therapies are the more-recent cognitive therapies. We will consider Albert Ellis's rational-emotive therapy as a representative of this movement. The third force, which is the most diverse of the three, is described as the existential-humanistic tradition. The three names we have chosen from this tradition are Carl Rogers and his person-centered therapy, Fritz Perls and his Gestalt therapy, and Viktor Frankl and his logotherapy.

We will not try to be exhaustive in our description of these approaches. Further details on each may be obtained by consulting any of a number of readily available secondary sources (e.g., Patterson [1973], Corsini [1979], or Corey [1982]) or by reading the primary source writings (the works of Freud, Skinner, etc.). What we will do is identify their basic assumptions about reality and persons and then provide a preliminary evaluation of each in light of Scripture. We will also consider how they can assist a Christian to better understand and help people.

Psychoanalysis

Freud's classic method of psychoanalysis and the less intense forms of psychoanalytic therapy which have subsequently been developed share several basic assumptions about the nature of reality and the nature of persons. Throughout his life Freud declared that reality is composed of matter alone and that God does not exist. Although he asserted a one-story view of reality, he never was able to free himself of the annoyance of his early contacts with Christianity and his own Jewish heritage. Troubled at times though he was with the question of a realm beyond this world, he never embraced a two-story view of reality. He remained a naturalist who asserted that the world functions as a closed system of cause and effect. He explained the concepts of religion and the divine in terms of human projections of unconscious conflicts onto the cosmos.

With regard to persons Freud said that all behavior comes from one or the other of two basic drives: sex and aggression. All other drives are derivatives of these two, which are predominantly irrational and often self-destructive. He reduced the aesthetic, moral, and religious aspects of personality to expressions of the sexual and aggressive drives. We possess no higher motives. The problems humans struggle with are expressions of underlying unconscious conflicts which have their origin in childhood. The goal of therapy is, therefore, to help the individual understand his or her unconscious conflicts. This serves to break the tyranny of the unconscious and allows the individual freedom of choice.

Behavior therapy

More of a researcher and theorist than a therapist, B. F. Skinner is one of the most prolific and prominent behaviorists. He has significantly influenced the rise of the second force in psychology and encouraged the application of behavioral perspectives and principles to the clinical practice of psychology and psychiatry. Skinner has never hesitated to express his view of prime reality. Reality is nothing more than a materialistic existence in which there is a uniform deterministic system of cause and effect. There is no second story, there is no God, and there is no possibility of a reordering of the present cosmos from the outside. Although Freud at points struggled with his view of reality, Skinner has never blinked an eye when faced with seemingly incompatible data. Instead he has either rejected them or refashioned them in behavioral terms.

With regard to persons, Skinner and behavior therapists in general have considered humans to be only sophisticated and complex evolved animals. Human animals are basically hedonistic in nature and therefore gravitate towards that which gives the greatest pleasure and enjoyment. They are animals that have learned to function in certain ways based upon the interlocking of stimuli, responses, and reinforcements. Behavior therapy has tended to deemphasize thinking, feeling, and exercising free choice for the purpose of focusing attention on behaviors, which are determined by the interaction of personal and environmental causes and effects. Behaviorists see the basic human problems as being unpleasant behaviors which are supported by current psychological and environmental determinants. Behavior therapy is therefore an attempt to change the unpleasant behaviors by instituting different psychological and environmental factors. The goal is to alleviate human suffering through changing unpleasant behaviors and whatever factors support them.

Rational-emotive therapy

In contemporary classification, Albert Ellis and his rational-emotive therapy are usually considered part of the second force in psychology. We will emphasize Ellis because his therapy is currently the best known of a group of approaches referred to as cognitive therapies. Ellis has been just as outspoken as Skinner on the subject of reality. He conceives of reality as nothing more than what we presently know through our senses and through our reflections. Reality is basically a one-story structure with no God, no absolutes, and nothing beyond this natural order.

Rational-emotive therapy views persons as highly evolved beings who are not locked into a deterministic system of cause and effect, but possess the capacity for freedom, choice, and reason. However, notes Ellis, while we are free to choose to be rational, we usually choose the irrational. This curious propensity to irrationality, that is, our refusal to use reason and our consequent belief in foolish propositions, is the basis of all psychological problems. To Ellis, the most basic determinant of what we feel and how we act is what we think. Quoting the early Stoic Epictetus, Ellis notes, "Men are disturbed not by things, but by the views which they take of them." The task of the rational-emotive therapist is first to examine what the client believes and then to attempt to change those beliefs that are judged to be irrational and thereby destructive.

Person-centered therapy

As we stated earlier, the third force in psychology is the most diverse of the three and has broadly been termed the existential-humanistic stream. We have chosen three diverse representatives of this perspective in psychology. Carl Rogers founded a therapeutic approach known today as person-centered therapy. His impact on modern psychotherapy has been profound and cannot be easily overlooked. Like Freud, Skinner, and Ellis, Rogers also has basic beliefs about reality. In his early years he held a basic belief in God and a material world, but with the onset of adulthood he turned from Christianity to liberalistic humanism, largely, it seems, in reaction to the rather harsh religious convictions of his parents. With liberalistic humanism came a naturalistic world-view that had no place for God and conceived of the present cosmos as a closed system of causes and effects.

With regard to human nature person-centered therapy rejects Freud's pessimism, Skinner's determinism, and Ellis's belief that the key to our behavior is our willful irrationality. It instead proposes that the basic human drive is to fulfil one's potential, to become fully functioning as a human being. At the core of personality Rogers sees the pull towards actualization and wholeness. In this he exhibits a faith in an innate human goodness, and his therapeutic approach reflects this optimism. As Rogers sees it, we develop problems when people important to us accept us only conditionally. As children we are told to be good or else we will displease our parents and they will withhold their love. We continue to face conditional acceptance from others right on into adulthood. According to Rogers, this is at the heart of all psychological problems: it forces us to deny the parts of ourselves we feel others will not accept. The task of the person-centered therapist is to accept each client unconditionally and nonjudgmentally. The client will then be able to accept himself or herself and be free to rediscover and accept those parts of his or her personality which have been denied and lost. This in turn will free the client to progress towards the goal of self-actualization and full human functioning.

Gestalt therapy

Fritz Perls developed Gestalt therapy in the 1940s, and it has rapidly evolved into an important and popular form of treatment in the third force of psychology. Perls's therapy is a unique blend of humanistic and existential psychology, and with it he took a view of prime reality which excludes a concept of God and places emphasis on material existence. The cosmos exists as a system of cause and effect with no potential for outside intervention simply because the material world constitutes the whole of existence. Perls's naturalistic assumptions about reality led him to see the cosmos as ultimately a one-story structure without any relation to a Being beyond; there is no God, no Creator.

Perls's view of persons begins with the humanistic assumption that individuals have within themselves all they need to achieve personal wholeness and live effectively. The ingredient missing in most peoples' lives is courage, courage to become fully aware of their feelings and experiences. Without the courage to be aware of what is presently happening within and without, one experiences anxiety and suspension of growth. The major goal in Gestalt therapy is to teach the client to become more aware of the present. This heightened awareness is accomplished through a variety of techniques: active questioning by the therapist, group interaction, and a range of experiences orchestrated by the therapist. Through an increased awareness of the present the person can regain the parts of his or her self which were misplaced or lost by focusing on either the past or the future. Through this rediscovery of the lost parts of oneself, the individual is freed to achieve wholeness and effectiveness.

Logotherapy

Viktor Frankl developed a uniquely existential approach which he termed logotherapy. The term is derived from two Greek words, *logos* (word or meaning) and *therapeia* (healing). Logotherapy, then, is providing or experiencing healing through meaning. Frankl does not, however, view the meaning which brings healing as derived through a relationship with a realm beyond the natural order. He sees reality instead as no more than material existence. Frankl is a naturalist in that he sees reality as only material, thus excluding a divine realm. There is no God. Nothing exists but the present world.

Frankl views persons as free agents who are responsible, unique, and unified. As agents they are self-determining and self-actualizing. This enables them to transcend environmental factors which hamper their search for meaning. Humans are able to transcend because they, uniquely among all other species, are spiritual. By "spiritual" Frankl does not mean that they are able to commune with a Being beyond the natural order, but that they have a capacity for discovering, deciding, and actualizing their own existence. This spirituality cannot be taken away from a person. It is this dimension which makes life meaningful and purposeful. The primary motivation in humanity is their search for meaning. This involves ideals and values that draw rather than push an individual. Problems in living occur when the person experiences a loss of meaning, a lack of purpose, an existential boredom, and frustration with life itself. The ultimate goal of logotherapy is to help clients accept responsibility for themselves through their spiritual capacity. This allows them to make choices and thereby discover the meaning of life. Logotherapy is a form of treatment which encourages the person to discover and in fact create personal meaning in this world of meaninglessness.

In discussing the difference between a Christian and non-Christian world-view we noted that the non-Christian framework is built on the basis of the human perspective alone. And now, as we compare the several therapies we have just mentioned, we note that each one is based on the human perspective alone and assumes a view of reality which is naturalistic. For each, God is not a key factor. The key factor is the present material cosmos with its complex array of causes and effects.

Although these approaches agree in general on the nature of reality, they are in great disagreement over the nature of persons. They describe us in a variety of ways: we are in constant unconscious conflict, we are determined by psychological and environmental factors, we are thinking beings who nonetheless tend to irrationality, we are striving for fulfilment, we are in need of an awareness of the present, and we are in search of ultimate meaning. Looking at the vast array of ambiguous data about human nature and functioning, each system of psychotherapy interprets and orders them differently. From the naturalistic perspective there is an absence of consensus about the basic nature of persons. This may be because persons are simply unintelligible from an exclusively naturalistic and materialistic perspective.

A Christian World-view

What does Scripture teach us about reality and persons? The Bible provides us with a corrective in our view of reality. Without God's point of view we would have a strong inclination to see reality as a one-story structure, as a material cosmos alone. But God does not leave this to chance. Through the Bible he gives us his perspective, which presents reality as a two-story structure consisting of both himself and the material existence which he has created. This view of reality we call supernaturalism, that is, there is something beyond the material realm.

The Bible not only tells us that there is a God out there, but it also tells us what he is like. God is infinite and yet personal, transcendent and yet immanent, sovereign and yet merciful. By infinite and personal we mean that God is beyond scope and beyond measure, but at the same time he is not just a mere force or energy—he has personality. He is also transcendent and yet immanent. While he is beyond us, other than us, and radically different from us, he is also close to us and very much with us. Finally, he is sovereign and merciful. He rules over his creation, but in ruling he is also generous toward and concerned for his creation.

Along with revealing the existence and character of God the Bible tells us in a broad way about the nature of our world. God created the cosmos by his spoken word, and he sustains it continually of his own choice. In creating the cosmos he designed it to operate with a uniformity of cause and effect, but also with the possibility that he might be continually involved with it and reorder it if he chooses to do so. This means that the created world is not prime reality, but in fact the one who made it is. God has always existed; he is the source and sustainer of our present world, and has constituted it in such a way that it is both orderly and yet open to be divinely reordered.

The Bible also speaks of persons in a broad way. In the first three chapters of Genesis we have a sketch that is at the heart of the scriptural view of the human race. In Genesis 1:26–27 it is declared that persons are created in the image of God. Any view of human beings that calls itself Christian must start with the truth that God fashioned them in his own likeness. This doctrine means that God placed humans at the pinnacle of creation, designing us to be in personal relationship with him and express him in the rest of creation. This doctrine also suggests that human beings cannot be fully understood unless seen in relation to the Creator. Something fundamental to human nature will be overlooked if persons are considered apart from their relationship with God.

The second creation narrative (Gen. 2:4–25) contains further details about what it means for human beings to be formed in God's image. God forms a human being from the dust of the earth and breathes into his nostrils the breath of life (2:7). This fact illustrates the unique place persons hold in God's creation. We are like God in terms of being constituted in his image, but we are also unlike God in that we are finite creatures made of earth's dust. Human beings not only have a unique relationship with their Creator, but also have a unique relationship with the rest of creation. We are like God in that we are personal, but unlike God in that we are creatures. We are like the rest of the created order in that we are creatures, but unlike the rest of creation in that we are capable of personally relating with God.

Another point made in this narrative is that human beings were created as free, independent agents, capable of ultimate choices. This is implied in 2:16–17, where the first human is told not to eat of a particular tree, and cautioned as to the consequences should disobedience occur. As agents persons have certain motives, which are rooted in their values, loves, and hopes. To ultimately understand human actions we must understand human motives, purposes, and values. As agents we are also rational, capable of evaluating various options and calculating a plan to accomplish the way chosen. In addition, as agents we are not free of responsibility. Human beings were created in relation to God and were to live in accordance with divine values and guidelines. But human ability to evaluate and choose was later abused in rejecting the special relationship to God, thus further demonstrating the extent of human free agency.

We cannot talk very long about persons' being created in God's image without considering the truth of their sinful rebellion as recorded in Genesis 3. While none of our worth was lost in the fall, the doctrine of total depravity asserts that all aspects of our nature now bear the mark of sin. This is not to suggest that we are as evil as we could be, or that all that was good about us has been lost. However, we are now thoroughly sinful, no aspect of our personality being free from the effects of sin.

Here we must make a subtle distinction. Because persons still bear God's image we can still accurately describe them as good with regard to their standing in creation. We have not lost our value but continue to stand as creatures of incalculable worth. However, we cannot accurately describe human beings as good with regard to their moral standing or even to their capacity to choose ultimate good. The Old Testament asserts that the human heart is deceitfully wicked (Jer. 17:9), and this theme is carried into the New Testament, where it is stated that evil has its origin not in the external environment but in the human heart (Mark 7:15).

It is important to realize that while this fall into sin resulted in alienation from God, human beings still necessarily had a relationship with God, and were responsible to him even in their rebellion. God's image in persons was broken and marred, but not obliterated. Had it been, we would no longer be human, for at the very heart of humanness is likeness to the personal God.

As a result of the fall, however, persons lost both their place and their identity. Like a puzzle with the most important pieces missing, human beings are incomplete until they stand once again in intimate communion with their Creator. However, unlike the inanimate puzzle, human beings constantly search for the missing parts, for their elusive place and identity. When we understand that persons are striving to find their place, we understand both their fundamental drive for meaning and their innate religiosity. Humans were created to be self-transcendent, to lose themselves as they serve God and others. This is what it means to be innately religious. Humans were created to serve; and their most crucial choice, indeed the only choice of real consequence, is whom they will serve. We must see our religious nature, then, as a fundamental part of personality. All human beings are religious; some serve the true God and others serve false gods. It is very much as Martin Luther said, "Man either has God or an idol."

Persons have lost their proper place in the world and seek continuously to find it again. This produces what we recognize as both strivings for meaning and incurable religiosity. Yet we also see ambivalence combined with these strivings rooted in God's image. Due to our chosen rebellion, we also hate God or actively reject him, and so are trapped in contradictions. We sense that a critical piece is missing though we often do not realize that the missing piece is fellowship with God. In fact, we may turn our strivings to the worship of false gods, self, other humans, or various philosophies.

Although because of our sin we have trapped ourselves in conflict and contradictions, we are redeemable and have been redeemed. The story of creation and the fall is told in the first three chapters of Genesis. The story of God's redemptive activity takes the rest of the Scriptures to unfold. The Bible records God's love for persons in searching them out, finding them locked in contradiction, and redeeming them by the sacrifice of his own Son, Jesus Christ. Through the great grace of God, human beings have been given the possibility of a new life, a life involving a substantial restoration to their place and identity in God, and subsequent healing from the results of their rebellion and alienation.

That God has provided the missing pieces does not mean human beings play no role in this salvation. They were not forced to fall. They are not forced to return to their place in God's order of things. And yet most Christians would agree that God is the primary agent in salvation. (It is, of course, not possible for us at this point to discuss the issue of predestination versus free will.) The human role is to respond by repentance and to accept God's provision of restoration and healing through taking Jesus Christ as Lord and Savior.

Comparison and Evaluation

We have sketched the world-views of six psychotherapies and also have outlined the world-view presented by Scripture. Now let us compare these world-views and begin to evaluate the psychotherapies. As Christians we measure everything by the biblical statements on reality and persons; we assert that the Christian world-view is superior. We judge it to be superior to alternate world-views primarily as an act of faith. However, we also observe that the Christian world-view gives us a more adequate way of orienting our lives, bringing all the data of our world into clear focus, and ordering our experience.

In comparing the views of reality we note a major disagreement between the naturalism of the six psychotherapies and the supernaturalism of the Bible. As Christians we believe in a God who has created, who presently sustains, and who intimately interacts with our world. We believe in a material world which was created by God to operate with a system of causes and effects but which is open to God's interventions. We must therefore reject any view of reality which asserts that matter exists eternally and which denies the possibility of a divine Being beyond the natural order. We also must reject any conception of a material world composed simply of causes and effects without the possibility of divine intervention.

In comparing the Christian perspective with the diverse views of persons proposed by the six secular therapies we note both similarities and differences. The Bible asserts that human beings are made in God's image and that this is what makes them unique. Also, the Scriptures declare that humans are made of the dust of the earth and in this they are closely related to the rest of creation. None of the therapies have such a wide perspective in viewing humanity although they do note both our divinelike and animal-like dimensions. None of the therapies assert a belief in God or the possibility of humans' being fashioned after such a model. But some of the therapies do recognize in human beings a uniqueness which distinguishes them from the rest of creation. Rogers, Perls, and Frankl all assert that we are of great worth and clearly different from the rest of the creatures constituting the animal kingdom. Although they would not go so far as to identify these distinctive aspects with God's image, they do in fact recognize our specifically human characteristics. What they fail to recognize is their meaning and significance.

On the other hand, Freud and Skinner focus upon the animal-like aspects of persons. In focusing on the unconscious dimensions of humans, Freud came to see persons in terms of the basic animal drives which push them toward certain goals and behaviors. Skinner notes the close resemblance between animal and human responsiveness to environmental stimuli and to reinforcement. From such observations he posits that human behavior is determined.

The Bible also asserts that in addition to being created in God's image, humans were created as free, independent agents capable of choice. In conceiving of them as agents it asserts that they are rational and evaluating beings as well. Ellis focuses on the rational agency of persons and notes that problems result when persons choose to think and act irrationally. Ellis, although rejecting the concept of God, has noted this important dimension in us which the Scriptures link to the image of God. The Scriptures constantly stress that thinking is foundational to human life (e.g., Prov. 23:7) and that it is essential to choose a pattern of thinking which will renew our minds so that we grow in Christ (Rom. 12:1–2).

Rogers's humanistic emphasis has led him to hold a strong view of the human capacity to evaluate and choose from various options. This capacity is hindered when we lack acceptance by others and consequently reject part of ourself. If we come to be unconditionally accepted by another, however, we can accept ourself and can then choose what is best for us in an unhindered manner. Perls's blend of humanism and existentialism leads him to see persons as moral agents who, by gaining an awareness of their present existence and courageously embracing it, can be freed to achieve wholeness. Frankl also perceives persons as free agents who are responsible for seeking and discovering their own meaning in life, this being the route to liberation from anxiety and frustration.

Freud's view on the issue of human agency is not easy to define. His focus was not on the rational and conscious, but on the irrational and unconscious aspects of persons. Within the unconscious he identified powerful sexual and aggressive drives which in large part determine human behavior. Freedom from these determining influences and a capacity for choice come, in Freud's view, only by awareness and understanding of these unconscious forces and the conflicts associated with them. Skinner goes even further than Freud in limiting human freedom and agency. He asserts that freedom is an illusion; humans are locked into a deterministic system of stimulus-response patterns.

Scripture also declares that persons have fallen into sin and that the impact of sin has been felt in every dimension of personality. Freud's pessimistic view of human nature, which asserts that the closer we look into human motivations, the more we see evil and destructiveness, clearly indicates his awareness of sin even though he does not label or understand it as such. Ellis's consciousness of the human proclivity toward irrationality shows that he also recognizes a negative dimension in human motivation which we Christians associate with sinfulness. And Skinner, in asserting that humans are determined and bound by habit, is recognizing that which the Bible describes as human beings' habitual slavery to sin. Persons are not free to live in the ultimate sense because, apart from God's intervention, they are locked into a pattern of sinfulness. These more pessimistic views of persons are in radical contrast to the rosy optimism of the existential-humanistic therapies which turn a blind eye to the negative aspect of human nature.

As a result of the fall human beings lost their place and identity. The fundamental drive in human personality is to regain our place, to find our identity. Our religious and spiritual nature is not something added on to our personality, but is, rather, at the core of our humanness. Saint Augustine's familiar point that we were created for God and are restless until we find our place in him depicts the drive for meaning which Frankl has noted in his logotherapy. Although Frankl recognizes the human need for meaning, he denies that it is God who provides that meaning. Perls's and Rogers's views that persons constantly reach toward wholeness and self-fulfilment are very similar to this concept of our longing for meaning, but they still fall far short of the human search for God and the need to find a place in him. In contrast, Freud and Skinner acknowledge no higher human aims than the gratification of basic hedonistic urges. Meaning and purpose seem to have no place in the psychoanalytic and behavioral views of human beings.

A biblical look at the views of reality and persons held by these representative psychotherapies suggests several conclusions. First, the naturalistic view of reality is opposed to the biblical supernaturalism. On the basis of the superior biblical perspective we must reject the view of reality proposed by these therapies. Second, none of the six therapies correspond exactly to the biblical picture of persons; in fact, all six differ from it in some important ways. However, each of the six does contain at least one aspect of the biblical view and brings that aspect into particular focus. Thus we shall neither completely reject as unbiblical nor unreservedly accept as entirely biblical any of these approaches. Third, the Bible has much to say about reality and persons, matters on which any Christian who wishes to help people must have knowledge. We should also note, however, that the biblical teachings on persons become much clearer when we consider them in light of current psychotherapeutic theories. And this, of course, is the major reason why Christians who are not directly involved in the mental-health profession should gain a knowledge of these theories. They will learn more about what questions to ask Scripture and thus greatly increase their understanding of human nature.

Christian Psychotherapy

We have considered how our Christian faith can provide a basis for evaluating various therapies so as to assist us in gaining insight and techniques for helping people. But what about the possibility of the Christian faith itself providing a novel approach to counseling? This question is different from the previous issue of learning from secular therapies. It asks whether there is a uniquely Christian psychotherapy, one which is fundamentally different from all those approaches not classified by the adjective *Christian*. The issue of a Christian psychotherapy addresses the nature of the Bible itself and of the integration of theology and psychology. In the final portion of this chapter we will deal with the nature of divine revelation and integration as they relate to three general attempts to work out a uniquely Christian approach to

therapy: biblical therapy, therapy by a Christian, and biblically informed therapy.

Biblical therapy

A number of Christians who work in the area of psychology assume
that the Scriptures contain a clear model of personality development,
psychopathology, and psychotherapy, including techniques and goals.
In other words, they assert the Bible contains a unique and comprehensive anthropology and theory of psychotherapy. For example,
Jay Adams (1977) argues that the Bible is the only textbook necessary
for the Christian to learn all that is needed for counseling. He asserts
that "if a principle is new to or different from those that are advocated
in the Scriptures, it is wrong; if it is not, it is unnecessary" (p. 183).
Others (Carter [1980], Crabb [1977]) have avoided the assumption that
apart from the Scriptures nothing useful can be learned about counseling, but have retained a high degree of confidence that the Bible
contains a unique personality theory and an implicit model of counseling. The striking thing, however, is that seldom do these people agree
as to just what the Scriptures suggest to be this unique theory and
model. Perhaps these individuals are approaching Scripture with
wrong expectations. Out of a deep concern to be completely biblical
and thoroughly Christian in their practice of therapy, they have
pressed the Bible beyond what it is intended to bear.

The problem of expecting too much from Scripture in terms of a
unique anthropology and approach to therapy arises from a confusion
over the purpose of divine revelation and the nature of biblical language itself. The general judgment of biblical scholars has been that
the purpose of special revelation is to present God's claim on persons,
the truth about their condition before their Creator, and the provisions
he has made for their personal restoration. It is not the purpose of
Scripture to consider persons alone as unique entities in themselves or
to convey the fine inner dynamics at work within them. Rather, when
Scripture describes persons, they are seen in their total relation to God
the Creator and Redeemer (Berkouwer [1962]).

This revelation of God came in and through the languages of particular cultures. These biblical languages were not scientific but popular; the words were those of the common people, used in the
marketplace, at social gatherings, and in casual conversations. God's
chosen vehicle of popular languages was intended to make the Bible a
book for all people of all ages, and therefore it is improper to seek
technical terminology in it or to assume it is inadequate because it is
not packed with scientific jargon (Ramm [1954]).

The language of the Bible is not only popular but also phenomenal. By phenomenal we mean language limited to what is apparent. It descibes what is seen, heard, thought, felt, and generally experienced by the average person, not what is scientifically postulated or theorized. This suggests that when biblical writers refer to psychic functions, they do not speak in scientific psychological phraseology but in descriptive popular language. For example, the Bible occasionally speaks of psychic functions in terms of physical organs such as the heart or kidneys. This is popular and phenomenal language, never intended to be interpreted literally. In the same way the Scriptures speak of the sun rising and setting. Although we in the post-Copernican world know that the sun does not go around the earth but rather the earth around the sun, we are not to treat the biblical phraseology as scientific error. Rather, we are to treat it as figurative language describing what is apparent.

Now the Scriptures were no more given as a textbook of psychology than as a textbook of astronomy (Ramm [1954]). They were given by God to reveal his purposes and provisions for humanity. Accordingly, in the Bible humans are understood in the context of their relation to the Creator and Redeemer. The language used to express these truths is not scientific or technical but popular and phenomenal. The Scriptures were never intended to provide a unique scientific anthropology or a technically sophisticated theory of psychotherapy (Berkouwer [1962]).

Therapy by a Christian

Others who work in the area of psychology have asserted that Christian psychotherapy is no more than a Christian doing therapy. This perspective limits the Scriptures to addressing spiritual and theological concerns which at best may provide a resource for the therapist personally. Never should they be expected to provide content for the theory and practice of Christian therapy. For example, Rodney Vanderploeg (1981) argues that "there is no difference between Christian and non-Christian therapy. The goals are the same . . . the means are the same. . . . The difference lies not within therapy but within the therapists themselves. One group is Christian and the other is not" (p. 303). Others (e.g., Jansma [1960]) argue that to talk about Christian psychotherapy is ridiculous as it suggests that there is a unique kind of theory or procedure that a Christian should hold or employ. At most a Christian psychotherapy is a formal helping relationship which involves a Christian therapist.

This view that Christian psychotherapy is simply therapy by a Christian is the opposite of the first view we discussed. While those seeking a unique and comprehensive theory of therapy from the Scriptures expect too much of the Bible, this approach expects too little of the Scriptures. We agree that Christian therapy is therapy administered by a Christian, but we believe it is more. It is more because the Scriptures, although not providing a comprehensive theory of personality or psychotherapy, do contain a view of persons that is most essential to the individual wishing to provide Christian therapy. In fact, whatever else Christian psychotherapy is, surely it must be based on and informed by the biblical perspective on human nature.

Biblically informed psychotherapy

We have seen that some Christian psychologists have suggested that a uniquely Christian therapy will be based on the Bible alone, while others have based it on the Christian therapist alone. We find these extreme views inadequate because they expect either too much of God's revelation or too little. A Christian approach to therapy is both different from secular approaches in some ways and yet quite similar in other ways. Christian psychotherapy takes biblical revelation seriously and recognizes the need to evaluate everything in its light. But Christian psychotherapy also recognizes the limits of biblical revelation and the need for the added input and insight found in psychology. To illustrate how Christian psychotherapy is both different from yet similar to other forms of therapy we will look at three parts of a biblically informed therapy: its theory, goals, and techniques.

Theory. Although the Scriptures do not provide a comprehensive theory of personality or psychotherapy, they do tell us much about persons which is essential to developing a Christian theory. Three biblical themes which seem particularly relevant are the doctrines of creation, the fall, and redemption. Albert Wolters (1985) argues that the Christian should look at all of life through the framework of the original good creation as provided by God, its perversion through sin, and its restoration through Christ. Some of this we discussed earlier in constructing a world-view by which to evaluate various therapies. It may be helpful at this point to briefly consider how these themes inform a Christian approach to psychotherapy.

As noted earlier, human beings were fashioned in God's image. This fact is foundational for understanding persons. Part of being in God's image is the human ability to make ultimate choices, to interact socially, and to seek meaning, purpose, and self-transcendence. These aspects as revealed in God's Word provide a unique perspective in developing a Christian anthropology. If persons are created in God's image, then they must be understood in the context of a relationship with God. Accordingly, any strictly psychological view which excludes the divinely oriented dimensions of human beings is self-limiting. If persons are agents, then we must not hesitate to incorporate human responsibility into our Christian anthropology. If persons are of a social character, then we should include social and interpersonal dimensions in our theorizing. And if human beings are spiritual, we should ensure that our view of persons makes room for the human propensity to seek meaning, purpose, and self-surrender to someone or something beyond.

As created by God, persons were and are a unity of psychological, physical, and spiritual functions. Many have attempted to understand the scriptural teaching about persons by analyzing their parts (heart, soul, mind, etc.); this has led to debate over whether human beings are composed of two parts (soul-body) or three parts (body-soul-spirit). But most biblical scholars now agree that the primary biblical emphasis is on the unity of personality. While the Bible does present a number of aspects of the human being, these were never intended to be interpreted as components or parts. Always they are to be seen as perspectives on the whole. This unity means that persons do not have spirit but are spirit. Similarly, persons do not have soul or body, but are soul and are body. Further, this means that since we do not have distinct spiritual or psychological parts, neither do we have problems that are purely spiritual or purely psychological. And because no problem is strictly spiritual or psychological, the Christian psychotherapist must resist the temptation to artificially categorize problems as strictly psychological or spiritual.

While the fact of our creation in God's image validates the good and noble aspects of human functioning, the Christian view of persons must be balanced by recognition of the reality of sin. More than just a tendency to fail to meet our personal expectations or those held by others, sin is active rebellion against a holy God. This rebellion results in alienation from God, self, and others. These consequences of sin are ultimately, although not necessarily personally or directly, at the root of all our problems. This reality of sin and its consequences must also inform a Christian approach to therapy. For example, we must recognize that, sin being a reality, guilt may not always be neurotic. Sometimes it is a reality either because of our condition of being born in sin and separated from God or because of sinful habit patterns that require the divine provisions of forgiveness and healing.

The third major doctrine which must inform a Christian understanding of persons is the doctrine of redemption. God is active in this fallen world, restoring his good creation. Redemption is God's work of grace, setting the prisoners of sin free and restoring us to communion with himself. Redemption is grace restoring nature, making it whole again.

Psychotherapy is not redemption. However, Christian psychotherapy participates in God's redemptive purposes. Because Christ is the reconciler of all things, including our minds (Col. 1:19–22), and because we have been entrusted with the "ministry of reconciliation" on his behalf (2 Cor. 5:18), psychotherapy by a Christian can be a unique way of participating in God's redemptive work.

This view of persons as created in God's image, polluted by sin, and pursued by a God of grace who is in the process of reconciling all things unto himself must be at the foundation of any theory of personality that calls itself Christian. However, this view is far from adequate as a complete personality-theory. While we therefore should not expect the Scriptures to yield a comprehensive anthropology, it is nevertheless clear that they do contain perspectives that are foundational for Christian psychotherapy.

Goals. What goals should guide Christian therapy? The goals of the Christian therapist must be both immediate and ultimate: immediate in terms of addressing the symptoms which have brought the client in for help, ultimate in terms of growth toward human wholeness. But the fact is that few clients are concerned with the ultimate goal of wholeness. Instead they desire immediate intervention which will relieve them of their discomfort. This is usually followed by a decision to discontinue therapy. Because the Christian view holds that humans are capable of personal choice and morally responsible, Christian psychotherapists are not in a position to force the client into dealing with ultimate concerns if his or her only focus is on immediate relief. While Christian therapists will have the ultimate spiritual welfare and growth of the client as a part of their concerns and goals, they will be willing to work with less than ultimate concerns if this is therapeutically appropriate. Christ's own ministry clearly demonstrates that ultimate concerns do not need to be a part of every healing contact. The parable of the good Samaritan and the frequent healings which occurred apart from an explicit verbal presentation of the gospel show Christ's concern to meet people at their point of need. His ministry was not always in ultimate dimensions, although he never lost sight of what those ultimate dimensions are.

In setting goals the Christian therapist will always keep in view the scriptural portrait of the whole mature person that is the result of Christian growth. Thus, for example, the Christian therapist will seek to encourage the development of interdependence, this in contrast to the autonomy and independence valued in many therapeutic approaches. Similarly, the Christian therapist will encourage self-transcendence and ultimate self-surrender to God, viewing as less than wholeness a life that is self-encapsulated or idolatrously invested in other gods. It is likely that the Christian therapist will share many goals with the non-Christian therapist, particularly in terms of immediate symptom reduction. However, the ultimate goals that direct Christian therapy will grow out of the overall Christian view of persons we discussed above.

J. Harold Ellens (1980) adds a note of warning. He points out how easy it is for Christian therapists to substitute private philosophy for sound psychotherapeutic practice. He states that "the practice of the helping professions which is preoccupied with the final step of wholeness, spiritual maturity, will usually short circuit the therapeutic process" (p. 4). Christian psychotherapy is not the same as evangelism or discipling. Whatever else it is, it is first of all excellent psychotherapy.

Techniques. Is Christian therapy unique by virtue of its employment of certain techniques? Are there uniquely Christian techniques? Adams (1977) answers these questions affirmatively and, assuming every technique to be bound to a presuppositional base, has judged the techniques of secular therapies to be inappropriate for the Christian therapist. As we briefly stated early in this chapter, however, the relationship between most techniques and the theory with which they are primarily associated seems to be very loose indeed. One has only to note the diverse therapies using the same techniques to see this point.

Most techniques seem to be neither Christian nor non-Christian. Therefore, they should be judged not on the basis of who first described them but rather on their efficacy. Do they achieve the therapeutic goals? Also, they should be evaluated for their consistency with the overall theoretical framework guiding the therapy. The Christian therapist will thus be cautious of adopting a pragmatic eclecticism in deciding which techniques to employ. Some Christian therapists do employ explicitly religious resources such as prayer, Scripture reading, or even laying on of hands. While any of these interventions may well be appropriate under some circumstances, the responsible therapist will, before using them, determine clearly their significance for the client and the therapy process.

In summary, Christian psychotherapy is best viewed as therapy offered by a Christian who bases his or her understanding of persons on the Bible and allows this understanding to shape all aspects of theory, goals, and techniques. This suggests an ongoing process rather than a finished product. Defined thus, Christian therapists are not those who practice a certain type of therapy, but, rather, those who view themselves in God's service in and through their profession and who consider their allegiance and accountability to be primarily to God, and only secondarily to psychology.

References

Adams, J. (1977). *Lectures on counseling*. Nutley, N.J.: Presbyterian and Reformed.

Berkouwer, G. (1962). *Man: The image of God*. Grand Rapids: Eerdmans.

Carter, J. (1980). Towards a biblical model of counseling. *Journal of Psychology and Theology* 8: 45–52.

Corey, G. (1982). *Theory and practice of counseling and psychotherapy* (2d ed.). Monterey, Calif.: Brooks/Cole.

Corsini, R., ed. (1979). *Current psychotherapies* (2d ed.). Itasca, Ill.: Peacock.

Crabb, L. (1977). *Effective biblical counseling*. Grand Rapids: Zondervan.

Ellens, J. H. (1980). Biblical themes in psychological theory and practice. *Bulletin of the Christian Association for Psychological Studies* 6.2: 2–6.

Jansma, T. (1960). Christian psychotherapy. *Christianity Today* 4.19 (20 June 1960): 9–10.

Patterson, C. H. (1973). *Theories of counseling and psychotherapy* (2d ed.). New York: Harper & Row.

Pepper, S. (1966). *World hypotheses: A study in evidence*. Berkeley: University of California Press.

Ramm, B. (1954). *The Christian view of science and Scripture*. Grand Rapids: Eerdmans.

Sire, J. (1976). *The universe next door: A basic world view catalog*. Downers Grove, Ill.: Inter-Varsity.

Vanderploeg, R. (1981). *Imago Dei* as foundational to psychotherapy: Integration versus segregation. *Journal of Psychology and Theology* 9: 299–304.

Wolters, A. (1985). *Creation regained*. Grand Rapids: Eerdmans.

Psychotherapy as a Spiritual Enterprise

Clinton W. McLemore and David W. Brokaw

The orthodox Christian believes in the efficacy of prayer, in the power of the Holy Spirit to bring healing and growth, in the divine enabling of all Christians to pursue righteousness, and above all in the reality of the atoning death of Jesus Christ and the necessity of each individual's embracing the person of Christ to receive salvation.

How should such beliefs affect how a Christian does psychotherapy? Do we have an obligation to seek to heal the deeper spiritual wounds of a person preoccupied only with temporal suffering? If the Holy Spirit is the Healer and Comforter, must the Christian recognize and incorporate that work in some formal way in doing Christian psychotherapy? Is true health to be found only in the pursuit of holiness, and how should the counselor's religious beliefs interact with the client's moral behavior? This chapter will help the reader begin to sort out these issues.

Clinton W. McLemore (B.A., Adelphi University; Ph.D., University of Southern California) is an adjunct professor at Fuller Theological Seminary Graduate School of Psychology. His book The Scandal of Psychotherapy *(Wheaton, Ill.: Tyndale, 1982) has been helpful to many Christians struggling to relate their Christian faith and the mental-health professions. Among his other writings are* Good Guys Finish First *(Philadelphia: Westminster, 1983),* Honest Christianity

178

(Philadelphia: Westminster, 1984), and several contributions to professional journals, including American Psychologist. *David W. Brokaw (B.A., Wheaton College; M.A., Ph.D., Fuller Theological Seminary Graduate School of Theology) is an adjunct professor of psychology at Azusa Pacific University. Both authors are principally affiliated with the Relational Dynamics Institute of Pasadena, California.*

When individuals decide to undergo psychotherapy, they are usually asking for help with strong and unresolved feelings. Summing up their problem, they might state, for example, "I feel terminally depressed," "I can't seem to get over my ex-boyfriend," or "I'm terrified of heights!" This chapter is concerned with the spiritual dimensions involved in the treatment of such feelings. Among the questions addressed are: How, if at all, do feelings relate to life in Christ? Feelings being the central concern of psychotherapy, where do God and the supernatural come in? What are the religious issues that weave themselves into the fabric of virtually every psychotherapeutic encounter, regardless of whether the client is a believer or an atheist? What does the ever-present spiritual dimension of therapy imply for the conduct of therapy by a Christian? To put all of this a little differently, in this chapter we will examine what is inescapably religious about conducting psychotherapy.

God and Human Feelings

The idea that emotions are irrelevant to life, or that they are intrusions into the otherwise smooth business of living, is perhaps the most tragically mistaken belief currently alive within Christendom. Nothing about us is more spiritually diagnostic than the condition of our hearts, the feelings and feeling processes that characterize us.

As argued in *Honest Christianity* (McLemore [1984]), affective states are the very essence of spiritual life and therefore of human life. God cares more about our feelings, and the feelings of others, than we usually dare imagine. From Cain's wrongheartedness in Genesis 4 to Laodicea's complacency in Revelation 3, the Creator-Provider-Sustainer shows a keen interest in our coronary health.

The Old Testament Scriptures speak of God's preferring a right heart to acts of sacrifice. In the New Testament, Jesus was most upset with the very proper but coldhearted Pharisees, and it appears that our Lord often looked past ostensibly flagrant sin because he saw someone's earnest love, repentant faith, and interpersonal openness; that is, he saw the condition of the person's heart.

Psychotherapists as Doctors of the Heart

Whether or not a particular therapist understands it, he or she is a heart doctor. Therapists treat the emotional core of the human person and, therefore, what they do is *by nature* spiritual. While one can build a bridge or even a city without much in the way of concern with the heart, it is impossible to minister to the psychological needs of another without addressing the heart in some way. The heart, after all, is where the hurt and therefore the need are. But how does the therapist minister, and what does therapy have to do with what God desires for our hearts? To answer these questions, we must first ask, What exactly is God up to when he works in our lives? As the ultimate heart surgeon, what operation is he attempting to perform?

God wants us to love him. Loving God and other people is what life is ultimately about. We have, in other words, been created expressly to develop certain dispositions of the heart. Unfortunately, regardless of how genteel we may appear on the surface, genuine *agapē* love, the giving, sacrificial love of God himself, is not easy for us. Try as we might, we continually fall short of what we painfully understand to be mature love.

Spiritual growth is fraught with contrast and seeming paradox. It appears, for instance, that we can grow in love only to the extent that we reckon with our imperfections in *agapē* love. To love more, we must begin to see that, in fact, we love less. To draw closer to God, we have to grasp just how very far away we are. To know the truth about ourselves, we are forced to understand that we have hidden the truth from ourselves, to hear the stark message that we have been cultivating pride, and therefore false security, through defensive lies.

All good therapists, no matter what their personal beliefs and quite aside from whether they comprehend the psychospiritual nature of what they do, help people face themselves. Even if such words as "sin" and "atonement" never enter the psychotherapeutic conversation, the successfully treated client will come away with a keener sense of his or her inner being. The effectiveness of psychotherapy, in fact, almost always hinges on the client's encountering previously unrecognized personal realities; it hinges on his or her willingness to look inside at those not so nice things that most of us would prefer to pretend are not there. Psychotherapy, in its essence, is the benevolent pursuit of truth; responding to this truth is, in the end, what changes us.

We conclude that all good psychotherapy is essentially interrelated with the spiritual core of life, and must therefore be seen as a spiritual enterprise. This is not to say, however, that psychotherapy is an exclusively pastoral task, one which can be done only under the authority and ministry of an official church. Rather, psychotherapy is spiritual in that it deals with the unified psychological and spiritual core, the heart, of the person. Given this spiritual nature of psychotherapy, we must inquire further as to its relationship with other forms of spiritual ministry, especially evangelism.

Is Psychotherapy Evangelism?

Some Christian psychologists have come to the conclusion that psychotherapy is, at its best, evangelism. They believe that the Christian therapist's job is somehow to convert people to Christ. That psychotherapy by a competent Christian practitioner may be coincidentally evangelistic we do not dispute. By "coincidentally" we mean that the purpose of evangelism may be served by the client's being motivated to investigate the Christian faith further and to convert, even though the therapist never explicitly witnesses to the client. After all, if someone helps us to change our life for the better, it is only natural for us to be at least interested in his or her personal philosophy. A patient lifted from the depths of depression may be unusually open to the therapist's religion. Nevertheless, the plain fact that philosophical-religious persuasion sometimes attends psychotherapy does not imply that such persuasion is intrinsic to the therapeutic process.

The therapist's role as defined by a common societal understanding (transmitted by such means as the media, public pronouncements by members of the profession, and so forth) is to help people know their own inner psychological workings (their existing thoughts, feelings, and impulses) and, then, to come to terms with them. Coming to terms customarily means resolving conflicts between competing desires, which in turn typically results in the person's acting more effectively and expending less energy to keep unwanted material out of awareness. In a sense, it means facing one's sin.

A Christian medical doctor might well share his or her faith during the course of treating a physical ailment, but the bearing of such witness is only tangentially related to the medical treatment per se. Similarly, while a Christian therapist might share his or her faith with a client, such sharing is not an inherent part of psychotherapy—unless, of course, we redefine therapy to mean a binding up of emotional wounds in order that we may have the opportunity to enact our ultimate agenda: evangelism.

The problem is that the only clients regarding whom the concept of evangelism is relevant are those who are not believers. These clients generally do not expect and frequently do not desire to be evangelized by their psychotherapist (unless, of course, the Christian therapist has indicated beforehand an intention to so minister and the client comes for that very reason). Thus, to slip in explicit religious witness, Christian or otherwise, apart from the client's request for such witness, is tantamount to fraud. The therapist promises one thing, conventional therapy, while intending all along to deliver another, the gospel.

It is perhaps worth remarking that evangelism as many conservative Christians conceive it may be different from how Jesus Christ conceived it! All through the New Testament, Jesus drew people to himself. He did not constantly repeat verbal solicitations or resort to slick sales tricks in order to win people to God. To the contrary, his calls to faith were built upon true human contact, upon genuine person-to-person relatedness.

As more and more psychotherapists are recognizing, the vehicle— or perhaps we should say the means—of therapy is the relationship between doctor and patient. Like Jesus, good therapists meet people where their needs are. Now, if the therapist is a Christian, and if an occasion arises for a nonintrusive presentation of the gospel because of the therapist's personal healing impact on the client, the most wonderful evangelism possible will ensue (quite apart from whether the client becomes a Christian).

At the end of John's Gospel (21:1–13), one morning after the resurrection, Jesus bids his disciples, who have been fishing unsuccessfully all night, throw their net on the right side of the boat. The result is a massive catch of fish. When they come ashore, he very humanly says to them, "Come and eat." It is clear from the passage that Jesus cooks for them and serves them. He addresses their basic temporal needs. Competent Christian psychotherapists also meet basic needs, emotional ones. Having done so, they are in a position to share their personal experience of Christ Jesus ("all I know is that while once I was blind, now I see"). However, even though such sharing is among the highest forms of evangelism imaginable, it is not of itself psychotherapy. Rather, it remains evangelism that has been spawned in the waters of a healing relationship.

We will now discuss with more precision some of the considerations in deciding when the sharing of a therapist's personal faith is proper and when it is improper. As discussed elsewhere (McLemore [1982]), the prime existential directive for any Christian may well be Christian witness. Christians believe that all persons need to reckon with God through Christ Jesus and, in the process, to allow God to reorient their lives (they must turn from their sin). Paul describes all Christians as being ambassadors for Christ who carry the message of reconciliation (2 Cor. 5:17–21). Thus, we are all to be his witnesses. The rub comes when we try to determine the nature of the witness we are to bear. Just how forceful should it be? Are we derelict in our discipleship if we do not become fervent door-to-door evangelists? Here, of course, we are turning to the question of whether traditional evangelical conceptions of witness are, in fact, always God's will.

Our first consideration is that some persons are genuinely called and gifted by God to be evangelists, whether through public speaking or one-to-one contact. God has not only given them the desire to evangelize but has also equipped them with the communication skills needed to do so effectively. Doing deliberate evangelism is for these persons a *specific* ministry and a commission that is to receive a significant portion of their personal energy. We would argue that Christian psychotherapy, while calling for a general attentiveness to the need for evangelism of all people, is also a specific form of ministry for the emotional healing of persons—a task different from evangelism.

Probably few Christians are called and gifted as both therapists and evangelists, but if a person is truly called and gifted in both areas, he or she is going to live in a certain amount of tension, in that he or she has dual callings that are not identical. As in the case of a person called to be a physician and an evangelist, there are times when the two tasks can be combined, but there will also be many times when the two activities must remain separate. The person with such a dual calling must be aware, for example, that explicitly sharing one's faith with a client might on occasion interfere with the therapeutic process (here we enter the ambiguous territory between clinical and spiritual judgment). Accordingly, the therapist-evangelist must take special pains to maintain a very high standard of ethics.

Dual commissions to concurrent explicit careers as an evangelist and therapist seem, while not impossible, unlikely. Why, for example, would a person who knows that he or she is called and gifted as an evangelist endure all the years of training necessary to become a qualified therapist? After all, little if any of this training is relevant to evangelism, and there are easier ways to acquire that little which is. On the other hand, if a practicing therapist becomes aware of God's call to evangelize, why would he or she continue to practice psychotherapy?

Still, God might call a practicing therapist to become an evangelist and yet also wish this person to continue in a psychotherapeutic healing ministry. Who is to say what God will and will not do (Isa. 40:13–14; John 3:8)? Similarly, God might call an evangelist to a concurrent psychotherapeutic ministry, in which case it would make sense for the evangelist to undertake formal professional training to become a therapist.

In either case, because of the public's expectations of what psychotherapy is and is not, any person who is commissioned to be both therapist and evangelist must, to maintain integrity, be extremely careful not to misrepresent his or her intentions with clients; indeed, to avoid fraud, these intentions should properly be declared to clients *before* the beginning of treatment (this has to do with the client's legal-ethical right to give informed consent for a given treatment procedure). We feel quite certain that God does not want, much less require, deceit from his witnesses. Here, surely, the ends do not justify the means.

The discussion above has dealt with the unusual case of a person who feels a call to a dual ministry as both a therapist and an evangelist. But what about the more common situation of the Christian in psychology who, while not explicitly called to and gifted in the special ministry of evangelism, nevertheless has a general sense of obligation to evangelize because of God's charge to all Christians to do so ("Go therefore and make disciples of all nations"—Matt. 28:19, RSV) and because of a genuine caring for the eternal fate of the client? How does this person handle potentially conflicting urges?

First, the Christian therapist should recognize that it is impossible for psychotherapy to be conducted in a value-free fashion. All human interactions are instances of interpersonal influence. Sometimes in a psychotherapeutic situation the nature of the influence is blatantly obvious (as in a widely discussed case in which the therapists worked on changing the religious beliefs of a client to reduce her pathology; see Cohen and Smith [1976], and the responses by London [1976], Halleck [1976], and McLemore and Court [1977]). At other times, the nature of the influence is much more subtle, leading to vigorous debates as to whether personal (including religious) values have a valid place in psychotherapy (see, e.g., the exchanges involving Bergin [1980a, 1980b], Ellis [1980], and Walls [1980]).

Given that therapists can validly influence their clients, we must still struggle with the appropriate limits of such influences. We note that while God might well lead a Christian therapist to share his or her faith with a client, in such cases the therapist is caught in tension between the American Psychological Association's code of ethics (and, by implication, the state licensing board) and his or her own sense of Christian duty. This is because the code of ethics (correctly, in our opinion) prohibits dual-role relationships. Simultaneously maintaining two or more types of relationships with a client (e.g., the therapist may also be a friend, lover, or business partner) potentially blurs the therapist's judgment through loss of objectivity. Worse, such relationships may introduce motives that run counter to the client's well-being ("I'd better not offend Mr. Smith with this therapeutic interpretation since, if I do, he may not let me in on his new condominium deal"). It is worth noting, in passing, that a strict avoidance of all dual-role relationships would probably put most therapists out of business (being members of the same church or country club is, strictly interpreted, a relationship). At the same time we recognize that the prohibition of dual-role relationships, as it is intended by the code of ethics, is an important and valid ethical consideration, and who should be more ethical than a Christian? Other issues to the side, we insist that once a therapist begins to share the gospel with a client, he or she at least temporarily ceases to be a therapist in any conventional sense of the word.

Second, we insist that all therapists, but especially Christians who desire to be above reproach, clearly state to their potential clients, at the outset, the general nature of their personal beliefs if those personal beliefs could in any way impact the process and focus of therapy. No reasonable person seeking to become more adept in business would continue with a therapist upon finding out that the therapist is a Communist, and no one seeking to develop a sense of pride in his or her African ethnic heritage would continue with a therapist discovered to be a member of the Ku Klux Klan. Unfortunately, a lot of people feel the same way about religion, and some are particularly ill-disposed toward Christianity. Whether we like it or not, people have a right not to be upset by unnecessary surprises.

Religious-philosophical persuasion by a psychotherapist is blatantly unethical (and by implication sub-Christian) when it is intrusive, coercive, or dishonest. Persuasion is *intrusive* when it offends the client's sense of autonomy, provoking reactions like, "I didn't come here to hear this!" Such intrusions are unethical for a variety of reasons, including the fact that they subvert the client's goals for the therapeutic relationship, substituting in their place the hidden agenda of the therapist. Awkwardly introducing political concerns into therapy is equally inappropriate. Attempts at persuasion are *coercive* when they involve the use of power to impose beliefs or induce behavior. For example, communicating to a client that treatment will be discontinued if he or she does not attend church or read the Bible is coercive. Attempts at persuasion are *dishonest* when they are either denied or hidden. As we intimated above, to conduct therapy with an avowed atheist without revealing that there will eventually be an attempt to persuade him or her of the truth of Christianity is simply fraudulent.

As a final point, we note that the Christian therapist must constantly beware of complacently ignoring Christ's call to share the gospel for fear of exercising undue influence or playing a dual role. Although, as we noted above, Christian therapists necessarily live with some tension in these areas, that does not permit them to be spiritually negligent by avoiding Christian witness when led to bear it.

A case in point involves our work with a young man whom we shall call Peter. Peter reported significant difficulties in his attempts to form close personal relationships, despite strong desires for intimacy. He described himself as feeling socially awkward, shy, and undesirable. Furthering his difficulties, he would often attempt to lessen the pain of his loneliness through the use of mind-altering substances, a strategy that was self-defeating in a variety of ways.

As Peter developed trust, he began to share his uneasiness regarding Christianity, his disdain for the hypocrisy he saw in Christians, and his strong doubts about his own salvation. At this juncture the value of Peter's working with Christian therapists should be pointed out. Unlike secular therapists, Christian therapists offer a familiarity with particular religious issues. It appeared, however, that Peter was raising questions that begged for more than a sharing of knowledge, accurate therapeutic reflection, or insightful interpretation. His concerns seemed to require a personal disclosure from those who had gained his trust. Although some might argue that, technically, Peter should have been referred to a pastor to discuss spiritual issues, we felt that Peter was directing his questions specifically to us, as a result of our attempts to minister to his needs in a Christ-like fashion. It is clear that in cases like this a clinical judgment and spiritual counsel are required. Evangelistically minded therapists must take care, however, not to hear pleas for personal disclosure where there are none. Only a critical self-examination and consultation with a colleague can sharpen our awareness of our own biases. Even when the client raises spiritual issues, we would do well to ask ourselves what sort of information is most appropriate at this time and in this particular case.

After considering his personal history and his concerns, we chose to meet with Peter at a later date in a capacity other than therapists. At that time we noncoercively shared our relationship with Christ and attempted to direct Peter beyond the shortcomings of other Christians to the person of Christ. From a psychological viewpoint, this time represented therapy aimed at helping Peter to relate in an intimate manner—an area in which he was seeking help. Far more important from our perspective, however, was the result of that meeting: Peter left with a better understanding of the gospel and indicated that he now, on the basis of our time together, felt secure in his relationship with Christ. Three months later Peter died tragically and unexpectedly. This event reconvinced us of the importance of responding quickly to the urging of the Holy Spirit.

There are no pat, easy answers to the questions of when evangelism is appropriate and when it is not, and of exactly what form such interactions should take. We have argued that the therapeutic relationship, intended as it is to produce healing and growth, should be zealously protected from the potentially devastating effects of violated expectations, deception, dual-role relationships, abuses of power, and undue intrusiveness. On the other hand, a genuine caring for the client and a true allegiance to the Creator-Redeemer will give us the desire to minister to the total welfare of the client, and this may well include evangelistic sharing.

The Role of the Holy Spirit

We have suggested that God may sometimes prompt a Christian therapist to put himself or herself at risk in relationship to professional organizations and government licensing agencies by entering into a dual-role relationship with a client (i.e., therapist and evangelist). With this suggestion, we are alluding to the work of the Holy Spirit in the life of the therapist, especially his call to share the gospel. Without an awareness of the active involvement of God's Spirit in our lives, we become spiritual zombies. Christian therapists without a moment-to-moment sense of the transcendent are, at best, spiritually dormant if not numb.

In addition, we would argue that the Holy Spirit is also active in the lives of clients. We have worked with at least two people whose psychological conditions were radically transformed by their Christian experiences. Both were psychiatric casualties in the sense that years of therapy—with a variety of practitioners—had done little to improve their conditions. Through vital religious experiences, however, they changed—and much for the better! While we would not necessarily contend that they had previously been mastered by evil, they were certainly filled with God's goodness after their spiritual renewals. So, from time to time at least, God does seem to perform something on the order of a psychological miracle.

To write of the power of the Holy Spirit in filling us with goodness raises the question of evil, a topic that has received much attention over the past few years as a result of Scott Peck's (1983) *People of the Lie*. Peck is a psychiatrist with solid credentials (Harvard, B.A.; Case West-

ern Reserve, M.D.) who in the late seventies wrote a best seller called
The Road Less Traveled (1978) and subsequently became a Christian. In
People of the Lie, Peck suggests that some people are, in fact, evil. There
is something of a theological problem with identifying certain people
as evil, in that even the best and worst of us are admixtures of both
good and evil. Further, we can never summarily judge the heart of
another—not even Adolf Hitler's or Genghis Khan's. Jesus instructs us
to "judge not" precisely because, as C. S. Lewis wrote in *Mere Christianity*, in evaluating someone else's bad behavior, we can never know
for sure how much to attribute to moral perversity and how much to
faulty raw material (including one's psychosocial history).

Nevertheless, we respect Peck tremendously for caring enough
about spiritual matters to put his reputation on the line for Christ.
There is a veiled battle between good and evil under way (Eph. 6), a
cosmic drama of sorts (Col. 1), and all of us play an important part in
this drama as it unfolds both in our own lives and in the lives of other
people. For a Christian therapist to attempt to write the presence and
work of God (the Holy Spirit) out of the therapeutic script is to flirt
with becoming an agent of evil. The struggle between good and evil can
be subtle, and a therapist can unwittingly contribute far more to the
outcome of this struggle than most of us realize. This is why Christian
therapists cannot afford to be lulled hypnotically into a spiritual
slumber.

The Law of God and Mental Health:
A Complex Relationship

Discussing the issue of evil leads us to consider the complex matter
of the relationship between personal evil, that is, sin, and one's mental
health. How should the Christian understand the relationship between
moral behavior and personal well-being? Should the Christian counselor influence clients to follow his or her notions of what is right in a
given situation?

Exactly what God's law entails and a Christian's relation to it are
matters of debate among learned theologians. For the sake of our short
discussion here, we will understand the law to signify the Ten Commandments, and we will assume that Christians ought to keep these
commandments. It should be noted, however, that when keeping the
law becomes an end in itself, the *familial relationship* a Christian enjoys
with God becomes obscured. Indeed, by concentrating primarily on
behavior rather than the heart we run the risk of crucifying Christ
afresh (Heb. 6:6). When we keep the law (as God intends), it should be
because we want to, not because we fear the final judgment. This

judgment, like God's other judgments, will be of the heart. We suspect that, to our Father, behavior matters primarily as an index of what is going on in the heart (except, of course, as it affects his other beloved beings).

Before we can summarize our general position regarding the law and mental health, we must make a few comments which will reveal some of the great complexities involved in this relationship. First, because (and only because) we live among fallen creatures in a fallen world, from time to time we find ourselves having to make what theologians term tragic moral choices, situations in which whatever we do will be characterized by at least some evil. The classic example is those brave souls who hid Jews during World War II. If the Gestapo came to one's home and asked if any Jews were inside, to say yes would have resulted in murder, while to say no was to lie. In such dilemmas, we bear the sometimes excruciating moral responsibility of attempting to determine the lesser of two evils (see McLemore [1982], ch. 4, for additional examples).

Second, the tragic moral choices confronting individuals and their therapists are sometimes between keeping the law and emotional survival. Some individuals may literally be psychologically unable at a given time to obey the law of God. None of us, of course, are able to perfectly obey the law, but some may be less able than others. Take, for example, Ephesians 6:4, which commands fathers not to provoke their children to anger. It is possible that a father who struggles with a very limited tolerance for frustration may, at a given time, be unable to survive emotionally unless he becomes verbally abusive with his children, thereby tearing down their self-esteem. Although he may not be able to prevent his outburst, he is still held responsible by God to recognize and admit the sinfulness of his actions and to seek spiritual growth which will enable him to do better in the future.

Third, contrary to the simplistic formulas of some teachers, life is a good deal more complicated, emotionally and morally, than any of us would like. God designed it this way! Moral ambiguity is built into much of what we do, in order for us to learn to live in faith and rely on the Father in the face of uncertainty. Rules are easy to articulate in the abstract, but when we confront the incredible complexities inherent in a great many real-life human struggles, deciding what to do can become mind-boggling.

Please understand that we are *not* arguing that since grace covers us we might as well do whatever feels good. We are not to do God the dubious favor of making him look good by showing the world how forgiving he can be (see Rom. 6). To live in this way is, as it were, to throw God's grace back at him. It is the quintessence of bad faith.

Having looked at some of the complexities involved, we can now summarize our position regarding the law and mental health. First, it appears in general that spiritual health and mental health are closely related; God's laws are not capricious, but are descriptive of human life as God originally intended it. We are most likely to find spiritual and psychological fulfilment by living according to his will. On the other hand, we should also note that research comparing the mental health of Christians and non-Christians has generally found no real differences between the two. Although there are a number of problems inherent in attempting to distinguish what constitutes a spiritually healthy Christian, the research at least suggests that becoming a Christian does not necessarily provide an immediate cure for ongoing emotional conflicts or difficulties.

Second, it appears that situations sometimes arise in which morally right choices do not lead to immediate psychological fulfilment; in fact, there are times when breaking God's law may actually seem to enhance emotional well-being, at least temporarily (see "The Not-Too-Unusual Case of Robert," in McLemore [1982], pp. 69–72, where the client's immoral sexual behavior led to a dramatic reduction in his fear of women and enhanced his overall interpersonal adjustment). In all fairness, we must acknowledge that we can never know what would have occurred in such ambiguous cases if the individual had chosen not to disobey God's law. After all, God says he blesses those who walk in the paths of the righteous (Ps. 112; Prov. 2–3).

Quite apart from any debate about the above point, our bottom line is that *Christians are called to obedience to God's law*. However, moral dilemmas, whether in psychotherapy or life in general, may not always be settled by simplistically attempting to follow the letter of the law. Christ directly addressed this issue when he deliberately broke the Mosaic law by working on a Sunday, picking grain and healing the man with the withered hand (Luke 6). At times, several lawful principles may stand in conflict (Is there greater good in Christ's healing a man and feeding himself and his disciples, or in keeping the Jewish Sabbath law? Is it more righteous for a woman to remain in a marriage where she is physically beaten daily, or to break the law by obtaining a divorce to remove herself from the emotional and physical trauma inherent in such a situation?). Such tensions are all around us in this fallen world, and result in moral fogs, where the best choice is simply not clear.

As Christian therapists, we have chosen not to encourage clients to break God's moral law, even when it appears that some apparent good might come of such action. We also respect the client's right (free will) to make his or her own life decisions, even if they include what seems to us to be a mistake (e.g., breaking God's law). Some Christian parents have not yet grasped this in relation to their own children, hoping to protect their children from the pain that they, the parents, have gone through. Failing to realize that the greatest learning sometimes comes through our most painful mistakes, they try to make all of their children's moral choices for them. By contrast, our primary role as therapists is to help our clients tease out the probable consequences, both positive and negative, of their decisions.

Finally, as noted elsewhere, "while it is easy, in the abstract, to assert that ends do not justify the means, excessive concern with the moral purity of means, to the neglect of the ends these may produce, seems foolish, irresponsible, and inhumane" (McLemore [1982]). Rather, we would argue that both mental and spiritual health are best fostered by a balanced application of the law, tempered by such grace, love, and compassion as we see modeled by Christ. Further, it seems to us that a judgmental or legalistic application of God's law might actually be destructive to the emotional and spiritual well-being of others.

We conclude this section with a second case study. We believe that it illustrates the complexities involved in attempting to understand the role which the Holy Spirit and religious truth are to play in psychotherapy, as well as the difficulties encountered in trying to determine the relationship between psychotherapeutic growth and the cosmic (and human!) battle between good and evil, sin and righteousness.

Recently, we began to see a husband and wife in individual therapy supplemented by conjoint marital sessions (where the couple is seen together). We are still seeing this couple at the time of writing this chapter. He is a gifted surgeon who for some years has been involved not with medicine but with a small business. She is a beautiful and talented singer. They are wonderful people who have been married for about fifteen years and have two fine children. In many ways, they seem extremely compatible, and yet their marriage has been close to dissolution. Neither the woman, whom we shall call Katherine, nor her husband, whom we shall call Gregory, is in any fundamental way different from other serious Christians who believe in the sanctity of marriage. They have a basic respect for each other, which comes out clearly during the conjoint sessions. There is little in the way of character assassination, although the sessions occasionally become intense and expressive. Nevertheless, Katherine has been extremely frustrated with Gregory for years. She complains of his being emotionally distant and in general feels as if she is going to die if she stays with him. Katherine has been honest with Gregory about her dissatisfactions and wants a separation and possibly, eventually, a divorce. Gregory, for his part, has done everything he can to please Katherine, including joining one of our therapy groups in order to enhance his emotional expressivity. From our vantage point, while he is not as emotionally intense or expressive as his wife, neither is he unconcerned or without deep feeling. In spite of this, she is dissatisfied with him as a person and feels that she absolutely must get some space. Like her husband, a person of basic goodness, she aches over the reality of her dissatisfaction and truly wishes it were not so. She confesses to wanting him to be something he is not, something more than, or at least different from, what he is.

Several aspects of this case make it a clinical-spiritual dilemma. First, we struggle with the reality that as Christian psychologists we are committed to holding marriages together whenever possible. Our bias, in the face of ambiguity, lies strongly in the direction of caution, restraint, and conservative values. Gregory and Katherine know this and agree with us. That is why they came to us in the first place. Second, if we were to tell Katherine that because she is a Christian she should stay with her husband no matter what, she would most certainly regard us as weighing her down with law. She knows as much of the theology of marriage as we do. Third, we are uncertain to what extent her desire to separate from Gregory represents the acting out of unresolved psychological conflicts within her, and we have told her so. We have also done everything we might reasonably do to caution her against any such acting out. Remember, we do not know if in fact there are any unresolved conflicts. All we know is that, having said for some time that she is desperate (some mild to moderate suicidal ideation), she now is intent upon a separation.

To many people, this case may seem straightforward. Some people, for example, are of the opinion that Christian therapists ought to tell their clients never to separate. This we feel is an oversimplification of a complex ethical problem and confuses the roles of the pastor and the psychologist. Others would maintain that since Katherine says emphatically that she wants a separation, to oppose her desire in any way is professionally inappropriate.

However, the reality is far more subtle than this. For one thing, we believe in their marriage. As far as we can tell, they are far more compatible than incompatible; and beautiful though she be, if Katherine divorces her husband, we do not expect her to find anyone who, overall, will be better for her. Yet, having treated her for some time now, we take her desperation seriously. Concerns for the children aside, she is and for a long time has been acutely miserable in the marriage, and nothing we know of is likely to change this.

What complicates matters all the more is that her husband understands all this. He loves her. Naturally, he wishes we could do something to make her contented with him, but he is an extremely intelligent man who well comprehends that we cannot. We have probably prayed more for them than for any other client with whom we have worked. We have counseled, advised, and cried. Silently we shout at the heavens, "Why does this have to be?"

What is the proper course? Should we tell Katherine to wait a few more months, in the hope that something will happen, perhaps some breakthrough, to restore her to marital happiness with Gregory? Should we use our influence and professional skills to cause her to doubt her decision? Or should we commend her for her candor, which we greatly admire, with the attending risk that this might only reinforce her plans for separation? (Actually, we did so commend her, and there seems to have been no effect other than to enhance their mutual respect.)

This case, we believe, brings into sharp focus the distinction between preaching and psychotherapy. And yet, for complex reasons, this distinction is routinely missed by a large number of Christians. While a therapist is a heart doctor, in the sense that he or she helps people know and constructively simplify their emotional lives, a therapist is not, per se, either an evangelist or a preacher.

The Therapist as Christ's Representative

"Come to me, you who are loaded down with burdens, and I will give you rest." This is what the good therapist says. Like the good Samaritan, an effective therapist lifts up hurting people and tries to improve their human conditions. To the extent that this is true of particular therapists, they are serving as Christ's representatives to their patients. Well-conducted psychotherapy is, for many people, the closest they will ever come to experiencing what God's love is really like. This being the case, we must ask, "What exactly does a therapist do?"

Psychotherapy is, in large measure, a client's self-disclosure to a wise advisor. While certain schools of thought contend that therapy should not involve the giving of advice, all interpersonal communications, and certainly everything a therapist says and does with his or her patients, carry with them a certain amount of recommendation:

"Perhaps it would be good for us to continue talking about how you felt when your best friend died."

"Say a little more about your emotional situation when your father left for the service."

"It seems almost as if, with your directors and perhaps even your wife, you tend to put yourself into a position of resentful vulnerability—you become both angry and submissive."

These statements, which are representative of what most therapists might say, are subtle forms of advice, and rightly so. What antiadvice theorists are really trying to get at is that blatant advice is often superficial and threatening to the client and, therefore, not typically helpful. But in the words of the interactional theorists, all human communications are both reports and commands. Therapy of whatever sort, then, does seem to embody the giving of advice.

We have said that psychotherapy involves self-disclosure to a wise advisor. The responsible therapist will show wisdom through both the nature of the advice given and the way it is communicated (it can, e.g., be communicated in a controlling or in a freeing manner). It seems self-evident that the content of a Christian therapist's advice, and perhaps to some extent also his or her style of communication, are going to differ from the content and manner of communication of a non-Christian's advice. In other words, even though psychotherapy is most definitely not evangelism or proclamation, the fact that a practitioner is a Christian can and should make a difference. At the risk of oversimplification, we suggest that Christian therapists, on the whole, will tend to differ from non-Christian therapists in the following ways:

1. Christian therapists will be more concerned with values; and, beyond this, they will, by and large, affirm the values traditionally endorsed by the Christian church.
2. Christian therapists will be more interested in spiritual matters and, therefore, will honor a client's desire to explore such matters, at least to the extent that the desire does not seem inherently pathological and such exploration is not a way of avoiding therapy (of facing up to some truth).
3. They will care more about relationships. They will be interested in promoting peace between people; and, understanding that we have been created to be intimate with God and with each other, they will be more likely to focus on ways to enhance intimacy.
4. They will love their patients more—they will be more committed to the ultimate well-being of those who come to see them.

This is an exciting time in church history! More and more Christians recognize the enormous benefits that professionally responsible psychology can bring to the church, and increasing numbers of Christian college students desire to devote their lives to the ministry of psychological healing. It is our hope that this chapter will be an encouragement to Christians interested in the mental-health field to struggle courageously with the complexities of relating their religious faith with psychotherapeutic practice.

References

Bergin, A. (1980a). Psychotherapy and religious values. *Journal of Consulting and Clinical Psychology* 48: 95–105.

———— (1980b). Religious and humanistic values: A reply to Ellis and Walls. *Journal of Consulting and Clinical Psychology* 48: 642–45.

Cohen, R., and F. Smith (1976). Socially reinforced obsessing: Etiology of a disorder in a Christian Scientist. *Journal of Consulting and Clinical Psychology* 44: 142–44.

Ellis, A. (1980). Psychotherapy and atheistic values: A response to A. E. Bergin's "Psychotherapy and religious values." *Journal of Consulting and Clinical Psychology* 48: 635–39.

Halleck, S. (1976). Discussion of "Socially reinforced obsessing." *Journal of Consulting and Clinical Psychology* 44: 146–47.

London, P. (1976). Psychotherapy for religious neuroses? Comments on Cohen and Smith. *Journal of Consulting and Clinical Psychology* 44: 145–46.

McLemore, C. (1982). *The scandal of psychotherapy: A guide to resolving the tensions between faith and counseling.* Wheaton, Ill.: Tyndale.

———— (1984). *Honest Christianity: Personal strategies for spiritual growth.* Philadelphia: Westminster.

————, and J. Court (1977). Religion and psychotherapy: Ethics, civil liberties, and clinical savvy—A critique. *Journal of Consulting and Clinical Psychology* 45: 1172–75.

Peck, M. S. (1978). *The road less traveled: A new psychology of love, traditional values, and spiritual growth.* New York: Simon & Schuster.

———— (1983). *People of the lie.* New York: Simon & Schuster.

Walls, G. (1980). Values and psychotherapy: A comment on "Psychotherapy and religious values." *Journal of Consulting and Clinical Psychology* 48: 640–41.

10

Psychology of Religion

Glenn D. Weaver

The psychology of religion, in broad terms, is the subfield that attempts to better understand the human religious experience by applying the scientific methods of psychology to this aspect of life. It has addressed such questions as whether there are particular predictors or causes of religious conversion, whether and how religious experience affects personality and behavior, and what the commonalities among all forms of religious expression are.

Christians vary in their response to such studies. Some welcome scientific analysis as an asset to understanding their own religious experience. Others see in any study of the psychology of religion the inevitable press by humanists to reduce religious experience to mere psychological events having nothing to do with divine realities.

This chapter surveys the history of the field of the psychology of religion, categorizes and critiques various approaches to the task of understanding religious experience, and offers insights as to where the field as a whole needs to go.

Glenn D. Weaver (B.A., Wheaton College; M.Div., Princeton Theological Seminary; M.A., Ph.D., Princeton University) is professor of psychology at Calvin College. An ordained Presbyterian minister and trained social psychologist, he has published a number of monographs and articles, and is preparing a book on the psychology of religion.

When I began my graduate study in psychology, I expressed an interest in the psychology of religion to a senior faculty member. The professor was nonplussed. He shrugged off the idea with the comment, "I have no interest in religion," and advised me that I was about sixty years too late to find investigators who were seriously interested in that area.

The professor was at least partially correct, because at that time in the late 1960s there were very few psychologists actively developing theories of religious belief and action. In the United States the golden age of the psychology of religion spanned the period 1890–1920 and thereafter largely passed from the scene as a valid theoretical concern at American universities. It is instructive to consider the cultural context in which this interest flourished and then died. Even a brief consideration of this history will raise questions about what the crucial issues for a psychology of religion are and what the prospects for its future development might be.

At the beginning of the twentieth century, mainline Protestant churches were experiencing a theological shift. The increasing acceptance of the Darwinian theory of evolution made it difficult for many educated persons to accept the biblical account of creation as a trustworthy record of the work of a transcendent God. About the same time, prominent European theologians were proposing that humans know God not through historical and scientific fact, but through a somewhat more mystical sense of community with other persons and the conviction of moral duty which accompanies it. For many, these ideas seemed to offer the prospect of being religious without surrendering intellectual honesty and scientific rigor. The result was a movement toward a liberal theological position in the major Protestant denominations.

Unlike the European theologies which had influenced it, American theological liberalism had a social-activist slant. Preachers exhorted their flocks to follow the moral example of Jesus, the man who had become fully conscious of his own dependence on God. If men and women collectively chose to obey his example, they could bring about a new society, the very kingdom of God on earth. From this viewpoint, the evangelical task of the churches no longer lay so much in bringing souls to repentance as in developing personalities adequate to change the culture. The newborn field of psychology seemed a natural ally for this task.

Psychology had only recently separated from the fields of philosophy and physiology. It was searching for an identity as an independent, empirically based discipline. Just as the theory of evolution gave rise to a theological shift, the Darwinian model of human development suggested a direction for psychology. From a scientific viewpoint, it made sense to study the interaction between persons and their environments through which uniquely human patterns of sensation, thought, and feeling were selected for survival. A number of the newly prominent American psychologists became concerned with identifying the roles which psychological processes played in human adaptation to different environments, and hence the value of those psychological processes for survival. This diverse movement in psychology subsequently became known as functionalism.

A surprising number of the early functionalist psychologists had ties to mainstream Protestant liberalism. For example, G. Stanley Hall, who decidedly shaped the nature of psychology in the United States, attended Union Theological Seminary in New York, a center of liberal theological thought, and later took it as his responsibility to reinterpret the message of Jesus Christ to the world in terms of the new psychology (Hall [1917]). Although most functionalists vigorously rejected orthodox Christian beliefs, many advocated a religion of high moral sensitivity and considered it a professional obligation to uphold an ethics of brotherhood among all persons and to encourage societal reform.

The functionalists were concerned with understanding religion in a way which entailed no necessary conflict for their evolution-based psychology. They were also concerned that their psychology support their religious values and moral convictions. They believed that human action necessarily involves processes of conscious moral judgment and a goal-directed exercise of the will. It was their further belief that all acts of the will result from a more basic, controlling instinct to survive, but that this does not reduce the significance of moral consciousness and resolve. Rather it indicates that the evolutionary process itself involves a larger pattern of moral significance by which humankind is being carried progressively toward greater possibilities for survival through cooperative living. The functionalists' research methods were fashioned within this framework—methods that took goal-oriented actions as appropriate data and accepted conscious judgments and willful intentions as explanations of specific human behavior.

Thus, at the beginning of the twentieth century, conditions existed which supported development of an empirical psychology of religion. Many who held vested interests in religious life viewed psychology as a useful aid in their mission of reforming the social environment. Those who held vested interests in psychology saw no clear reason for hostility between psychology and a naturally defined religion of human moral consciousness and social reform. Psychology of religion was embraced by both university and church (Jentz [1976]).

However, by the 1920s the cultural conditions which supported this interest had begun to change. Optimism that moral progress would result simply from the psychological nurturing of human moral instincts was shaken by the human destruction of World War I. The growing fundamentalist-modernist controversy in American Protestant denominations encouraged some in mainline churches to become more suspicious of Darwinian thinking, pushing them away from psychology, while it moved others farther toward a secularized worldview and away from any concern with psychological understandings of the symbols and practices of the church.

Changes in the field of psychology had an even greater effect. The broadly defined, inclusive empirical methods of functionalist psychology gradually gave way to the more narrowly conceived behaviorist approach of John Watson. Watson's behaviorist methodology accepted only those concepts that can be translated into terms of physical measurement, that is, stimuli in the environment and the patterns of muscular response that they provoke. Reference to experiences of conscious judgments or willful intentions, the common way of understanding morality and religion, was not acceptable in behavioral science. Like any other behavior religious experiences, the behaviorists thought, are reducible to simple physical stimulus-response sequences; and so psychologists simply lost interest in any specialized pursuit of the psychology of religion. Accordingly, there has been a relative silence in the field of psychology of religion from the 1920s until recently.

Once again, however, ground swells have begun to shake the foundations of psychological science. In the context of new understandings of psychological methods, it appears that interest in the psychology of religion is being reborn. Before discussing these new directions, we will consider some connections between the golden age and the present renaissance by reviewing the work of two thinkers, Sigmund Freud and William James, who developed original psychologies of religion which continue to receive wide attention to this day. In both cases their psychologies of religion are important parts of their larger views of science and their beliefs about the meaning of human life.

Freud's Psychoanalytic Understanding of Religion

Sigmund Freud's training as a physician presupposed a larger philosophical vision of reality and the way in which we come to know it. He was taught a form of analytic biology that reduced the functional units of human anatomy to their smaller constituent parts. Thus, the operation of the heart or brain was understood to be the result of simple physical, chemical forces present in the atoms and molecules of human cells. The basic processes of human life were reduced to interactions in the material world.

Freud initially based his understanding of scientific method on the positivist empirical viewpoint which understands science to be exclusively the search for impersonal laws of relationship between events in the physical world. It is not surprising, then, that Freud looked for the causes of human personality in materially based processes which are controlled by physical laws and can be observed by scientists. (It may be argued that this approach to science dominated the whole of Freud's thought despite apparent inconsistencies in some of his writings; see Sulloway [1979].) Freud proposed that personality is the product of instincts, or drives, the most important of which is the libido. Although the libido is often associated only with sexual feelings, Freud thought of it more broadly as a basic life drive which motivates our attachments to other persons, to those objects which bring us gratification, and to our developing ideas of what is real. Libido begins in the physical processes of cells in the body and ends in ideas and actions which provide energy release. Its eventual reduction is accompanied by a sensual quality of satisfaction.

Early in life we acquire libidinal satisfactions largely through relationships with our parents. We experience our parents in a manner controlled by our drive-based feelings rather than by an objective view of what people are really like. The frequently mentioned Oedipus complex presents a clear example. When a five-year-old boy begins to feel awakening sensations in his sexual organs, he will be attracted toward his mother in a new, more sexually possessive way. For a time, these emotional dynamics strongly influence his beliefs about his father, the major competitor for the mother's sexual attention. The boy may think of his father as a hard taskmaster, the parent to be feared, yet because of his adult strength, he is also viewed as the parent who can provide protection and as an ideal to be emulated. This image may or may not correspond to what the father is really like. The important point is that the basis of the image is situated within the mind of the boy himself, to a large degree within his unconscious, rather than in the actual situation without.

Young children attempt to gratify their desires without much thought or worry about the constraints of reality. However, as we develop beyond childhood, our drive-based impressions of the world are (or should be) progressively replaced by ideas, beliefs, and actions which are determined by external realities. If libidinal satisfactions have been achieved in normal structured relationships with the parents during the first five years, then children should be prepared to sacrifice the immediate gratification of their fantasies for a longer-term imperfect but sometimes effective control of the world as it is. If early frustrations have been the rule, however, neurotic processes may develop in adulthood and cripple a person's life.

In *The Future of an Illusion* (1927), Freud suggested that religious belief can be explained as a general regression to the drive-controlled experience of earlier childhood. Feeling helpless before the cruelties of natural disasters and forced to deprive themselves of pleasure because of the moral demands of society, some persons have an overpowering need to fulfil unconscious wishes for security and reward. These wishes are fulfilled in part by a form of cultural, obsessional neurosis, religion, which promises eternal satisfaction in an omnipotent, loving God. Belief in God is constructed from childhood feelings of dependence upon the strength and protection of one's human father. Freud concluded that religion is an illusion, meaning that its primary source, its basic authority, lies in our unconscious drives within.

Most of Freud's arguments about religion are best understood as speculative developments of his positivist views about science and his materialist assumptions about personality. From this perspective religious claims about divine revelation which cannot be explained in terms of universal laws of cause and effect are obviously false. The truth claims of religion, then, are not worthy of further consideration, and religious experience must be explained completely in naturalistic terms. Since human personality is nothing more than physical processes, human belief in God must also be reducible to these processes. The universal laws of personality not only explain how some persons may come to believe in God, they offer the only explanation of why a person comes to believe in God. The childhood drives we all have experienced with regard to our parents are the sole reality from which religious persons construct their faith in God.

These convictions guided Freud's search for empirical evidence for his theory. He attended to those aspects of religion which easily compare with the other clearly drive-dominated experiences of adult life—clinical neuroses. For example, he examined the similarities between obsessive-compulsive rituals to remove anxiety (e.g., hand washing) and religious rites to remove guilt (e.g., the Lord's Supper). But in looking only for parallels to clinical disorders, he failed to examine the similarities between what he would accept as mature psychological processes and aspects of the Judeo-Christian faith, such as belief in an orderly creation and the call to give witness to this order in all areas of life. We are presented with presumed evidence of Oedipal strivings in the Judeo-Christian belief in a holy Father. But no attention is given to Jesus' anti-Oedipal example of a life without hatred and rebellion against the Father, a life motivated by love and humility rather than by pride, sexual desire, and guilt (Vitz and Gartner [1984]). Freud's empirical observations and his theory reflect the controlling influence of his prior antireligious beliefs.

James's Functionalist Understanding of Religion

Most of those who presently do research in the psychology of religion have taken their orientation from William James. James was the most prominent figure in the functionalist movement, which gave birth to the mainstream of American psychology. He was vitally interested in determining the effects of various experiences, including religion, on the evolutionary development of human life. He also believed that psychology, like the other experimental sciences, must employ a method involving systematic, controlled observation of data.

However, James's intellectual commitments were more far-reaching than the narrow empiricism of positivist philosophy. He also studied and appreciated the idealist philosophers of the late nineteenth century and was sympathetic to the broad religious and moral heritage of his own family. His understanding of the human condition was also profoundly influenced by a personal psychological experience. During his twenties James fell into a prolonged episode of physical weakness and depression. About this time he came to sense that immense energies within himself were being mysteriously blocked. He discovered that the only way to release them was through a strong exercise of his will against all of the determining circumstances of fate. He chose the path of what he called "the vigorous life" by accepting a lectureship at Harvard and by throwing his effort into a highly productive period of writing on both the natural sciences and philosophy. He became convinced that by this willful commitment to act he had opened himself to a higher experience of reality which would otherwise have remained closed (Barzun [1983]).

Stressing the efficacy of the human will, James rejected the widely held belief that human identity can be explained as nothing more than material interactions in the body. Scientists must first consciously will to give their attention to material events before those events can be known. Therefore an empirical psychology should find its data in any events of consciousness which take on an identifiable form. Experimental observations of nerve cells in the laboratory and the feelings of spiritual well-being one experiences in church are both irreducible real data. It is the business of psychology to observe all identifiable experiences throughout the human species in order to determine the extent of their contributions to human survival.

Bringing this background of methodological concerns to the study of religion, James (1958) defined religion as "the feelings, acts and experiences of individual men in their solitude as they apprehend themselves to stand in relation to whatever they may consider the divine" (p. 42). The divine is whatever reality men and women take to be of such fundamental importance that they respond to it with ultimate solemnity and seriousness.

As James observed case study upon case study of religious experiences, a pattern emerged. The most intimate and personal experience of self-identity occurs in those moments in which individuals reflect upon their taking responsibility for themselves by a clear act of the will. When the religious persons whom James studied became aware of self-identity in this fashion, they sensed that there was something wrong or incomplete about themselves in their natural condition. They felt themselves opened to higher potentials of the self, which sometimes led to the perception of continuity with a larger Self, a Something More. The experience of an expanded self is the way to what religious persons of different persuasions call the divine. Although he did not consider himself highly religious, we can see this psychological description of faith as very similar to James's own discovery of meaning in his life. Whereas Freud related religion to the whole experience of personality in neurotic individuals and primitive cultures, James identified religion with those rare realizations of self-acceptance and personal power which form peak experiences in our lives—the experiences of mysticism, life-changing conversion, and intimate prayer.

A functionalist psychology inquires whether religious experiences perform the larger function of fostering human survival. James's observations led to the conclusion that religion typically produces the positive results of a movement beyond selfish concerns, a new energy in living, and a feeling of peace and joy. Thus, religion serves a particular need of the human species and so enhances species survival. In James's pragmatic philosophy, empirical recognition that a particular religious belief performs this function in human life is a necessary condition for accepting that belief as true (James [1963]).

While religion serves a particular need in human life (i.e., the need to get beyond self), it nevertheless does not serve all of the interests and needs of human life. There are other experiences which serve quite separate interests and needs. For example, common moral experience conveys a sense of oughtness, inducing one to accept responsibility for wrong actions. This is distinct from religious experience, which gives persons an assurance of forgiveness and release from the hard demands of conscience. Although every person may have some potential to be religious by affirming higher energies of the self, religion does not necessarily touch all of the needs of life, and it is possible to go through life without manifesting any religious attitudes in one's psychological functioning.

The functionalist viewpoint continues to influence a majority of the contemporary studies in the psychology of religion. Typically researchers employ some type of empirical method in order to draw generalizations about all religious experience. They seek to determine the ways in which uniquely religious phenomena (meditation, glossolalia, conversion) relate to human survival and health. For example, researchers have recently examined the changes which religion can work in the areas of one's sense of purpose in life (Paloutzian [1981]), racial prejudice (Spilka and Reynolds [1965]), one's need to achieve (Kim [1977]), and basic personality (Lovekin and Malony [1977]). These studies make no overt judgments about the truth of religious beliefs, but are concerned merely with the observable effects of religious attitudes and beliefs on present action.

There are criticisms to be made of this approach. The most significant problem for our present consideration is James's limiting of religion to exceptionally strong acts of the will. This belief encouraged him to focus his studies primarily on supernormal cases of rare piety and self-transcendence. It prevented him from perceiving religious significance in the more everyday experiences of the individual. It may be a major reason why subsequent studies in the psychology of religion have not made important contributions to the development of a broadly focused, genuinely human science of psychology.

The Relationship Between Psychology and Christian Faith

Our discussion of Freud's and James's psychologies of religion has argued that each thinker proceeded on the basis of presuppositions which deeply influenced his development of investigative methods and explanatory concepts. Since these presuppositions involved beliefs about the nature of reality, the human condition, and the ways in which we come to have knowledge of both, we may consider them to be presuppositions of a religious nature. So then, if we are to understand, and perhaps take steps toward developing, psychologies of religion from within a context of Christian faith, we must ask more specifically what the relationship between psychology and religious presuppositions should be.

Important work has already been done to address this issue. Chapter 1 of this book explained C. Stephen Evans's (1982) conceptual scheme for understanding different approaches to the integration of Christianity and psychology. We will draw upon that framework here.

The position of the territorialists

Limiters of science are those who believe that the task of integration begins with an informed separation of the different domains addressed by science and theology, which is the confessional language of our Christian faith. The way to establish a proper relationship between the two is to recognize the powers and limitations of each and then carefully maintain the boundaries between them. Evans identifies two primary expressions of this viewpoint, the territorialists and the perspectivalists.

The territorialists think of science and religion as separate regions of reality. This position has been most appealing to Christian thinkers who believe that the Scriptures provide a dualistic picture of the nature of persons. The body is the material substance of our human existence. Its form and operations are publicly observable and can be explained in terms of universal laws of causation. The soul is the nonmaterial core of the person that provides our special relationship with God. The soul is essentially private and has the ability to choose obedience or disobedience to God. This reality is the domain of all true religion and is not accessible to empirical investigation nor explainable by scientific law.

Most territorialists respond to the psychology of religion in one of two ways. The first, and probably the more common, response is outright suspicion and rejection. Psychology is understood to be a behavioral science the sole data of which are automatic, reflexlike responses which are direct manifestations of the workings of the body. It investigates conditioned reactions in organs of the body under autonomic control, for example, the processes of color vision. Psychology has little or nothing to contribute to our understanding of the soul, that is, it can tell us little or nothing about our experiences of obedience or disobedience to God. Attempts to bring psychological explanations to bear upon these experiences can only distort our understanding of their real nature and by so doing encourage false understandings of religion and disobedient responses to God. Among those who react in this way to psychology of religion is Jay Adams.

Some have taken the territorialist viewpoint to a different conclusion. Especially in the Catholic churches, where a strong tradition of philosophical dualism persists, there has been a perceived need for psychological concepts which can explain just how the soul experiences God. Psychology is here defined as a discipline which deals with the experience of spiritual meaning rather than with behaviors which can be measured in physical terms. Accordingly, it is not considered primarily an empirical science, but is instead reconstructed as an adjunct to the branch of theology that deals with spiritual practices.

Morton Kelsey (1976) bases his explanations of religious experience on the theological teaching that every person is in contact with two different worlds—the material and the spiritual. Christians are called to place themselves in communication with the spiritual dimension of life, where the Holy Spirit speaks to us. Since scientific rationalism and empiricism close one's mind to this reality, we need to seek psychological experiences that transcend these limits. Christian meditation is one such technique. In a meditative state one's mind is open to receive images emanating from the unconscious. Kelsey believes that these images are our personal experience of the spiritual world. How this spiritual discipline uniquely brings one closer to God can be psychologically explained by carefully reflecting upon one's own experiences of meditation and the church's teachings about meditation.

Kelsey (1982) reports his own experience of an episode of "active imagination." Upon waking during the night after a dream, feelings of anxiety about meeting a deadline overwhelmed him and took form as a mental image of himself walking close to the edge of a steep cliff. He then imagined a conversation between God and himself. When he took God's part in this conversation, the voice said: "You are in a beautiful spot with One who truly loves you. Let go and flow with the current of My life and love." This message changed Kelsey's reaction to the image of the cliff from fear to a feeling of security. He reflectively interpreted the message to be an expression of his unconscious self-identity. Inasmuch as the experience agreed with Kelsey's theological beliefs and brought feelings of completion, peace, and relief to his life, it was considered a valid psychological insight into human personality.

The position of the perspectivalists

The perspectivalist separates psychology and theology by suggesting that psychology as an experimental science provides one valid type of explanation about every human experience, including religious belief and practice. While it may completely explain an experience from its own perspective, it nevertheless offers only one kind of explanation about that experience. By identifying a series of observable causes and their necessary effects, psychology will answer the question of how a given experience came about. Christian theology, on the other hand, explains the original cause and the ultimate significance of any experience for a person's relationship with God. When these two very different sorts of explanation are properly developed within the boundaries of their own logic, they present themselves as independent yet complementary theories, each of which has its own peculiar explanation about the same sample of human life.

Raymond Paloutzian (1983) speaks for many psychologists who are evangelical Christians when he summarizes his perspectivalist viewpoint on the psychology of religion:

> As a science psychology operates on the assumption that behavior, including religious behavior and the things that we choose to do of our own free will, is the result of the operation of cause-effect laws. . . . At the outset it should be made clear that the notion that natural cause-effect laws exist and regulate what we do is not a fact of science. It is a working assumption inherent in the scientific method. . . .
>
> This naturalistic assumption says nothing about who or what creates and sustains nature, just as the rules of a football game say nothing about who or what created the game or the rules. However, the possibility that we might understand religious behavior from a natural perspective in no way detracts from the validity of a religious or supernatural perspective. Both can be valid at the same time. [pp. 46, 53]

Many perspectivalists employ traditional experimental methods to determine whether events in the environment affect religious experience in rigorous cause-and-effect patterns suggestive of scientific law. In a study mentioned earlier, Paloutzian (1981) investigated the changes in a person's sense of purpose in life at different intervals following conversion. He divided a sample of Christian converts into four experimental groups, each representing a specific period of time since their conversion experiences. Each group was given standardized questionnaires in order to measure the degree to which they now found life worthwhile and satisfying. Comparison of the test scores indicated a greatly increased sense of purpose in life one week following conversion, a significant decrease one month later, and a gradual recovery of sense of purpose to the period of six months and beyond.

Another study examining the effects of time focused on the willingness of seminary students to offer help to a stranger in need (Darley and Batson [1973]). The students were asked to read either the biblical story of the good Samaritan or material dealing with ministerial vocations. They were then told to proceed to a building next door in order to make a presentation of the material they had just read. Some of the students were instructed to hurry; others were told that there was no reason to rush. Along the way each student encountered a person who acted as though he were experiencing a medical emergency. The study found that the material which the students had just read and rehearsed (the parable of the good Samaritan or vocational literature) did not significantly influence whether or not they stopped to help. As the experimenters had predicted, the students were more likely to offer help if they were not under time constraints to get to their destination.

Both of these studies examined how an environmental variable, time, can affect religious experiences. They both employed experimental methods and statistical analyses to determine whether a regular pattern of behavior on the order of scientific law might be expected in all subjects. Traditional scientific procedures were followed in order to ensure that the resulting explanation of behavior would not be directly influenced by the view of persons developed in Christian theology.

The position of the humanizers of science

The major alternative to limiting the sciences as territorialists and perspectivalists do is to suggest that science and religion must have some more direct influence upon one another. Evans calls those who take this position humanizers of science. Humanizers of science do not wish to deny psychology its status as a science. That is, they generally accept the idea that psychology should be constructed as a discipline with sets of common investigative methods and rules of explanation which can be shared by a community of researchers. Many would accept the idea that psychology must remain an empirically based science. However, they reject the assumption that the methods and explanatory logic of all of the sciences must be alike. For some humanizers, the direction for constructing new methods and rules of explanation which will make psychology a genuinely "human" science is to be found exclusively through reflection on the existential meaning of our common experiences, the universal necessity of making choices which shape the course of our lives. This conviction functions as a control-belief guiding their judgments as to what makes for an acceptable theory in the area of psychology in which they work (Wolterstorff [1976]). For Christian scholars who confess that an accurate understanding of human significance can be found only in the higher authority of God's revelation, the content of their Christian faith will function as a control-belief in their creation and weighing of theories.

Although theologians will assume the leading role in defining the meanings of the core assertions of the Christian faith, the need to identify important Christian control-beliefs suggests work for scholars in all fields of inquiry. According to the Christian humanizer of psychology, for example, there is a biblically based view of persons which Christians must either theologically confess or psychologically assume if they are to carry out their responsibilities of discipleship.

This view of persons provides significant control-beliefs which necessitate revisions in the positivistic, experimental approach to psychology.

For example, humanizers may question whether traditional experiments in which a researcher manipulates environmental conditions of his or her choosing and then looks for a predetermined response in the subjects do justice to our belief that persons are capable of interpreting and directing situations in a variety of different ways. Some psychologists of religion have developed alternative research procedures which address this concern. In his studies of religious thinking in children David Elkind (1964) employs an interview process in which the child participates fully in guiding the direction of the conversation. To encourage spontaneity, Elkind asks children questions about religion which seem so absurd to adult thinking that most children have never heard them before. This prevents them from simply reciting well-learned responses and encourages them to develop their own interpretations of the issues. As an illustration, after the death of President Kennedy, Elkind heard one of the children whom he was observing ask, "Are they going to shoot God too?" This suggested that the child associated God with high offices and that pursuing a conversation along this line might help to reveal how children think about God's authority. "Can God be President of the United States? Why or why not? Who chooses the President? Who chooses God to become God?" Through this sort of structured dialog Elkind has identified various methods of interpretation which children of different ages employ as they develop their understandings of religious belief.

Chapter 1 discussed some of the considerations important to deciding among the different models of integration. According to a growing number of philosophers of science, the sciences have developed not so much through the progressive accumulation of data as through significant changes in control-beliefs about what observations should be made, how they should be interpreted, what data present real problems, and how these problems should be dealt with. Philosophers have supported this viewpoint primarily by citing examples drawn from the history of the physical sciences. Even stronger evidence can be found in the development of psychology. Our review of the early approaches to the psychology of religion provides an illustration. Freud and James were pioneers in the psychology of religion because each worked through certain assumptions about the nature of reality and the human condition to arrive at a new way of systematically observing religious experience. Some of the most important of these assumptions we would consider to be of a religious nature. Thus the history of psychology itself lends support to at least a modified version of the position of the humanizers.

There is another way for us to consider the relative merits of the approaches of the territorialist, the perspectivalist, and the humanizer of science. Since each of these models seeks to view psychology in such a way as to preserve authentic Christian commitments, they may be fairly judged by evaluating their compatibility with relevant Christian beliefs. The Scriptures themselves provide some clues regarding the proper relationship between psychology and religion.

The Genesis account presents the view that the creation of human beings was continuous with God's ordering of the physical world— "The LORD God formed a man from the dust of the ground and breathed into his nostrils the breath of life. Thus the man became a living creature" (Gen. 2:7, NEB). In older versions of Scripture the term *creature* is sometimes translated "soul." It is a term which in other Old Testament passages refers to a person's throat, neck, desire, or the vital processes that uphold physical life. Passages in the New Testament which speak of the Christian's hope of an eternal identity refer to the creation of a resurrection body rather than the continuance of a disembodied soul. When all of these references are considered, it seems that although a person's identity manifests different aspects, yet that identity may be spoken of as a single entity, one creature, rooted in the processes of the body.

This emphasis on a unified spiritual-physical identity presents difficulties for the traditional territorialist viewpoint. It offers little support for the idea that two wholly separate types of data, physical and spiritual, can be distinguished in our observations of human persons. The biblical evidence appears more clearly compatible with the idea of the perspectivalist and the humanizer of science that all physically embodied psychological processes can be explained within the framework of an empirical science.

The biblical view also entails the belief that human beings were created to act as responsible agents. We were made "in the image of God" or, perhaps more accurate to the theology of the Hebrew text, we were created "imagers of God" to serve as his representatives in the creation (Gen. 1:27). This suggests that although continuous with the natural world in our substance, we are also unlike the rest of the natural world in our capabilities and in our calling. Humans alone have the capacity to govern the creation. Humans alone have the capacity to distinguish that which is good because God has redeemed it from that which is evil because it is ruled by sin. And humans have the power to make real decisions about how they will act in response to God.

The Christian acceptance of human agency, both in our confession and in the way we live, is difficult to harmonize with the claim that psychologists can explain all human behavior in terms of universal laws of cause and effect. The positivistic understanding of science demands that the events being studied be seen as fitting into a specific observable sequence of behavior which can be deduced from the law of causation and therefore can be realized in no other form. In this type of approach, significant data are recognized purely in terms of their occurrence in a specific sequence of observable events. But Christian psychologists, and indeed many other psychologists without clearly stating what they are doing, take an interest in meaningful patterns of experience enacted by free agents and regard them as data requiring their explanation. These patterns are recognized by the purpose or meaning which they have in our lives.

For example, it would be foolish to regard prayer as nothing more than a specific observable sequence of kneeling, clasping hands, and uttering a particular set of verbal sounds. We identify the experience which we call prayer by our intention toward God when we pray. Furthermore, we cannot deduce from the law of causation a list of specific actions through which our intention must be realized in order to be an example of prayer. Persons pray in innumerable ways. To reduce prayer to a specific list of observable actions radically alters the way we identify it and probably makes a psychological investigation of prayer of little interest. Yet that is precisely what honest adherence to the traditional positivistic view of science requires.

This issue presents a problem for the perspectivalists, who maintain that psychology is simply the perspective of natural science independent of yet complementary to theological interpretations of the same experiences. It is another argument that the humanizer of science gives for suggesting some modifications in the rules of the psychological game. Since we are unified beings and the power of human agency is central to our personal identity, we must be understood as responding to God through all of our psychological functioning. Christ encounters us at the center of life and makes a claim on all of our being. No area of experience may be divorced from our relationship with him.

To summarize: we have argued that both recent philosophical understandings of science and elements of our Christian confession support the position of the humanizer of science. Our Christian understanding of human nature should actively influence the way in which psychological realities are explained. If the Christian understanding does not have this influence, other religiously significant control-beliefs will.

New Directions for the Psychology of Religion

As we seek to develop the psychology of religion as a science humanized by Christianity, the biblically based beliefs just mentioned will serve as control-beliefs for our theories. In this light, psychology of religion should not be primarily a matter of applying the accepted methods of natural science to explore that small set of behaviors that are usually considered religious. Rather, psychology of religion should seek to explain all of the basic psychological processes in a manner which is in keeping with our actual experience of those processes as responses to God. Thus, our theories of perception, cognition, emotion, and all other psychological processes should explain how it is that we perceive, think, and feel in ways which make our lives religiously significant—as unified identities possessing the power of agency and the capacity to relate to other humans and to God.

There are recent developments in mainline experimental psychology which offer promise for such projects in the psychology of religion. Consider the following illustration from the area of perceptual psychology:

For decades experimental psychologists have sought to explain perception as a simple process of cause and effect. Many of the models which have been formulated present perception as simply information processing (e.g., Lindsay and Norman [1972]). Perception is conceived to be much like the operation of a complex digital computer. Information is fed into the system at a stationary point, for example, the retina of the eye. This input, which has a particular physical pattern, is processed as it moves through the sequence of operations within the system. Each operation executes a program designed to detect just certain crucial features in the pattern. Data about these features are then passed on to higher centers of the brain. Here the data are sorted and combined with data previously stored in the memory. This eventually produces the image that the person consciously recognizes. The sequence has a clear beginning, input at the receptors, and a clear end, the conscious image. The steps in between are wholly determined by the structure of the system and the information (the stimulus) entering from the outside. The whole process can be explained in terms of universal laws of causation.

But this model leaves a number of important questions unanswered. How does it happen that in real life different people notice different aspects of the same situation? How are successive glances at the same scene integrated into patterns? Why are we often able to perceive the meaning of events immediately without having to work through the surface features contained in the sensory input?

Ulric Neisser (1976), who is often considered to be the father of modern cognitive psychology, proposes a different understanding. He begins with the assumption that perception is a process of continual interaction between the person and the environment. The person plays an active, creative role. Our perceptions are best understood not as linear sequences of causes and effects moving through the brain, but as meaningful experiences in which we are rather fully involved as we sample information from our present environments. These experiences do not have clear beginning and end points. They are continuous cycles of which we are aware to greater or lesser degrees as time passes.

The cycle of perceptual experience has three interacting aspects. First, we anticipate the sort of information which might be available in a given situation and which will be important to acting in a meaningful way in that situation. Neisser calls these anticipations our *perceptual schema*. Every particular schema is a small part of our larger understanding of the world and its possibilities.

The perceptual schemata are tools which we employ to direct our *sensory exploration*—the second aspect of the cycle. Unlike computer terminals which passively receive informational input, humans actively move about and make decisions about what they will look at and how they will then investigate further. These actions are part of the complete set of actions and situations unique to the individual life. Our explorations allow us to sample the information available in the environment which we have chosen at that moment of time.

The *environment*, of course, which is the third aspect of the cycle, has a real, ordered existence of its own. The information which we sample from our present environment is only part of the total information available in the actual real world. This sample typically presents features which will not exactly fit the anticipations of our schema and so may lead us to modify our schema to guide our explorations more helpfully in the future. Thus, often unawares, we are continually changing our perceptual expectations.

In this model, no one aspect of the cycle is thought of as a cause which brings about a necessary effect. We can choose to allow the process to be dominated by old acquired biases and prejudices or by the most obvious features of our present circumstances. Or we can choose to alter the shape of the process at any time. We can do this most quickly by trying out a very different set of anticipations or by experimenting with a different way of gathering information. For example, a scientist who toys with a different theory may soon discover surprising new information; or a frustrated lover who decides to exercise the power of positive thinking and seeks his beloved's company all the more may suddenly notice expressions of romantic interest that were there all along. A more difficult way of altering the perceptual process is to work hard to locate more information in situations which have already been examined in many different ways. An example here is the chess player who studies the games of the masters so as to be able to read the emerging patterns on a chess board in a single glance.

Neisser's theory holds that perception actively involves and influences human agency. Obviously, then, our perceptions have religious significance. I have a close friend who traveled the following pilgrimage. During his college years his study of Scripture led him to believe that genuine Christian discipleship involves concern for and service to the poor. This understanding influenced him to accept a mission assignment in Africa, which allowed him for the first time in his life to sample information about poor people directly. But his perceptual explorations were crude. His broadly defined schema regarding serving the poor led him to attend only to the extremely serious problems of hunger and disease. This overwhelmingly grim information challenged his original sense of calling—his belief that he could effectively serve the poor and his perceptual schema which anticipated clear evidence of success. It led him to anticipate failures and perceptually to focus attention on his inadequacies as well as on the poor around him. He began to see aspects of similarity between his situation and that of the people in the culture which he had come to serve. As he acquired more information about himself and other specific individuals, his understanding of his calling gradually changed. He no longer thought of his mission as serving the African poor, but as being a friend who could work with other Christians in that culture toward certain ends. A new perceptual schema took shape. His reading of Scripture resulted in new convictions about God's concern to establish international justice for the poor nations of the earth. His perceptual exploration of his work increasingly focused on the tasks which he and the people with whom he lived could address together. Although he may not view his experience in this way, I believe that he has grown, in part through perceptual changes, to be the type of servant he originally felt called to be.

This example suggests how a continuing cycle of perceptual experience can help us grow in response to God's demands. Systematic, empirical studies should be done on this issue. It should be noted, however, that persons whose perceptual cycles include no concern for the claims of Scripture and no attention to the needs of the poor will also respond to God, but in disobedient ways. Psychology of religion cannot concern itself exclusively with those who are models of religious piety.

Our discussion has come full circle. Since, as research suggests, our early understanding of the gospel and the way we decide to live influence the kind of information that we will subsequently find in the Scriptures and in the whole of God's creation, psychological theory must inform our theology and evangelism. Right practice is crucial to right belief. Our vision of God's revelation will be a reflection of the way in which we live. If we hope to understand the meaning of Christian discipleship more fully, then, Christian psychologists and theologians must in good faith pursue a dialog exchanging their learning.

References

Barzun, J. (1983). *A stroll with William James*. New York: Harper & Row.

Darley, J., and C. Batson (1973). From Jerusalem to Jericho: A study of situational and dispositional variables in helping behavior. *Journal of Personality and Social Psychology* 27: 100–08.

Elkind, D. (1964). Contributions to research method: Piaget's semiclinical interview and the study of spontaneous religion. *Journal for the Scientific Study of Religion* 4: 40–47.

Evans, C. S. (1982). *Preserving the person: A look at the human sciences*. Grand Rapids: Baker (originally published 1977).

Freud, S. (1961). *The future of an illusion*. New York: Norton (originally published 1927).

Hall, G. S. (1917). *Jesus, the Christ, in the light of psychology*. New York: Doubleday, Page.

James, W. (1958). *The varieties of religious experience*. New York: New American Library (originally published 1902).

———— (1963). The will to believe. In W. James, *Pragmatism, and other essays*. New York: Washington Square (originally published 1897).

Jentz, J. (1976). Liberal evangelicals and psychology during the progressive era. *Journal of Religious Thought* 33: 65–73.

Kelsey, M. (1976). *The other side of silence: A guide to Christian meditation*. New York: Paulist.

———— (1982). *Christo-psychology*. New York: Crossroad.

Kim, H. (1977). The relationship of Protestant ethical beliefs and values to achievement. *Journal for the Scientific Study of Religion* 16: 255–62.

Lindsay, P., and D. Norman (1972). *Human information processing*. New York: Academic.

Lovekin, A., and H. N. Malony (1977). Religious glossolalia: A longitudinal study of personality changes. *Journal for the Scientific Study of Religion* 16: 383–93.

Neisser, U. (1976). *Cognition and reality*. San Francisco: Freeman.

Paloutzian, R. (1981). Purpose in life and value changes following conversion. *Journal of Personality and Social Psychology* 41: 1153–60.

_____ (1983). *Invitation to the psychology of religion*. Glenview, Ill.: Scott, Foresman.

Spilka, B., and J. Reynolds (1965). Religions and prejudice: A factor-analytic study. *Review of Religious Research* 6: 163–68.

Sulloway, F. (1979). *Freud, biologist of the mind*. New York: Basic Books.

Vitz, P., and J. Gartner (1984). Christianity and psychoanalysis, part 1: Jesus as the Anti-Oedipus. *Journal of Psychology and Theology* 12: 4–14.

Wolterstorff, N. (1976). *Reason within the bounds of religion*. Grand Rapids: Eerdmans.

11

Social Psychology
David G. Myers

Some Christians say that our hearts dictate how we act; therefore, it is futile to try to change behavior without a preceding change of heart. Other Christians say that waiting for a change of heart is mere procrastination; God made us responsible beings so that we can obey him, and a change of heart will follow a faithful change of behavior. This chapter shows how recent findings of social psychology enlarge our understanding of these seeming contradictions.

This chapter also examines recent findings about the fallibility of human reasoning which are compatible with the biblical understanding of the person. Here we have a good model of creative examination of the interface between revealed truth and the findings of social science.

David G. Myers (B.A., Whitworth College; Ph.D., University of Iowa) is Werkman Professor of Psychology at Hope College. He is the author of several books relating the findings of social psychology to the Christian faith (including The Human Puzzle *[New York: Harper & Row, 1978] and* The Inflated Self *[Minneapolis: Winston, 1981]), of numerous articles in professional and popular journals, and of the popular texts* Social Psychology *(New York: McGraw-Hill, 1983) and* Psychology *(New York: Worth, 1986).*

This chapter is a revision of "Social Psychology and Christian Faith" by David G. Myers from *Behavioural Sciences: A Christian Perspective*, edited by Malcolm A. Jeeves (Leicester, England: Inter-Varsity, 1984). Reprinted by permission.

Exploring human nature is, for some of us, the most fascinating adventure imaginable. It becomes the more so when we explore simultaneously from two directions, scientific and biblical.

To simplify matters, we might say that God has written two books—nature and the Bible—and it is the task of professional scientists and biblical scholars to help us discern these two revelations. This discerning is always a human act; the natural and biblical data are both viewed through human spectacles and are therefore subject to bias and distortion. We should consequently be open to insights that come through either nature or Scripture (recognizing God to be the common source of both), while remembering that no one's interpretation of nature or Scripture is final truth. This being the case, we should view with some skepticism any attempts to subject theology to science—or science to theology.

The dangers of subjecting science to theology or theology to science are even more apparent when we realize that they are posing different questions. There is a sense in which religion takes over where science leaves off. The big questions science leaves unanswered: What are the ultimate source and destiny of nature? Who am I and why am I alive? What ought I to do? Where can I find hope? It will prove fruitful, then, to view human experience from multiple perspectives, each of which is incapable of answering questions raised by other, complementary perspectives. Use of a variety of perspectives will form a more complete picture, just as different two-dimensional views of an object may be assembled, without contradiction, into a more complete three-dimensional image. In this essay we will describe how some of the modern insights of social psychology (which are drawn from two research areas) illuminate the ancient biblical revelation of our human nature.

Social psychologists have their own special insights into human nature. Other insights into human nature have been independently discerned by biblical scholars. How well do these two realms complement one another? My overall answer is that while there are points of tension which deserve our attention, the ancient biblical view of human nature comes home with renewed force as we review the relevant findings of social psychology.

Behavior and Belief

What is the relationship between people's internal beliefs and attitudes and their external actions? This question has interested both theologians and social psychologists, and its answer has practical implications for anyone interested in influencing people. The prevailing assumption has been that internal beliefs and attitudes determine a person's public behavior, so anyone wanting to change the way people act had best change their hearts and minds. This is the implied theory behind the way in which most teaching, preaching, counseling, child rearing, and other endeavors involving efforts at persuasion are carried out. But if social psychology has taught us anything during the last twenty years, it is, as we will see, that the reverse is equally true: we are as likely to act ourselves into a way of thinking as to think ourselves into a way of acting. After considering the relationship of attitude and action, we will ask how this squares with the biblical understanding of faith and action, and we will draw practical implications for church life and Christian nurture.

Action and attitude

Social psychologists now know that attitudes and actions have a reciprocal relationship, each feeding on the other. In retrospect, this seems obvious. But some aspects of this relationship were, in fact, not obvious before the research was done. For conventional wisdom emphasizes the effect of attitude on action; people's acts are presumed caused by their thoughts and feelings. The way to reform their action is therefore to change their attitudes and beliefs. Given how widely this is believed, it is shocking to discover what little correspondence there often is between expressed attitudes and actual behavior. Students' expressed convictions about cheating, for instance, bear little relation to the likelihood of their cheating when they are given a convenient opportunity. Attitudes toward the church have only a modest relationship with church attendance on any given Sunday. Self-described racial attitudes predict little of the variation in behavior that occurs when people are confronted with an actual interracial situation. It is, therefore, hardly surprising that attempts to change people's behavior by changing their attitudes have usually achieved modest results at best. Smoking, television-watching, and driving habits, for example, are not much affected by persuasive appeals.

These surprising results sent social psychologists scurrying to find out why what people *say* so often fails to predict what they *do*. The luxury of hindsight enables us to make some sense out of this seeming contradiction. People's expressed attitudes may often disguise their real attitudes. Moreover, their action is usually the product of many influences—of social pressures and of various unmeasured attitudes that may be relevant to the specific situation. Whether one attends church next Sunday will be determined by multiple factors, not just one's attitude towards the institutional church. When these other influences are minimized, or when one's usual behavior across many situations is in view, or when the expressed attitude is very specifically related to the act in question (e.g., one's expressed political preference and actual vote), the attitude-behavior relationship is much closer. Thus it is now fairly clear that the relationship between expressed attitudes and actual actions can range from virtually nonexistent to substantial. Attitudes are, then, one determinant of our action.

While attitudes determine behavior to a lesser extent than is commonly supposed, the reverse proposition—that behavior determines attitude—turns out to be far more true than most people realize. We are as likely to believe in what we have stood up for as to stand up for what we believe. Let us quickly look at several of the mountains of evidence which have established this powerful principle.

Manipulated action and subsequent thinking. A variety of experiments have artificially altered people's actions and noted that the subjects' thinking easily adjusts to accommodate the altered actions. For example, Jose Delgado implanted an electrode in a patient's brain (Pines [1973]). When the electrode was stimulated by remote control, the patient would invariably turn his head. Unaware of the external stimulation, the patient thought his head turning was spontaneous and, when questioned, would offer a reasonable explanation: "I am looking for my slipper," "I heard a noise," "I am restless," or "I was looking under the bed." The act produced the idea, a phenomenon evident in other experimental research as well. For instance, hypnotized persons will often volunteer ingenious explanations for their outwardly induced actions.

Role playing. The same phenomenon occurs, although more subtly, when people perform acts prescribed by their assigned roles. Laboratory experiments indicate that people induced to play a temporary role will often later espouse increased sympathy for the attitudes they have acted out. Research outside the laboratory has likewise indicated that vocational roles have a substantial impact on the people who occupy them. One's chosen career determines far more than just one's activities while on the job; it also shapes attitudes congenial with those activities. Perhaps the reader can recall a time when he or she assumed some new role—as a college freshman or a military recruit, for example. At first one may feel a lack of genuineness in carrying out the actions appropriate to a new role. There is a feeling of artificiality, almost as if one were playing a theatrical role. The new routines feel alien—but probably only for a time, for the sense of sham and artificiality generally does not long endure. Soon the new role starts becoming internalized, and before long the feeling that one is playing a role diminishes. It becomes more difficult to distinguish the role from the real person.

The foot-in-the-door phenomenon. A number of experiments indicate that to get people to do a big favor, a good technique is to get them to do a small favor first. In a well-known demonstration, Jonathan Freedman and Scott Fraser (1966) found that California housewives who had been asked to sign a petition promoting safe driving were more likely to comply later with a bigger request to place a large, ugly "Drive carefully" sign on their front lawns than were women who had not first been approached for the small favor. Note that in this situation, as in countless other experiments demonstrating the effect of action on attitude, the action (signing the petition) was a *chosen, public* act. Time and again, social psychologists have found that when people bind themselves to a public action *and* perceive it to be their own doing, they come to believe more strongly in the action. The brainwashing procedure to which prisoners of war are subjected includes techniques built on this phenomenon.

Note also that the effect on the housewives' attitudes was evident in their subsequent willingness to take an even more substantial action, thus demonstrating the reciprocal influence of action and attitude. Sometimes action and attitude feed one another in a spiraling escalation. In one of the best-known experiments of social psychology, Stanley Milgram (1965) induced adult males to deliver supposedly traumatizing electric shocks to an innocent victim in an adjacent room. The ostensible purpose of the experiment was to determine the effectiveness of punishment as a means of instilling learning. The subjects were instructed to deliver the shocks, which were said to be punishments for wrong answers, in gradually ascending steps from 15 up to 450 volts. The "shocking" result—65 percent of the participants complied right up to 450 volts even while the victim screamed his protests—seems partly due to the foot-in-the-door principle. The "teacher's" first act was innocuous—15 volts—and the next act—30 volts—was not noticeably more severe. By the time the supposed victim first indicated mild discomfort, the teacher had already bound himself to the situation through several acts; and the next act was, again, not noticeably more severe. External behavior and internal disposition can amplify one another to extremes, especially when social pressures induce actions by degrees. And so it is that ordinary people can become unwitting agents of evil.

The effects of moral and immoral acts. All this suggests the more general possibility that acts which are discrepant from one's existing moral values may set in motion a process of self-justification that leads ultimately to sincere belief in those acts. Experiments bear this out. As long as there is a feeling of having some choice in the matter, people who are induced to give witness to something about which they have doubts will generally begin to believe their little lies. Likewise, harming an innocent victim—by uttering a cutting comment or delivering shocks—typically leads aggressors to believe in what they are doing, especially if they have been coaxed rather than coerced into their harmful acts. Times of war provide the most tragic real-life parallels to these laboratory findings. Immoral acts corrode the moral sensitivity of the actors.

Happily, the principle cuts in the other direction as well. Moral action has positive effects on the actor. Experiments demonstrate that when children are induced to resist temptation, they will internalize their good behavior, especially if the deterrent is mild enough to leave them with a sense of choice. Moreover, young people who are actively engaged in enforcing rules or in teaching moral norms to small children subsequently follow the moral code better than do young people who are not given the opportunity to be teachers or enforcers. To generalize the principle, it would seem that one antidote for the corrupting effects of evil action is repentant action. Evil acts shape the self, but so do moral acts.

Interracial behavior and racial attitudes. If moral action is conducive to moral attitudes, might not the elicitation of more positive interracial behavior lead to improved racial attitudes? This was one of the arguments behind desegregation rulings and civil-rights laws. It was said that if we were to wait for the heart to change—through preaching and teaching—we would wait a long time for racial justice. But if we would go at it the other way around and legislate moral action, we could, under the appropriate conditions, indirectly improve attitudes.

And substantial changes in attitude have, in fact, followed on the heels of desegregation. Since the Supreme Court decision, the percentage of white Americans favoring integrated schools has about doubled. Furthermore, in the ten years after the Civil Rights Act of 1964, the percentage of white Americans whose neighborhoods, places of business or employment, and schools were exclusively white declined about 20 percent. During the same time the percentage of white Americans who said blacks should be allowed to live in any neighborhood increased from 65 to 87 percent. Throughout the United States, uniform national standards have been followed by decreasing regional differences in racial attitudes. As we have come to act more alike, we have come to think more alike.

While these findings are consistent with the principle that attitudes follow behavior, the real world is so complicated that we can speculate about other factors which may instead be responsible for these changed attitudes. Fortunately, laboratory experiments have isolated and measured the effects of positive behavior towards another individual. Doing a favor for a person, or helping a person in need, does indeed tend to increase one's liking for that person.

Political socialization. The apparent effect of a society's racial behavior on its racial attitudes suggests that the same general principle might be used for political education on a mass scale. The Nazis did so: participating in mass meetings, demonstrating, wearing uniforms, and repeating the enforced public greeting "Heil Hitler" created for many people an uncomfortable inconsistency that was resolved by coming to believe in what they were saying and doing. American political rituals—saluting the flag, singing the national anthem—likewise build private commitment to country through public action. Observers of the American civil-rights movement during the early and mid-1960s and the radical student movement during the late 1960s and early 1970s have noted that both were intensified by public acts. It took an idea whose time had come to initiate the first demonstrations and marches; these public acts in turn helped drive the idea more deeply into the souls of the participants.

Action therapies. A striking common denominator of many of the new psychotherapies is their emphasis on the client's chosen actions. In contrast to the older insight therapies like psychoanalysis, which basically engage the client above the neck, the newer therapies assume that the client must be induced to act in healthier ways. Reality therapy, behavior therapy, assertiveness training, and many types of group methods all, in their own way, activate the client. Judging from the research we have been reviewing, we would expect these procedures to be most successful if the client is encouraged to own responsibility for the new actions, rather than to attribute them to pressure from the therapist or the group.

In this brief overview we have seen that several independent streams of observation—laboratory experiments, social history, and therapeutic interventions—merge to form one river: all demonstrate the powerful effect of overt action on internal disposition. This phenomenon, now an accepted fact in social psychology, is more clearly established than its explanation. And so social psychologists have been busy playing detective, trying to track down clues that might eventually reveal why action affects attitude. One suggested explanation is that human beings are motivated to justify their actions in order to relieve the internal dissonance that exists when an action is noticeably discrepant from one's prior attitude. An alternative explanation is that when our attitudes are weak or ambiguous, we observe our actions and then infer what attitudes we must have, given how we have acted. What we say and do can sometimes be quite self-revealing. Neither of these views necessarily implies that the effect of action on attitude is a mindless, irrational process. Thinking is stimulated by commitment to action. The reasons developed to justify or explain the action can be real and intellectually sound.

Regardless of what explanation is best, there is a practical moral here for us all. Each time we act, we amplify the idea lying behind what we do. If we want to change ourselves in some important way, we had therefore better not depend exclusively on introspection and intellectual insight. Sometimes we need to get up and act—to begin writing that paper, to make those phone calls, to go and see that person—even if we do not feel like acting. If Moses had waited until he *felt* like doing what God was calling him to do, his mission would never have been accomplished. (Indeed, if not acted upon, the idea often begins to fade until recharged by new action.) Fortunately, we often discover that, once we have written that first paragraph, made that first call, or whatever, our commitment and enthusiasm for what we are doing begin to take hold of us and to drive us forward under their momentum.

Action and faith

The social psychological evidence that action and attitude generate one another in an endless chain affirms and enlivens the biblical understanding of action and faith. Depending on where we break into this spiraling chain, we see that faith can be a source of action or a consequence of action. Both perspectives are entirely correct, since action and faith, like action and attitude, feed one another. Christian thinking has usually emphasized faith as the source of action, just as the conventional wisdom has insisted that our attitudes determine our behavior. For the sake of balance, we will therefore emphasize the complementary proposition: faith as a consequence of action. Throughout the Old and New Testaments we are told that full knowledge of God comes through actively *doing* the Word; faith is nurtured by obedient action.

The contribution of action to religious knowledge and faith. Reinhold Niebuhr and others have called attention to the assumptions of Platonic thought, which permeates our Western culture today, and of biblical thought. Plato presumed that we come to know truth by reason and quiet reflection. This view, translated into Christian terms, equates faith with cerebral activity—orthodox doctrinal positions, for example. The contrasting biblical view assumes that reality is also known through obedient commitment. Otto Piper (1962) comments:

"This feature, more than any other, brings out the wide gulf which separates the Hebraic from the Greek view of knowledge. In the latter, knowledge itself is purely theoretical . . . whereas in the Old Testament the person who does not act in accordance with what God has done or plans to do has but a fragmentary knowledge" (p. 44). In fact, the Hebrew word for "know" generally connotes observable action. To know love, we must not only know about love, we must act lovingly. Likewise, to "hear" the Word of God means not only to listen but also to obey.

We read in the New Testament that by actions of love one knows God, for it is the person who does right who is righteous. Jesus declared that those who do the will of God will know God, that he will come and dwell within those who heed what he says, and that we find ourselves, not by passive mystical contemplation, but by losing ourselves as we take up the cross. The wise man—the one who built his house on rock—differed from the foolish man in that he acted upon the Word. Over and over again, the Bible teaches that the gospel power can be known only by living it.

The theological understanding of faith is built upon this biblical view of knowledge. Faith grows as we act on what little faith we have. Just as experimental subjects become more deeply committed to that for which they have suffered and witnessed, so also do we grow in faith as we act it out. Faith "is born of obedience," said John Calvin (1975, p. 75). "The proof of Christianity really consists in 'following,'" declared Søren Kierkegaard (1944, pp. 87–88).

C. S. Lewis captured this dynamic of faith in one of his *Chronicles of Narnia*. The great lion Aslan has returned to Narnia to redeem its captives. Lucy, a young girl with a trusting, childlike faith in Aslan, catches a glimpse of him and eventually convinces the others in her party to start walking toward where she sees him. As Lucy follows Aslan, she comes to see him more clearly. The others, skeptical and grumbling at first, follow despite their doubts. Only as they follow do they begin to see what was formerly invisible to them—first a fleeting hint of the lion, then his shadow, until finally, after many steps, they see him face to face. As Dietrich Bonhoeffer (1963) concluded in *The Cost of Discipleship*, "only he who believes is obedient, and only he who is obedient believes" (p. 69). Christians surely understand and communicate their faith as a rationally defensible entity. Yet when Jesus counseled that the kingdom of God belongs to those who are like children, he reminded us that intellectual understanding need not precede the beginnings of faith.

Implications for church life and Christian nurture. We have seen that the modern social psychological view of how action nurtures attitude is paralleled by the ancient biblical understanding of knowledge and faith. How might this consensus be usefully applied in church renewal and in the development of personal faith? Anyone who understands the principle is capable of brainstorming its application. Just remember: behavior which is public and personally chosen is especially likely to stimulate internal change.

First, a top priority for churches must be to make their members *active* participants, not mere spectators. Many of the dynamic religious movements of today, ranging from sects such as the Jehovah's Witnesses, the Mormons, and the Unification Church, to charismatics and discipleship-centered communities, share as a common denominator an insistence that *all persons on board be members of the crew*. This is a Reformation idea, that all believers are to be priests, and it makes both psychological and theological sense. It is easier said than done, but it does provide a criterion by which to evaluate our standards and procedures for admitting and maintaining members, and a principle to apply in implementing programs of parish life. As a local church makes decisions and administers its program, it should constantly be asking, Will this activate our members and make priests of believers? If research studies on persuasion are any indication, this will best be accomplished by direct personal calls to active commitment, not merely by mass appeals and announcements.

In worship, also, people should be engaged as active participants, not as mere spectators of religious theater. Research indicates that passively received spoken words have surprisingly little impact on listeners, and that any attitude changes which do result are less likely to endure and influence subsequent behavior than are attitude changes which emerge from active experience. This points to the desirability of stimulating listeners to rehearse and act upon the spoken word, and of enabling the congregation to participate actively in the liturgical ritual. The public act of choosing to get out of one's seat and kneel before the congregation in taking communion is but one example. When the people sing responses, write their own confessions, contribute prayer, join in the reading of Scripture, take notes on the sermon, utter exclamations, bring their offerings forward, make the sign of the cross, and sit, stand, or kneel, they have made the liturgy their own work.

The action-attitude principle can also inform Christian education and Christian nurture. There is now ample evidence that mere head knowledge about religion, even when it is totally orthodox, often has little effect upon actual behavior. One recent review of pertinent research concludes bluntly: "As far as moral behavior is concerned, religion appears to have little effect." Since attitudes formed by experience are more likely to effect positive action, we might consider new methods of faith development. For example, few Christians even begin to realize the potential benefits of rituals within a family setting. Rituals practiced by Old Testament families helped them to remember the mighty acts of God. When today's Jewish family celebrates the Passover by eating special foods, reading prayers, and singing psalms, all of which symbolize the historical experiences of Israel, the family members are helped to remember and know who they are. Such practices, done without question, renew deep convictions and feelings. As Tevye exclaims in *Fiddler on the Roof,* "Because of our traditions every one of us knows who he is and what God expects him to do. . . . Without our traditions our lives would be as shaky as a fiddler on the roof." Among American Christians, family celebrations are becoming more common during special seasons, for example, Advent. With a boost from the church, home-based activity could be extended to celebrate all the great themes of the church year.

To sum up: recent social psychological research on action and attitude reinforces an ancient but underappreciated biblical truth. Biblical and psychological perspectives link arms in reminding us that faith is like love: if we hoard it, it will shrivel; if we use it, exercise it, and express it, we shall have it more abundantly.

Illusions of Human Thought

Social psychological research in the area of cognition reminds us of another biblical truth, that human wisdom is, as Paul indicated, not nearly so wise as God's foolishness (1 Cor. 1:25). During the late 1970s this new research on the foibles and fallacies of human thought was rolling off the presses faster than anyone could read it. These experiments gave new insight into how it is that people come to believe things which are not true. For proud individuals living in a self-righteous culture it is shocking to discover that one of the brute facts about human nature is that it is permeated with illusions, self-deceptions, and false beliefs.

A cautionary preface is needed here. This will not be the whole story of human thinking. Just as Christians believe that humanity is created in the very image of God and yet also fallen, so also does psychological research picture both the grandeur of the human intellect and the ease with which it forms and perpetuates false convictions. Portraying the glass of human reasoning as half empty, the new research actually balances our natural optimistic tendency to see it as half full. Understanding the frailty of our wisdom can move us to a better and more accurate evaluation of our thinking. It may, for instance, help deflate our arrogance and amplify our humility—reminding us of the vast gulf which distinguishes the omniscient mind of God from our own finite capacities. Here, then, is a reminder that, contrary to Hamlet's paean of praise, humans are not always "noble in reason" and certainly not "infinite in faculty."

Pride—the tendency to view oneself as better than average

It was noted earlier that people generally come to believe in the acts they have committed; hence, they are likely to perceive their evil acts as morally justified. This process of self-justification is complemented by a self-serving bias: people remember and interpret events of their lives so as to take personal credit for positive outcomes and avoid blame for negative outcomes.

Experiments have revealed this self-serving bias time and again. During the 1970s, the most active research in the field of social psychology concerned "attribution"—how we explain our own and others' behavior. One widely accepted conclusion is that people generally attribute their positive behaviors to themselves and their negative behaviors to external constraints. This, of course, enables them to take credit for their good acts and to deny blame for their bad acts. (Recall that most ancient of attributions, Adam's excuse that "the woman you gave me . . ." [Gen. 3:12].) Although Thomas Harris may imagine that most people suffer from the "I'm not OK—you're OK syndrome," the evidence suggests that William Saroyan is much closer to the truth: "Every man is a good man in a bad world—as he himself knows."

A few examples will indicate how widespread the self-serving bias is. A teacher or therapist who is trying to influence someone else tends to take credit for a positive outcome, but to blame a poor outcome on the other person. Hence a therapist may surmise, "I helped Mrs. X get better, but Mr. Y got worse despite my help." After working on a problem, people generally attribute their successes to themselves, ascribing them to personal factors such as ability and effort, while attributing failures to external factors such as bad luck and the difficulty of the task.

When two parties both exhibit the self-serving bias—by blaming the other party for his or her bad deeds while excusing one's own—open hostility is the usual result. It happens all the time in marriage and in aggressive confrontations involving the police. Each party sees its own toughness as a reasonable response, but attributes the other party's toughness to its evil disposition. John attributes Mary's hostility to her nastiness, but sees his own hostility as entirely justified.

An impressive series of experiments by Barry Schlenker (1976) shows how egocentric perceptions can poison a group. Schlenker had people work together on some task, and then gave them a false evaluation as to whether the group had done well or poorly. In every one of his studies, the members of the groups that were told (falsely) they had done well claimed more responsibility for their performance than did members of the groups that were told they had failed.

Schlenker's findings are complemented by other research which consistently reveals that people are more likely to accept and recall positive information about themselves than negative information and tend to see themselves as better than average. Most people see themselves as more ethical than their average peer and as less prejudiced than the typical individual of their community. Most people view themselves as healthier than average, and most college students believe they will outlive by about ten years the life span which actuarial tables predict for them. (It has been said that Freud's favorite joke was about the man who told his wife, "If one of us should die, I think I would go live in Paris.")

Jean-Paul Codol (1976) conducted similar experiments involving subjects ranging from twelve-year-old schoolchildren to professional adults. A perceived superiority of the self was consistently present, regardless of those involved and the experimental methods. For example, Codol found that the more we admire a particular trait, the more likely we are to see it in ourselves but not in others.

The self-serving bias can be demonstrated by having a group of people anonymously fill out questionnaires concerning their relative standing with regard to a variety of socially desirable traits. I have in fact asked some of my own students to participate in just such an experiment. A typical item on the questionnaire was, "My hunch is that about _____ percent of the others in this class are more *sympathetic* than I am." Bias seems to operate most freely when one is assessing subjective traits such as sympathy or morality, where objective comparison is difficult. My students typically rated themselves in the top third of their class. Consciously, at least, a superiority complex predominates over an inferiority complex.

The self-serving bias can have unfortunate consequences. Corporation presidents widely predict more growth for their own than for competing firms, and production managers similarly overpredict performance. As investigator Laurie Larwood (Larwood and Whittaker [1977]) has observed, such overoptimism can produce disastrous consequences. If those who deal in the stock market or in real estate perceive their business intuition to be superior to that of their competitors, they may be in for some rude awakenings.

Larwood also surveyed homes in a northeastern city and found that the typical citizen professed to be more concerned than others about ensuring clean air and water and believed he or she used less electricity than did other city residents. The typical individual was a self-proclaimed better-than-average citizen. As Larwood notes, if most people "are merely the average persons that they must be statistically, but behave as though they are superior, their goals and expectations must inevitably conflict" (p. 197). Each of us will continue to use more than his or her fair share of resources.

The better-than-average phenomenon affects not only our self-images, but also our perception of the groups to which we belong. Codol found, as have other researchers, that people see their own groups as superior to comparable groups. The children in each of several school classrooms, for instance, saw their class as surpassing the other classes in desirable characteristics. Irving Janis (1982) has noted that one source of destructive international conflict is the tendency of both sides to believe in the moral superiority of their acts. Americans say that the United States built missile bases in Turkey near the Russian border to protect the free world from communism, while the Soviet Union sought to put missiles in Cuba to threaten American security. The Soviets, of course, switch the motivations.

Modern research on self-serving perceptions confirms some ancient wisdom about our human condition. Something is awry with the way we see ourselves. The tragic flaw portrayed in Greek drama was *hubris*, pride. Like the subjects of our experiments, the Greek tragic figures did not consciously choose evil, but, rather, thought too highly of themselves (they were better than average), with consequent disaster. In the biblical account, pride is self-deceit, ignorance of the truth about ourselves. Søren Kierkegaard lamented that becoming aware of our own sin is like trying to see our own eyeballs.

Yes, social psychology is here, too, dusting off some ancient wisdom about our human condition. The self-serving bias is the social psychologist's modern rendition of the forever underappreciated truth about human pride. "There is," said C. S. Lewis (1953), "no fault which we are more unconscious of in ourselves. . . . If anyone would like to acquire humility, I can, I think, tell the first step. The first step is to realize that one is proud. And a biggish step, too" (p. 99).

The tendency for expectations to control our interpretation and recall of events

The self-serving bias is but the first of many examples of what Herbert Simon has called our "bounded rationality." Some of these illusory thinking processes raise troubling questions about certain beliefs and practices in popular Christianity. In this and the following two sections we will be considering a few such illusions in human thinking.

In every arena of human thinking our prior beliefs bias the way we view, interpret, and remember the new information that comes to us. Most of us already know this, but we generally fail to appreciate the degree to which it is true. Our inclination to perceive events in terms of our expectations is one of the most significant facts about the human mind. Our processing of information is, in the words of today's researchers, "theory driven."

The tendency to prejudge reality on the basis of our beliefs has implications for science and for biblical interpretation—or so philosophers and theologians have been arguing lately. Less well known are some new experimental studies which systematically manipulate people's presuppositions, with astonishing effects upon their interpretation and recall of objective information. One category of these experiments has involved implanting in people's minds a belief which is not necessarily true and then trying to discredit that belief. Demolishing such a belief turns out to be surprisingly difficult, especially after the subject conjures up a rationale for it.

For instance, Craig Anderson and his colleagues (1980) invited their subjects to consider whether a person who is inclined to take risks would make a good or bad fire-fighter. They were given only two concrete cases to inspect: one group was shown a risk-taking individual who was a successful fire-fighter and a cautious person who was an unsuccessful one; the other group was shown the reverse. After deciding that risk-taking people make either better or worse fire-fighters, the subjects wrote an explanation for their conclusion. Those who were induced to believe that a risk-taking person makes a good fire-fighter typically reasoned that such an individual would have the bravery to save occupants from a burning building. Those who believed the reverse explained that successful fire-fighters are careful rather than impulsive and thus less likely to risk their own and others' lives. Once formed, each of these explanations was viable independent of the initial information which led to the conclusion. Thus when that information was discredited (the subjects were informed that the cases were merely manufactured for the experiment), the conclusion nevertheless survived mostly intact. The subjects retained their self-generated explanations and therefore continued to believe that risk-taking individuals really do make better or worse fire-fighters.

These experiments go on to indicate that, paradoxically, the more closely we examine our theories and understand and explain how they *might* be true, the more closed we become to cogent discrediting information. There is every reason to suspect this phenomenon is true of scientists as well as lay people. Scientific theories are sometimes amazingly resilient to disconfirming evidence. Consider also the implications of this phenomenon for religion. What are the likely consequences of inventing and then explaining and defending a religious doctrine (or, for that matter, an antireligious doctrine)?

Erroneous beliefs are also sustained by another potent phenomenon. Our memories are largely reconstructions, not copies, or even fuzzy pictures, of our past experiences. Like a paleontologist inferring the appearance of a dinosaur from bone fragments, we reconstruct our past from fragments of information. The extent to which our current beliefs control our attempts to remember the past is evident in a study of conflicting eyewitness testimonies which was conducted by Elizabeth Loftus and John Palmer (1973). They showed their subjects a film of a traffic accident and then asked them questions about what they had seen. The subjects who were asked, "How fast were the cars going when they smashed into each other?" gave higher estimates than did those asked, "How fast were the cars going when they hit each other?" A week later they were asked whether they recalled seeing any broken glass (actually there was none). The subjects who were asked how fast the cars were going when they "smashed into" each other were more than twice as likely to report broken glass as were those asked how fast the cars were going when they "hit" each other.

The tendency to be persuaded by anecdotes and testimonies rather than factual data

Many recent experiments have found that people's judgments and attitudes are more influenced by vivid concrete examples than by reliable, but abstract, statistical information. This is true even when the concrete example is known to be of dubious validity.

Richard Nisbett and Eugene Borgida (1976) have explored the human failure to use statistical information. They informed their subjects of an incident in which most of the bystanders did nothing to help a seizure victim. The subjects were then shown videotaped interviews of some of the individuals who had supposedly been present. After receiving these two types of information, a statistical summary of how most of the bystanders behaved and a brief exposure to a few of the alleged bystanders, the subjects were asked to guess how the specific individuals had reacted. Knowing that most of the bystanders had done nothing had almost no effect on the subjects' guesses of how specific individuals had acted (nor, for that matter, on conjectures of how they themselves would have acted). The subjects placed almost total confidence in their intuitive reactions to the individuals: "Ted seems so nice that I can't imagine him being unresponsive to another's plight." The specific individual was the salient point, pushing into the background accurate information about how most people really acted.

Entrepreneurs capitalize upon this human foible. State lotteries (which typically return less than half of the money they take in) exploit the impact of a few conspicuous winners. Since the statistical truth always stays buried in the back of people's minds, the system seduces them into perceiving a lottery ticket as having much greater potential to win than it actually does. The effects of a vivid anecdote are also well known to professional persuaders. Preachers, teachers, and writers know the power of engaging examples. There is a rich, compelling quality to emotional stories and testimonials—but so much so that we are often persuaded even when they are grossly unrepresentative of human experience.

We have all heard compelling testimonies of how lives have been changed by conversion or how prayer has been followed by God's performing miraculous feats. We do not wish to dispute all these claims— if God exists he is certainly capable of doing anything he well pleases— but one does wonder whether those who recount these stories are not inclined to reconstruct their experience to make it maximally newsworthy. The glamorizing of Christian experience in dramatic testimonies sometimes may give a falsely romanticized impression of what being a Christian is like. Better to base evangelism on truth than on unrepresentative claims. Exaggerated testimonies not only provoke a sense of inferiority in listeners who feel ordinary by comparison, they also set the stage for disillusionment among converts when their experience falls short of the purported personal benefits.

Illusions of causation, correlation, and personal control

One mistake of human thinking known by nearly every student of psychology is the virtually irresistible temptation to assume that two events which occur together are necessarily causally connected. For example, since there is a relationship between educational attainments and earnings, between certain child-rearing styles and the personalities of children exposed to them, and between health practices and longevity, we too readily jump to the conclusion that education always pays financial dividends, that specific parenting styles have inevitable observable effects, and that life expectancy can automatically be increased by changes in nutrition and exercise habits.

Sometimes a merely accidental association between two events can induce a fallacious conviction that one is causing the other. Various experiments demonstrate that coincidence often results in superstitious behavior. If an act, say some good-luck ritual, just happens to be performed before a desired event occurs, it is easy to get the idea that the act must have *caused* the desired event, the reward. This inclines the subject to perform that act more frequently, thus increasing the probability that once again the act will have been performed just before the reward comes. Of course, it will be only very occasionally that a reward will indeed follow the specific act. But this erratic "intermittent reinforcement," as experimental psychologists call it, is especially conducive to persistence. If a hungry pigeon is given a food pellet every so often, regardless of what it is doing, the pigeon may develop some ritualistic behavior and, even after the pellets are discontinued, repeat that behavior ten thousand times or more before quitting. It is as if the pigeon believes that, in the past, persistence has eventually been rewarded.

The confusion caused by viewing correlation as causation is compounded by our susceptibility to perceiving correlation where none exists. When observing random events, people easily become convinced that, where they expect to see significant relationships, significant relationships do in fact exist. In one experiment, the subjects were shown hypothetical results of a cloud-seeding experiment (Ward and Jenkins [1965]). A chart was prepared covering fifty days. For each day it was noted whether the clouds had been seeded and whether it had rained. Shown a random mix of results (sometimes it rained after seeding, sometimes not; sometimes it rained on the other days, sometimes not), the subjects nevertheless were convinced—in conformity with their intuitive supposition about the effects of cloud-seeding— that there really was a relationship. This experiment, and others like it, indicate that people easily misperceive random data as confirming their beliefs. When we believe a correlation exists between two things, confirming instances are more likely to be noticed and recalled than are disconfirming instances.

Our tendency to perceive random events as though they were meaningfully related feeds the frequent illusion that chance events are subject to our personal control. Ellen Langer (1977) has demonstrated this with creative experiments which involve gambling. Her subjects were easily seduced into believing they could beat chance. Afterwards, those who were allowed to choose a lottery number for themselves demanded four times as much money for their lottery ticket as did those whose number was assigned by the experimenter. Moreover, when Langer's subjects played a game of chance against an awkward and nervous person, they were willing to bet significantly more than when playing against a dapper, confident opponent. The conclusion arrived at through these experiments was that people often act as if chance events are subject to personal control.

The phenomenon of "regression toward the average" often contributes to the illusion of control. People who rank extremely high or low in some type of classification are more likely to "regress" (fall back) toward the middle than to become even more extreme; when one is at the very bottom the only direction in which one can move is up. Said differently, after an unusual event, things return to their more usual level. College students who score unusually low on an examination to determine aptitude for graduate school or medical school may, before retaking the exam, study a book on how to score high on the test. They will likely score slightly higher the second time; this leads them to believe that the book was useful even if it had no effect. When things are desperately bad, we will try anything rather than sit passively, and whatever we try is more likely to be followed by improvement than by further decrement and thus seems effective. We therefore easily fall prey to an illusion of controlling power.

The illusions of causation, correlation, and personal control confirm the biblical image of the finiteness of the human mind. Their existence should also prompt Christians to wonder whether faith is ever displaced by superstition, giving people, for instance, an inflated sense of the power of their prayers. When a television evangelist declares that with ardent prayer "Jesus becomes like putty in your hands," one wonders if this self-deifying claim is faith or a counterfeit thereof, a glib caricature of true Christianity. The original sin, humanity's desire to be like God, still tempts all of us today.

The uses and superstitious abuses of prayer are discussed at length in my book *The Human Puzzle* (Myers [1978]). My hope for readers of this chapter is simply that they become sensitive to the possibility that prayer can be infected by superstition. Perhaps such a sensitivity might alleviate some of the arrogance which creeps in when people begin to think that their prayers are pulling the levers of an otherwise inactive cosmic vending-machine.

Other foibles of human thinking

Many other research findings testify to the magnitude of human folly:

1. We often do not know why we do what we do—we make false assertions about what we have done, why we did it, and what we will do in the future.
2. We convince ourselves that we actually predicted events which we now know have happened.

3. We also tend to be overconfident that our beliefs are accurate. This is in part due to our disinclination to seek information that might disconfirm what we believe.
4. Our beliefs, even if erroneous, sometimes generate their own reality. They may lead us to act in ways which will confirm them.
5. We underestimate the impact of social situations upon others' behavior—we are too quick to assume that their actions mirror their inner dispositions and attitudes.
6. We tend to believe repeated assertions, even if we know them to be of dubious credibility.
7. We overestimate the intelligence and competence of people who by chance are in positions of social power, even if we know they were assigned to their positions arbitrarily.
8. We often adjust what we say to please our listeners and, having done so, come to believe our altered message.

We could extend the list of thinking errors, but this has been a sufficient glimpse at the ease with which people come to believe things that are not true. Since we know that these errors creep even into sophisticated scientific thinking, it seems safe to conclude that none of us is exempt from them. Human nature apparently has not changed since the psalmist observed three thousand years ago that "no one can see his own errors" (Ps. 19:12, GNB).

Lest we succumb to the cynical conclusion that *all* beliefs are absurd, let us hasten to balance the picture. The elegance of the various analyses of the imperfections of human wisdom is itself a tribute to human wisdom. Were we to argue that *all* human thought is illusory, our assertion would be self-refuting, for it, too, would be but an illusion. The idea that reality is nothing but an inkblot onto which we project our invented beliefs self-destructs, because it necessitates that it is itself nothing more than another fabrication.

To conclude, research in cognitive social psychology mirrors the mixed review given humanity in the Bible. On the one hand, many research psychologists have spent lifetimes exploring the awesome capacities of the human mind. We image-bearers of the infinite, omniscient mind are capable of great achievements and impressive insights into the nature of things. In this humanistic age we already know this well. What we fail to appreciate is the extent to which people, motivated by pride and susceptible to the other illusions of human thought, will construct and perpetuate false beliefs.

In *The Inflated Self* (Myers [1981]) I have described how illusory thinking penetrates everyday life. For example, the difficulty we encounter in assessing the workings of our minds, the human tendencies to make false declarations about what we have done and why, to be overconfident about our intuitions, to take special notice of and recall events which confirm our expectations, to be too easily persuaded by unrepresentative anecdotes, and to miss the distinction between coincidence and causation—all these factors combine to convince gullible minds of phenomena, such as extrasensory perception, which may not exist.

Even within psychology there is now considerable evidence that clinicians are susceptible to erroneous convictions about the validity of their diagnoses and the effectiveness of their therapies. Indeed, because of their education and the respect they are paid, professional people may be the most susceptible of all to haughty pretension. Having created an imposing, intimidating aura about themselves and having convinced people to abdicate their own judgment to professional expertise, they of all people may need an occasional call to humility or even, sometimes, to have their pretension punctured.

Theologically, research on illusory thinking lends support to the Reformers' conviction that human reason is fallen, radically corrupted, and incapable of rationally weighing the evidence and deciding for God. The many demonstrations of the limits and errors of our reason are not at all congenial with the contrasting theological view which insists that people are capable of weighing all considerations and then rationally deciding on their own conversion. In this latter view, *I choose God*, an idea assumed in the title of the Billy Graham magazine, *Decision*. The Reformed perspective places less emphasis upon the human act of decision, insisting that there is also an important sense in which *God chooses me* as an act of his grace and enables me to respond with the help of illumination provided by his Spirit.

Evidence concerning the fallibility of human thinking also has implications for our attitude toward *all* theologies. While one may believe that Reformed theology fits remarkably well with the facts as social psychologists see them, one must also remember that God is not a monopoly or prisoner of any one theological school. Since theology is a human and fallible enterprise, its propositions must never be canonized as final truth. Christians would do well to adopt the attitude of science, which, in its ideal form, is profoundly humble. Theology at its best is like science at its best—ever reforming its always imperfect models. Insofar as human words are not God's words, we must view with suspicion those who propound their system of propositions about God with supreme certainty.

If evidence concerning the ease with which we form and perpetuate false ideas unsettles our confidence in our particular system of beliefs, it may also have the desirable effect of reminding us that Christians are called, first of all, not just to a system of words and beliefs, but also to obedient life. The most important truth is found not in propositions, but in relationship, the type of relationship Jesus had in mind when he said, "I am the truth," and "the truth shall set you free." This truth lies beyond the grasp of both empirical science and rationalistic theology. It is truth that can be known only through active personal experience.

Finally, the new research on illusory thinking drives home again the biblical teaching that human beings are, as Seward Hiltner (1977) put it, "creatures of God, beings other than he, and not as some religions have declared, pieces of or emanations of God. . . . The original sin appeared when human creatureliness and finitude were denied rather than accepted" (pp. 1, 5). Each of us peers at reality through a dark glass, glimpsing only its shadowy outlines. Therefore, the most certain belief we can hold is the conviction that some of our beliefs contain error—hence the need, at all times, to check our beliefs against the facts as we (to the best of our ability) discern them, to discipline our undisciplined credulity. This scientific spirit, this Christian humility, is an attitude that befits all human beings.

References

Anderson, C., M. Lepper, and L. Ross (1980). Perseverance of theories: The role of explanation in the persistence of discredited information. *Journal of Personality and Social Psychology* 39: 1037–49.

Bonhoeffer, D. (1963). *The cost of discipleship*. New York: Macmillan.

Calvin, J. (1975). *Institutes of the Christian religion*. Translated by F. Battles. Philadelphia: Westminster (original work published 1559).

Codol, J.-P. (1976). On the so-called "superior conformity of the self" behavior: Twenty experimental investigations. *European Journal of Social Psychology* 5: 457–501.

Freedman, J., and S. Fraser (1966). Compliance without pressure: The foot-in-the-door technique. *Journal of Personality and Social Psychology* 4: 195–202.

Hiltner, S. (1977). Sin: Theological and psychological perspectives. *CAPS Bulletin* 3.2: 1–5.

Janis, I. (1982). *Groupthink* (2d ed.). Boston: Houghton Mifflin.

Kierkegaard, S. (1944). *For self-examination, and Judge for yourselves*. Translated by W. Lowrie. Princeton: Princeton University Press (original work published 1851).

Langer, E. (1977). The psychology of chance. *Journal for the Theory of Social Behavior* 7: 185–208.

Larwood, L., and W. Whittaker (1977). Managerial myopia: Self-serving biases in organizational planning. *Journal of Applied Psychology* 62: 194–98.

Lewis, C. S. (1953). *Mere Christianity*. New York: Macmillan.

Loftus, E., and J. Palmer (1973). Reconstruction of automobile destruction: An example of the interaction between language and memory. *Journal of Verbal Learning and Verbal Behavior* 13: 585–89.

Milgram, S. (1965). Some conditions of obedience and disobedience to authority. *Human Relations* 18: 57–75.

Myers, D. (1978). *The human puzzle: Psychological research and Christian belief*. New York: Harper & Row.

―――― (1981). *The inflated self*. Minneapolis: Winston.

Nisbett, R., E. Borgida, R. Crandall, and H. Reed (1976). Popular induction: Information is not necessarily informative. In J. Carroll and J. Payne, eds., *Cognition and social behavior*. Hillsdale, N.J.: Erlbaum.

Pines, M. (1973). *The brain changers*. New York: Harcourt Brace Jovanovich.

Piper, O. (1962). Knowledge. In *Interpreter's dictionary of the Bible*, ed. G. Buttrick, vol. 3. Nashville: Abingdon.

Schlenker, B. (1976). Egocentric perceptions in cooperative groups: A conceptualization and research review. Final Report, Office of Naval Research, #170–797.

Ward, W., and H. Jenkins (1965). The display of information and the judgment of contingency. *Canadian Journal of Psychology* 19: 231–41.

12

Community Psychology
Stanton L. Jones

It seems that everywhere we turn these days, mental-health professionals (psychologists, psychiatrists, social workers, etc.) are shaping how we understand ourselves. They exercise enormous influence through the use of various media—radio talk shows, magazine articles, television interviews, and so forth. Less obvious, but no less dramatic, is the impact that these professionals have on our lives through their roles in shaping public policy and in creating and molding institutions which serve the public, for example, community mental-health centers, youth-outreach organizations, and the criminal-justice system.

This chapter examines the compatibility of one subdiscipline in psychology, community psychology, with Christian belief and tradition. The influence of community psychology is growing steadily. What is community psychology, especially in terms of its central vision of the person? Are there aspects of this field that Christians must be cautious about? Can the church in any way see itself as an ally with practitioners of this field? This chapter will help the reader to begin to grapple with these issues. Some of its ideas have been drawn from "Christian Faith and Community Psychology: The Case for a Limited Partnership," a paper coauthored with Kathleen Lattea and presented at a symposium on "Christian and Judaic Faith and Community Psychology: Potentialities for Partnership" at the August

240

*1983 convention (Anaheim, California) of the American
Psychological Association.*

Many psychologists have moved out of the consulting
room and laboratory into the real world, attempting to apply their
discipline for the enhancement of human welfare and performance
and the alleviation of suffering. Among the subdisciplines represented
in this move are industrial-organizational psychology, sport psychology, consumer psychology, and environmental psychology. The purpose of this chapter is to introduce the reader to another of these
subdisciplines of psychology, community psychology, and to examine
its relevance to the Christian studying psychology.

A Tentative Definition of Community Psychology

A relatively new subdiscipline in psychology, community psychology straddles the rather hazy boundaries between clinical psychology,
social work, sociology, ecological psychology, public-policy studies,
and public health. Because it is a new subdiscipline which is still in the
process of forging its identity, definitions of community psychology
must be made very tentatively. Like clinical psychology, community
psychology is concerned with mental health—both the alleviation of
psychopathology and the promotion of optimal adjustment. Community psychology differs from its clinical counterpart, however, in that
it attempts to understand and intervene at the level of the large group
(as opposed to the level of the individual or small group) and at the
earlier rather than the later stages in problem development.

Community psychologists are involved in a great number of activities. They tend to be research oriented due to their commitment to
empirical testing of the validity of their theories and the effectiveness
of their interventions. Some examples of community-psychology research will illustrate their work. Most people are aware that psychologists construct tests to assess the functioning of individual
personalities; community psychologists have constructed "personality" tests for organizations. For example, Kenneth Pargament, William
Silverman, and their colleagues (1983) have constructed a test to
measure the interpersonal climate of religious congregations. Congregations are scored in such areas as emotional expressiveness, stability, orderliness and clarity, and sense of community. The feedback
can be used by the congregations to help them determine if they are

creating the type of climate they intend. Other tests have been constructed to measure the interpersonal climate of schools, prisons, businesses, families, and volunteer organizations.

Bernard Bloom (1984, pp. 232–39) has summarized the work of one of the most well known community-psychology projects, the Primary Mental Health Project (PMHP) directed by Emory Cowen. Essentially, this program has involved the identification of children failing to adapt well to school long before there are any formal indications of psychopathology. Arguing that traditional psychology has been reactive to problems after they develop and become severe, Cowen has attempted to intervene earlier in the process, that is, before they become serious. The children identified as failing to adapt well have been targeted for special attention by teachers' aides, for special programs to teach them how to relate interpersonally and resolve conflicts, and so forth. Though evaluations of the program have not been uniformly positive, the Primary Mental Health Project is generally viewed as a model of how research and intervention can go hand in hand.

Other activities of community psychologists almost defy categorization. Some are attempting to understand the nature of stress, including how stress actually has an effect on people (Dohrenwend and Dohrenwend [1981]). Others are trying to find out how social support and the concern of others can make stress less harmful to us (Leavy [1983]). Some have attempted to find out what factors shape people's judgments of their quality of life, what can be done to make natural helpers such as neighbors, policemen, bartenders, and lawyers more effective, and how to change communities to decrease rates of crime among juveniles. Examples could be multiplied to fill this entire volume.

A Brief History

Understanding the history of this field will further illuminate its nature (the following summary draws upon Iscoe, Bloom, and Spielberger [1977], and Rappaport [1977]). The roots of the field lie in clinical psychology, the shape of which was basically forged in the two decades following the Second World War. The treatment of the emotionally disturbed during that time was heavily institutional in nature and dominated by the medical model of mental illness. Inpatient census at mental hospitals reached its peak in 1955 at 559,000 (Bassuk and Gerson [1978]). Most clinical psychologists at this time worked in such hospitals and related clinics, frequently under the supervision of physicians.

The period of the 1950s and 1960s was a time of tremendous change, including an incredible increase in governmental social-service programs, the birth of the civil-rights movement, an explosive growth of psychology as a discipline, and the development of more-effective psychoactive medication for the treatment of mental disturbance. In 1963, Congress passed legislation calling for the establishment of community mental-health centers across the nation, for the purpose of detecting and treating acute mental disturbances early in their development and of managing those with more-chronic problems, in the hope of avoiding costly and disruptive inpatient treatment at traditional mental hospitals.

A group of psychologists met in Boston in 1965 to discuss professional training for workers in the community mental-health system. Grave reservations were expressed by many at that conference that the implementation of community mental-health centers had merely moved the medical model from an inpatient to an outpatient setting, with no real revolution having occurred in the type of care delivered. They adopted the term "community psychology" to reflect their preference to focus on maladjustment as a cultural and sociopsychological phenomenon alone. They called for the community psychologist to be a "social change agent, a political activist, and a 'participant-conceptualizer'" (Rappaport [1977], p. 13). This job description is quite different from that of the typical clinical psychologist, and the skills needed are not usually taught in psychology graduate programs!

The church has been frequently mentioned in the ensuing literature as a possible vehicle through which community psychologists might develop innovative ways of rendering service (Pargament [1982]; Rappaport [1981]). Can the church learn from community psychology? Can it work with community psychologists who are not part of the church? What are the major roadblocks facing the Christian in studying and using community psychology? To answer these questions, we will first look ever so briefly at the recent history of the church to see if the church and community psychology share compatible goals. Then we will examine the nature of community psychology more closely and evaluate its distinctives from a Christian perspective.

The Church as a Helping Institution

The church has always been about the business of enhancing human welfare. Consider as evidence Jesus' summary of the law: "the great and first commandment" is "You shall love the Lord your God with all your heart, and with all your soul, and with all your mind. . . . And a second is like it, You shall love your neighbor as yourself" (Matt.

22:37–39, RSV). This remarkable passage suggests that the core of the gospel concerns our responsibilities in two dimensions: the vertical dimension of relationship to God and the horizontal dimension of relationship to fellow human beings. Note that clear priority is given to the vertical dimension.

The commandment to love our neighbor has been seen by Christians throughout history as providing the basis for social ministry on both the personal/individualistic level (or charity) and the societal/political level (or social action). Acts of charity or compassion to individuals have been universally praised in the church, and thus do not need to be examined further. But what about social action, which is the mode of intervention employed by the community psychologist?

The history of the church in America illustrates the different types of responses the church has made to the need for social action. Timothy Smith (1957) has documented the growth of social activism in the church of the early nineteenth century. Revival spread dramatically during the period between 1840 and the Civil War, accompanied by a resolve to revitalize the moral status of the country. Fueled by anticipation of an imminent establishment of the kingdom of God on the earth and believing that humans are perfectible through divine grace, many Christians of that day expended great energies in the pursuit of social progress. Many church leaders were in the forefront of this movement, pushing for reform on the issues of slavery, poverty, workers' rights, education, women's suffrage, and liquor traffic. Smith notes, "The vanguard of the movement went far beyond the earlier Christian emphasis on almsgiving [individual charity] to a search for the causes of human suffering and a campaign to reconstruct social and economic relations upon a Christian pattern" (p. 148). Revivalists stressed the idea that Christian love of God and neighbor is the principal fruit of conversion, and preached that the victory of the gospel over evil is not merely a personal victory, but extends to all of society as well.

After the Civil War, "the spirit of reform that had characterized ante-bellum Evangelicals ground almost to a halt" (Woodbridge, Noll, and Hatch [1979], p. 236). Faced with the monstrous devastation of the Civil War, the pernicious nature of the social problems they were attacking, and the influx of Catholic immigrants from Europe, Protestant evangelicals became discouraged and retreated into a quiet and privatized religion with little outreach to the world about them. Acceptance of rugged American individualism led in some circles to an emphasis upon material success and to ambivalence or even contempt toward the poor.

In the late 1800s, the social-gospel movement began to be the major agenda of the liberal Protestant church. It was proposed by Walter Rauschenbusch and other leaders of the movement that the core of the gospel is the *social* salvation of humanity; that is, care for the welfare of the individual here and now. In other words, the entire gospel began to be seen as comprising only the horizontal dimension of service to others (White and Hopkins [1976]). The social-gospel movement was eventually seen by more-conservative Protestants as a reductionistic one in which the critical vertical or transcendent dimension of the gospel was deemphasized.

The fundamentalist Protestants, seeing the erosion of their theological distinctives in the major seminaries of the day and an increasing lack of acceptance of their beliefs in the public forum, retreated to preserve their distinctives. In divesting themselves of every tinge of liberalism, they jettisoned the baby with the bathwater by rejecting social ministry as typified by social-gospel adherents (Smith [1957]). The zeal which had previously been directed toward social ministry in the local community was now directed toward private acts of charity and overseas missions, especially evangelistic, medical, and educational missions.

The situation in today's Protestant church is a distinctly complex one which bears the marks of this recent history. At the risk of oversimplification, three major responses of Protestant believers to the horizontal demands of the gospel can be seen today (after Samuel and Sugden [1981]). The first group might be called the privatizers; this group continues to be characterized by a retreat from confronting the social demands of their religious faith. Faith has become a private affair, with the person preoccupied with spiritual observances and private morality, but not with public issues. Sin, for example, is a matter of personal morality only, and must be dealt with personally through individual repentance. Another way in which faith is privatized is the formation of insular religious societies which minimize contact with others outside the fold.

The second group might best be seen as a continuation of the social-gospel movement, now represented in the extreme by the liberation-theology perspective. This group continues to see the gospel in essentially horizontal terms only: what matters is caring for people and doing justice in the here and now. This group sees sin principally in oppression of people, and only minimally (if at all) in personal terms.

The final group in the contemporary church consists of those who are retaining the spiritual core of the Christian faith, but are also reaffirming the social implications of the gospel. This last group differs from the second group in its retention of the concepts of individual sin and personal salvation. Nevertheless, this last group recognizes institutional evil as well as personal sin, and sees the mandate of the church as covering both the vertical dimension of concern for the spiritual life of the individual in relation to God and the horizontal dimension of care for and ministry to God's children on both individual and societal levels. It is this sizable last group that we will be focusing on in our discussion, in part because this position is the most compelling for the Christian and just as importantly because neither of the two other groups has any basis on which to interact with community psychology. In that it focuses on the temporal welfare of people, community psychology is not really a concern of the privatizers. By contrast, the social-gospel adherent tends to be unconditionally accepting of the field because of its commitment to similar ends.

The Nature of Community Psychology

Goals

The goals of community psychology were well summarized in the title of George Albee's (1982) article "Preventing Psychopathology and Promoting Human Potential." The foregoing discussion of the church as an agent of social change illustrates the historic interest of the church in the same goals as those expressed by Albee. But even at this broad level some tensions with the Protestant church can be pointed out. The church has throughout its history been working to further human welfare, a task which is basic to its purpose on earth. Many biblical passages charge God's people to care for and take the side of the poor and oppressed in society (e.g., Amos 5). In this social ministry the church has frequently been allied with nonchurch partners. But the social ministry of the church has always been embedded within the broader purpose of obeying and glorifying God, which includes the defense and promulgation of the faith. At the core, the assumption is that the furthering of the gospel will result in the enhancement of all aspects of human welfare, including both the religious and the temporal. Protestant Christians are likely, then, to see most of the concepts of human welfare espoused by community psychologists to be useful but limited, given their broader view of the human condition and need. The unique focus of the church (in comparison to psychology) is upon the transcendent needs of salvation and growth in faith. Yet even with its emphasis upon transcendent ministry, the church has constantly been reminded of the need to minister to the suffering, even when there are no obviously spiritual aspects to that ministry, because while spiritual ministry is the unique focus of the church, it is not the solitary focus.

Thus, the church and community psychology agree about the value of the goals of preventing psychopathology and promoting human potential. They differ, however, in that these goals are the *essential* and *exclusive* focus of community psychology, but are viewed by the church as *one among several* important dimensions of responsibility.

Conceptual distinctives

A field such as community psychology is defined in part by its goals, but is also defined by its conceptual distinctives, which are the characteristic ways of understanding the subject matter that distinguish one field of study from another. We will examine three of the major conceptual distinctives of community psychology and discuss their compatibility with a Christian world-view.

1. Ecological perspective. James Kelly (1981) tersely notes that "we and our settings are interdependent" (p. 248). In its essence, this concept calls for us to always look at people in their contexts in order to understand them properly. Charles Holahan (1977) delineates three aspects of this concept. The first is that all human behavior must be seen in its environmental context. That is to say, we cannot rightly understand the behavior of anyone without understanding the interpersonal, cultural, and even physical environment from which he or she comes. A mundane example of the consequences of failing to take this into consideration is the cross-cultural prejudices which occur when we do not view the behavior of others in cultural perspective. Thus, in assessing intelligence, we frequently are tempted to apply our Western academic standards of intelligence to all people, assuming that the only true mark of ability is academic credentials. A person from a primitive culture might appear quite unintelligent to us by this standard, and yet be an exemplary person of great ability in his or her own culture. Faced with the peculiar demands of that society, we in turn might appear the less intelligent due to our relative inability to meet its practical demands (e.g., food gathering).

Secondly, community psychology adopts a "social systems perspective in conceptualizing the environment" (Holahan [1977], p. 290). This means that the term *environment* is not understood narrowly as the physical environment, but all persons are seen in the context of a hierarchy of interlocking social systems. For example, I live in a particular environment composed of a work system (Wheaton College), a professional system (the American Psychological Association and the state board which licenses psychologists), a familial system (a nuclear and extended family), a neighborhood system, a church system (my local church), and so forth. Each of these systems radiates outward (I am part of an academic department, which is part of the college, which is part of a coalition of Christian schools, which is part of the private four-year college system, which is part. . .), and all of the systems interrelate and interpenetrate (as when my denomination takes an action that affects Christian colleges, or I meet a cousin at an APA meeting, or the state licensing board takes an action that affects what I teach at Wheaton).

Finally, community psychology sees psychological distress and subsequent adjustment as resulting from transactions between the individual and his or her environment. Social psychologists have established our sadly human tendency to attribute our own failings to circumstance, but to attribute the failings of others to enduring characteristics of their persons (see pp. 228–30). Why did I act nervous? Because I was preoccupied and having an off day. Why is the other person nervous? He is not made of such sturdy stuff as I! He is just the nervous type! Community psychology would call us all to be evenhanded in attributing the cause of distress. It calls us to consider all cases (ourselves and others) with a view to the interaction of the person with the environment.

An example of a major area of research today will serve to illustrate the ecological perspective of community psychology. In studying an occurrence of psychopathology (commonly called mental illness), the clinical psychologist is prone to ask individually oriented questions, such as "What are the unique characteristics of this person that have caused these problems?" But looking from an ecological perspective, the community psychologist is interested instead in the way that certain types of people interact with certain types of environments with the result that they experience real problems or are labeled as being a problem. One area of research along this line has been the work on stress (see Bloom [1984], chap. 6, for an excellent overview).

Researchers have produced persuasive evidence that stressful events increase one's chances of experiencing disturbances of both one's emotional adjustment and physical health. Some of the research has been targeted at identifying the types of events which are stressful. While individual variations are noted, some of the most stressful events include familial disruption (loss of spouse or parent through divorce or death, family conflict) and vocational disturbances (loss of employment, pervasive dissatisfaction). As the frequency of these stresses increases, so (in general) does the occurrence of emotional disturbance.

So the ecological perspective does have empirical merit, in that people are affected by the environment. Notice also that the major stressors are interpersonal in nature, supporting the notion that the primary influences in one's environment are the social systems. Researchers have also studied what factors minimize disturbance brought on by stress, and have found that these factors are both environmental and personal. Environmental factors that minimize disturbance include social-support systems; the individual with good interpersonal relationships can draw upon them in time of stress to help cope with difficulties. The personal factors that minimize disturbance include what have been called coping skills, the ability to so manage the demands on oneself as to make them less stressful. People differ in the effectiveness of their coping skills. The community psychologist generally believes that these skills can be enhanced.

At its core, the ecological view suggests that human experience is the product of the person's interacting with his or her world. Is such a perspective compatible with Christian theology? I would argue that in broad terms it is. There are two themes in theology which illustrate the compatibility. The first theme is that we find in the Scriptures a concern for the social environment and the influence it has upon both the individual and the community. Today, we tend to think of people individualistically, as solitary persons who stand on their own. But it was very different in biblical times. H. D. McDonald (1981) has stated that "in Hebrew thought the individual was not considered atomistically. . . . The individual was summed up, as it were, in the community; while the community itself was reflected in the individual" (p. 43). This marked interest in the social environment can be clearly seen in the preoccupation in the Old Testament with the theme of justice. God's concern, expressed in many passages, is not just with individual religious experience, but with political and social influences, because these factors were seen as shaping the character of God's chosen people both as individuals and as a group (see, e.g., Ps. 94; Isa. 10; Amos 5). Similarly, in the New Testament, emphasis is placed upon the unity of believers (see, e.g., John 17:20–23; 1 Cor. 1:10) and upon the importance of corporate worship and witness. It is assumed that environmental factors are important and serve to empower us to be more than we would be just by ourselves (Rappaport [1981]).

The second theme in Christian thought which parallels community psychology's emphasis upon human interaction with the environment is a dogged consistency in reiterating the responsibility of individual human agents despite environmental circumstance. Wright (in McDonald [1981], p. 44) states that in Hebrew society the "individual was not lost or submerged in this community order." In the Old Testament God is portrayed as condemning individuals for their personal behavior even though they were residing in societies which were thoroughly corrupt. These individuals obviously did not have an abundance of environmental alternatives. Nevertheless, while parents were to carefully discipline their children to prevent them from drifting into laziness or immorality, persons who were lazy or immoral as adults were held personally responsible for their behavior—they were not excused on account of having experienced poor parenting. Similar New Testament themes emphasize individual and corporate responsibility.

In summary, we see in the Christian Scriptures and, for the large part, in the history of the church a *dual* emphasis upon the importance of influences which shape or channel human choices and the importance of human responsibility or freedom; this is a true ecological view of persons. The Christian world-view is compatible with this distinctive of community psychology. Yet the theme of personal responsibility must always be emphasized because of the ever-present danger that an ecological view of the person and environment as balanced factors can drift into a pure environmentalism which regards the person as nothing but a product of the environment. Such a distortion which ignores or minimizes the person must be rejected.

    2. *Stress on human potential rather than defect.* Many community psychologists follow Albee (1982) in criticizing what he has called the defect model of human disturbance, the belief that emotional disturbance is the result of rather stable defects in the afflicted person, and thus that it is unpreventable and relatively unmodifiable. In opposition to this belief, community psychologists tend to emphasize the socioenvironmental causes of disturbance. They oppose the common practice of blaming the victim (Ryan [1971]). Blaming the victim occurs when an individual fails to fit in the mainstream of society because he or she has been denied access to the basic resources of that society, and consequently becomes a genuine eccentric, a street person, or perhaps a criminal. When someone fails to fit, we tend not to look at the conditions that created the problem in the first place, but rather to analyze the defects of the afflicted person and to attempt to change those defects through therapy or some other means. In this approach it is *not* the society, but the *victim* of the society, that is regarded as the problem.

    In counterreaction community psychologists believe that tremendous strides could be made toward enhancing the growth and development of all persons in a society through deliberate community interventions. They tend to focus on the competencies that could be developed in all persons, rather than the defects that certain persons have (Goodstein and Sandler [1978]). They also believe strongly in the possibility of preventing psychopathology (Cowen [1980]).

    Christian theology only incidentally addresses the issue of the origin of psychopathology by addressing the larger theme of the origin of all human suffering. Theology is fairly consistent in localizing the causes of suffering in *both* the person and his or her environment. When psychologists talk about person and environment (or nature and nurture), they most frequently mean by "person" the individual's genetic endowment and learning history, factors which do not seem to warrant holding the individual responsible for shortcomings. But Christian theology assumes that people are responsible for at least some of their faults and suffering. They are not merely the recipients of bad genes or victims of a bad environment, but are in some way personally culpable.

So then, Christian theology might assert three sources of human suffering: (1) the social and physical environment (which consists of other sinful persons and a fallen world); (2) potentially defective genetic, physically based, or other personal factors over which the individual has no control (e.g., learning history); and (3) the choices of the person as a responsible agent. Thus, Christian theology will be open to looking at genetic and environmental sources of suffering. But it will at times hold people responsible for their suffering in the belief that they are in fact not always victims of outside forces. Consider as an example that the Scriptures variously attribute poverty to each of the three sources we have mentioned. Isaiah 10 identifies the environment as the source—an oppressive government robs the people; John 9:1–12 speaks of genetic/physical factors—a man is forced to beg because of his blindness; Proverbs 6:6–11 points to personal responsibility—the poverty in view is attributed to sloth (laziness).

Albee (1982) has criticized Christianity for proposing the doctrine that some people are God's chosen, the "elect," and others are the damned. He claims that we blame the victim by assuming that those who do well in life, the successful, must be the elect and that those who do not fit in must be the damned. The damned are obviously the defective part of humanity. But does Christian theology really propose that the poor and the maladjusted are so because of a defect in them? Mainline church doctrine has never asserted this, and in this way is quite unlike the doctrines of many of the Eastern religions, which assert that people who have difficulties in this life are suffering for sins in their previous existence (the ultimate in pessimism and victim blaming!).

The church has historically, however, asserted that all humans are carrying a defect (their sinful nature) as well as living in a defective world. Notice that this defect is egalitarian in nature, in that it inflicts all persons. Because it is this defect that separates us from God, and because reparation of this disrupted relationship is the primary mission of the church, it is this personal defect which is emphasized in the church's ministry. Historically, though, when the church has been at its strongest, it has ministered to the whole person and has dealt with all three types of factors which produce human suffering: socioenvironmental factors are addressed by sociopolitical action, developmental missions, and the social ministry of the local church; genetic and physical factors are dealt with by medical missions; and personal factors are addressed through the spiritual and evangelistic missions of the church. Perhaps there is a place for a psychological ministry by the church to deal with the interface between uncontrollable personal factors (traumatic events like sexual or physical abuse, the divorce or death of one's parents) and those aspects of suffering related to maladaptive personal choices. (For a specific reply to Albee's charges, see Lantz [1984], or Muller and Vande Kemp [1985]).

So while Christian thought would not support the blaming of victims, it would at the same time assert that some of those who suffer are responsible for their condition. In concluding the previous section on the ecological view of community psychology, we argued that such a view is broadly compatible with the Christian perspective as long as it does not become totally environmentalistic. Unfortunately, we do find in community psychology's sociocultural explanations for emotional disturbance a decided tendency to ignore personal responsibility. This tendency must be corrected by the Christian studying and working in the field.

The community psychologist also emphasizes the enhancement of competencies and the possibility of human perfectibility. There is a general compatibility between this emphasis and church doctrine. The church has historically believed that all humans are created in the image of God. This image bearing has been marred and obscured by our rebellion against God, which is the essence of our fallenness. Nevertheless, a residual of the image remains. With salvation the image begins to be redeveloped through the gradual process of growth called sanctification (Berkouwer [1962]; McDonald [1981]). Note that the action of God in salvation is an essential element in this process. Thus, the church has historically been pessimistic about meaningful human change apart from a change of the heart (i.e., salvation), has been unabashedly optimistic about the change of individuals through divine grace, and has wavered between optimism and pessimism regarding the potential for the perfection of all of human society under the work of the Holy Spirit.

So, in summary, the church does not endorse the defect model of human disturbance as defined by Albee. All of humankind is viewed as struggling to overcome the effects of sin on the environment and on the person. Human perfectibility is viewed as impossible without divine intervention. This does not mean, however, that the church sees society as incapable of any progress whatsoever. Rather, the view is that beneficial societal change can occur according to God's providential will, but never merely through the work of humans apart from him. And further, any change occurring apart from a change of the heart may in fact be valuable but is necessarily limited.

3. *Diversity*. One implication which community psychologists draw from their ecological perspective (Rappaport [1977, 1981]) is that there is great value in creating a diversity of empowering settings to enhance the existing strengths and competencies of all persons: "In value terms an ecological viewpoint implies that differences among people and communities may be desirable" (1977, p. 3). One of the greatest problems in most present-day communities is intolerance of those who are merely different, whether that difference is intellectual (prejudice against the retarded frequently results in their being denied housing rights), social (those who violate behavior norms or merely look different are similarly rejected by the dominant community), or ethnic/racial/cultural (Rappaport [1977], chap. 2, documents how groups who differ from the mainstream of society have been labeled as deviant and mentally ill because of a lack of appreciation of their cultural heritage). Responding to these realities, community psychologists tend to emphasize the need for compassionate understanding and appreciation of the differences of others. Such a respect will lead the mental-health practitioner to shift away from attempts to provide therapy to change people who are merely different, in favor of creating settings where such people can find satisfaction in life without the stresses of attempting to conform themselves to the dominant culture. Accordingly, the community psychologist will frequently find it preferable to try to match the person with a supportive environment than to attempt to adjust or repair a personality. How does this fit with Christian theology?

The Protestant church has frequently been guilty of intolerance of cultures unlike its own. There has been a decided tendency among American Christians to inappropriately mix their Americanism with their Christianity. George Peters (1979), in discussing the missionaries of the last several centuries, states, "Unavoidably, unashamedly and unhesitatingly, they were bearers not only of the gospel but also of their Western culture. . . . All this and much more we regret and are penitent about" (pp. 10–11). Describing the attitudes of some of those missionaries as paternalistic, Peters notes that their spreading of their culture was often motivated by a sincere belief that their home culture had been deeply shaped by the Christian gospel and that the native persons being ministered to would necessarily benefit from their cultural efforts. Many conservatives today are struggling with how the church can respect the integrity of native cultures while adhering to an absolute core of gospel truth which transcends culture.

The church is likely to be in sympathy with the creation of diverse settings within cultures to optimize personal fit (Rappaport [1977]). Indeed, it is possible to view the church itself as a setting created and designed for the personal enhancement of its members. In addition, contemporary Protestantism's tremendous interest in the building of effectual community and interpersonal ministry has led to great diversity within the church: "The Church as a network of complimentary charismata (spiritual gifts) is a laboratory of social pluralism. The Church as an educational community is a nurturing ground for countercultural values. The Church as a community of forgiveness is a live alternative to a society structured around retributive sanctions" (Yoder [1974], p. 102). The church's role in the creation of a growth-enhancing social-support network has been well dealt with by Pargament (1982).

In summary, we would argue that the church, given its background, well understands the need for the creation of diverse settings for the enhancement of growth. Due to its confessed core of absolute truth, the church is, of course, likely to be less open to cultural relativity than is the community psychologist. For the latter, anything goes as long as people are satisfied with their lives. But the church maintains a commitment to the Scriptures as revealing not just truths about God, but truths about what the shape of our lives should be.

The Case for a Limited Partnership

Emory Cowen (1982) recently wrote an article on natural helping systems (including hairdressers and bartenders). While this effort was commendable, it is ironic how infrequently the church, in any form, is studied as a means for promoting human welfare. Pargament and his colleagues (1982; Pargament, Silverman, Johnson, Echemendia, and Snyder [1983]; Pargament, Tyler, and Steele [1979a, 1979b]) have been the major researchers in this area. The relative lack of study is most surprising given that in the United States:

Over fifty million adults report a life-changing religious experience with Jesus Christ.

Over one hundred million adults are members of a church or synagogue.

Increasing levels of personal piety are directly correlated with higher levels of social ministry (*Christianity Today* [1981]).

In times of crisis parishioners are more likely to consult members of the clergy (of whom there are more than one quarter of a million in the United States) than mental-health professionals (President's Commission [1977]).

Contrary to frequently expressed opinion, personal religiosity is not correlated with mental disturbance in any way (Bergin [1983]). In other words, religious people are no more and no less disturbed than the general population.

The church is an institution with a tradition of helping and a pool of potential helpers motivated by their religious faith (Pargament [1982]).

The church is financially self-sustaining and thus not subject to the uncertainties of government funding.

Despite the lack of study, the fact is that the church is very active in the task of enhancing human welfare. Major evangelical leaders have committed themselves to this task—witness, for example, the Lausanne Covenant (Stott [1975]) and the Chicago Declaration (Sider [1974]). The church currently provides an incredible array of helping services including child-care agencies, community-service centers, retirement and nursing homes, pastoral-counseling centers, chaplaincy services, rehabilitation centers and halfway houses, summer camps for the handicapped, Meals on Wheels, and soup kitchens. Churches are increasingly developing innovative self-help and social-support groups for the needy (President's Commission [1977]). The work of the Salvation Army and the various denominational social-service agencies in combating poverty is well known. In addition, several innovative programs in this area have been operating for years, including Sojourners communities in Washington and John Perkins's Voice of Calvary ministries in Mendenhall, Mississippi.

A number of ministries have been developed to enhance psychosocial competence; among them are the now widespread marriage- and family-enrichment programs offered in churches, including a variety of film series on parenting. Prison Fellowship, founded by Chuck Colson, evangelizes and supports prisoners as well as their families and provides help in restoring family relationships and finding productive work upon release. Proceeding on the belief that conversion as well as psychosocial support changes lives, follow-up studies are currently under way to determine the impact of Prison Fellowship on recidivism rates.

Finally, with regard to social justice, a number of church and religious groups maintain offices in Washington and in state capitals for the purpose of shaping public policy; these include the highly visible Moral Majority and less well known but active groups such as the National Association of Evangelicals, the Institute of Religion & Public Policy, the United Methodist Board of Church & Society, the Association for Public Justice, Evangelicals for Social Action, and numerous Catholic groups. Many churches are active in battling sexism and racism. We could continue to multiply our examples.

Albee (1982) has provided a useful and simple equation to guide us in reducing the incidence of psychopathology:

$$\frac{\text{Incidence of disturbances}}{} = \frac{\text{Organic factors + Stress}}{\text{Coping skills + Self-esteem + Social support}}$$

It is evident from this equation that reducing negative organic factors (such as hunger, birth defects, pollution) and stress (such as job dissatisfaction, prejudice, and discrimination) will result in a lower incidence of psychopathology, as will enhancement of coping skills, self-esteem, and social-support groups. All of the ministries mentioned above contribute in some way. Direct services offered by the church enhance personal coping. The diverse fellowship and social support (Pargament [1982]) of the church help to dilute stress. Efforts at social justice help create a more healthy environment and thus reduce stress on the individual. The strengthening of personal competencies, which has always been an outcome of church involvement, has lately become an intentional goal, since it is now recognized as a means of preventing spiritual and psychosocial disturbance.

The Protestant church probably sees ministry to the whole person as necessarily rehabilitative and preventive, necessarily individually and socially oriented. For the church views the causes of human suffering as lying inside and outside the person. Since a fundamental source of suffering is within the person from birth, ministry will always be in one sense rehabilitative even while effort is made to prevent future distress. This is not to imply that churches should necessarily shrink from involvement with projects of more limited scope than the whole person. It does imply, however, that the community psychologist should be aware that his or her project might well be seen as inherently limited in scope.

Does community psychology have anything to offer to the work of the church? We would answer with the same response that Seymour Sarason (1977) gave to a student critical of community psychology—community psychologists will not revolutionize the work of the church, but can supply an incremental gain by taking the same knowledge and principles as do those who work in the tradition of the church and, at least in the area of psychological adjustment, applying that knowledge and those principles "more consciously and expertly" (p. 43). The motivations, conceptions, and programs of the two groups are not equivalent, yet in many respects there is enough compatibility to warrant and even demand active collaboration. Thus Christians should maintain a limited partnership with community psychology.

References

Albee, G. (1982). Preventing psychopathology and promoting human potential. *American Psychologist* 37: 1043–50.

Bassuk, E., and S. Gerson (1978). Deinstitutionalization and mental health service. *Scientific American* 238.2: 46–53.

Bergin, A. (1983). Religiosity and mental health: A critical reevaluation and meta-analysis. *Professional Psychology: Research and Practice* 14: 170–84.

Berkouwer, G. (1962). *Man: The image of God*. Grand Rapids: Eerdmans.

Bloom, B. (1984). *Community mental health: A general introduction* (2d ed.). Monterey, Calif.: Brooks/Cole.

Christianity Today (1981). George Gallup polls America on religion. Carol Stream, Ill.: Christianity Today.

Cowen, E. (1980). The wooing of primary prevention. *American Journal of Community Psychology* 8: 258–85.

——— (1982). Help is where you find it: Four informal helping groups. *American Psychologist* 37.4: 385–95.

Dohrenwend, B. S., and B. P. Dohrenwend (1981). Socioenvironmental factors, stress and psychopathology. *American Journal of Community Psychology* 9: 128–59.

Goodstein, L., and I. Sandler (1978). Using psychology to promote human welfare. *American Psychologist* 37: 385–95.

Holahan, C. (1977). Community ecology: A tale of three cities. In I. Iscoe, B. Bloom, and C. Spielberger, eds., *Community psychology in transition*. Washington: Hemisphere Publishing.

Iscoe, I., B. Bloom, and C. Spielberger, eds. (1977). *Community psychology in transition*. Washington: Hemisphere Publishing.

Kelly, J. (1981). Tain't what you do, it's the way you do it. *American Journal of Community Psychology* 9: 244–61.

Lantz, C. (1984). Psychology's bias: A response to Albee. *American Psychologist* 39: 80–82.

Leavy, R. (1983). Social support and psychological disorder: A review. *Journal of Community Psychology* 11: 3–21.

McDonald, H. D. (1981). *The Christian view of man*. Westchester, Ill.: Good News.

Muller, R., and H. Vande Kemp (1985). On psychologists' use of "Calvinism." *American Psychologist* 40: 466–68.

Pargament, K. (1982). The interface among religion, religious support systems, and mental health. In D. Biegel and A. Naparstek, eds., *Community support systems and mental health*. New York: Springer.

Pargament, K., W. Silverman, S. Johnson, R. Echemendia, and S. Snyder (1983). The psychosocial climate of religious congregations. *American Journal of Community Psychology* 11: 351–81.

Pargament, K., F. Tyler, and R. Steele (1979a). Is fit it? The relationship between church/synagogue member fit and the psychosocial competence of the member. *Journal of Community Psychology* 7: 243–52.

_____ (1979b). The church/synagogue and the psychosocial competence of the members. *American Journal of Community Psychology* 7: 649–64.

Peters, G. (1979). The church and development: A historical view. In C. Henry and R. Hancock, eds., *The ministry of development in evangelical perspective*. Pasadena, Calif.: William Carey Library.

President's Commission on Mental Health (1977). *Report of the working group on religious support systems*, 15 November 1977.

Rappaport, J. (1977). *Community psychology: Values, research, and action*. New York: Holt, Rinehart & Winston.

_____ (1981). In praise of paradox: A social policy of empowerment over prevention. *American Journal of Community Psychology* 9: 1–25.

Ryan, W. (1971). *Blaming the victim*. New York: Random House.

Samuel, V., and C. Sugden (1981). Toward a theology of social change. In R. Sider, ed., *Evangelicals and development: Toward a theology of social change*. Philadelphia: Westminster.

Sarason, S. (1977). Community psychology, networks, and Mr. Everyman. In I. Iscoe, B. Bloom, and C. Spielberger, eds., *Community psychology in transition*. Washington: Hemisphere Publishing.

Sider, R., ed. (1974). *The Chicago declaration*. Carol Stream, Ill.: Creation House.

Smith, T. (1957). *Revivalism and social reform in mid-nineteenth-century America*. New York: Abingdon.

Stott, J. (1975). *The Lausanne covenant: An exposition and commentary*. Minneapolis: World Wide.

White, R., and C. H. Hopkins (1976). *The social gospel*. Philadelphia: Temple University Press.

Woodbridge, J., M. Noll, and N. Hatch (1979). *The gospel in America*. Grand Rapids: Zondervan.

Yoder, J. (1974). The Biblical mandate. In R. Sider, ed., *The Chicago declaration*. Carol Stream, Ill.: Creation House.

Index of Names and Sources

Subject Index